FIVE NOVELISTS OF

THE PROGRESSIVE ERA

FIVE NOVELISTS
OF THE
PROGRESSIVE
ERA

ROBERT W. SCHNEIDER

Columbia University Press   New York & London   1965

First printing April, 1965
Second printing November, 1965

LIBRARY OF CONGRESS CATALOG CARD NUMBER: 65-12110
PRINTED IN THE UNITED STATES OF AMERICA

ACKNOWLEDGMENTS

ONE or more of the several versions of this manuscript have been read by Merle Curti of the University of Wisconsin, Ralph Bowen of Northern Illinois University, and Clayton Ellsworth of the College of Wooster, and I am deeply obligated to each of them for the suggestions and criticisms which they offered. Portions of the manuscript were read and improved by the advice of my colleagues Charles George, Kenneth Owens, Richard Brown, and Richard Sewell. My greatest debt is to David W. Noble of the University of Minnesota, who has provided me with guidance, encouragement, and inspiration from the beginning. I wish also to express my appreciation to the College of Wooster for a summer grant, to Northern Illinois University for released time to complete the manuscript, and to Mrs. Ralph Bowen for valuable editorial assistance. My wife, Ann Schneider, performed so many varied functions in the realization of this work that my debt to her is beyond expression.

My appreciation is extended to the following companies and individuals for permission to quote from copyrighted material.

William Dean Howells: To Mildred and William W. Howells for Mildred Howells (ed.), *Life in Letters of William Dean*

Howells, 2 vols. (Garden City, N.Y., Doubleday, Doran and Co., 1928); and *Through the Eye of the Needle* (New York, Harper and Bros., 1907). To E. P. Dutton and Co. for *A Hazard of New Fortunes* (New York, 1952).

Stephen Crane: To Alfred A. Knopf, Inc., for Wilson Follett (ed.), *The Works of Stephen Crane,* 12 vols. (New York, 1925); *The Collected Poems of Stephen Crane* (New York, 1930); Robert W. Stallman (ed.), *Stephen Crane: An Omnibus* (New York, 1952); *Stephen Crane: Stories and Tales* (New York, 1955). To Appleton-Century-Crofts for *The Red Badge of Courage* (New York, The Modern Library, 1951). To Syracuse University Press for Corwin K. Linson, *My Stephen Crane* (Syracuse, 1958); and Edwin Cady and Lester G. Wells (eds.), *Stephen Crane's Love Letters to Nellie Crouse* (Syracuse, 1954). To Columbia University Press for Daniel G. Hoffman, *The Poetry of Stephen Crane* (New York, 1957).

Frank Norris: To Doubleday and Company for *Vandover and the Brute* (Garden City, N.Y., 1914); *Collected Works of Frank Norris,* 10 vols. (Garden City, N.Y., 1926). To The Book Club of California for *The Letters of Frank Norris* (San Francisco, 1956). To Hill and Wang for *The Octopus* (New York, Sagamore Press, 1957). To Stanford University Press for Ernest Marchand, *Frank Norris: A Study* (Stanford, 1942). To The Bodley Head for Isaac Marcosson, *Adventures in Interviewing* (New York, John Lane, 1920).

Theodore Dreiser: To World Publishing Company for *The Titan* (Cleveland, 1946); *The Financier* (Cleveland, 1946); *The "Genius"* (Cleveland, 1946); *Jennie Gerhardt* (New York, A. L. Burt and Co., 1911); *Moods Philosophical and Emotional Cadenced and Declaimed* (New York, Simon and Schuster, 1935); *Hoosier Holiday* (New York, John Lane and Co., 1916); *A Book About Myself* (New York, Boni and Liveright, 1922). To Harold J. Dies and Myrtle R. Butcher, co-trustees of the Dreiser Trust, for *A Traveler at Forty* (New York, The Century Company, 1920); *The Hand of the Potter* (New York, Boni and Liveright, 1918). To Hill and Wang for *Sister Carrie* (New York, Sagamore Press, 1957). To the University of Pennsylvania Library and The University of Pennsylvania Press for letters in the Dreiser Collection.

Winston Churchill: To the Macmillan Company for *Coniston* (New York, 1906); *The Inside of the Cup* (New York, 1913); *A Far Country* (New York, 1915); *The Dwelling Place of Light* (New York, 1917). To Holt, Rinehart, and Winston for Frederic T. Cooper, *Some American Story Tellers* (New York, 1911).

I also wish to thank *The Midcontinent American Studies Journal* and *Midwest Quarterly* for permission to publish revised versions of my articles on Stephen Crane, Frank Norris, and Winston Churchill.

ROBERT W. SCHNEIDER

DeKalb, Illinois
October, 1964

CONTENTS

Introduction   1

1 William Dean Howells: The Mugwump Rebellion   19

2 Stephen Crane: The Promethean Protest   60

3 Frank Norris: The Romantic Rebel   112

4 Theodore Dreiser: The Cry of Despair   153

5 Winston Churchill: The Conservative Revolution   205

Conclusion   252

Notes   259

Index   283

FIVE NOVELISTS OF

THE PROGRESSIVE ERA

INTRODUCTION

AMERICANS who came of intellectual age between 1890 and the end of World War I—the Progressive generation—found themselves engaged in a dramatic struggle between traditional dogmas and the forces of a new scientific and industrialized world. That struggle has affected most later American thinking. In a very real way the confusion of much current opinion reflects the similar confusion and ambiguity of thought during the Progressive era. Naturally, then, students in all fields of American culture have been expending time and energy trying to understand and synthesize the varied intellectual currents flowing from that period. Yet, in spite of great scholarly activity, the place of the Progressive generation in the development of contemporary American thought remains undefined and obscure.

The purpose of this book is to examine the problem from a different angle of vision. It is my contention that much of the difficulty scholars have found in analyzing the Progressive mind lies in the fact that the writers of the Progressive period were themselves convinced that they had liberated their minds from the shackles of the past and had gone, unencumbered, toward the future. Too often modern scholars have taken them at their word. Unduly impressed by the revolutionary aspects of Progressive thought, historians have paid too little heed to the residual commitment of the Progressive mind to the older ideals and values of the nineteenth century. They have tended to accept this self-proclaimed intellectual revolution as a fact because it provided historical antecedents for these historians' own views of mankind and the state. Therefore the majority of the scholars have agreed with Henry Steele Commager in thinking that the years 1890–1917 saw an abrupt intellectual change, in saying that the traditional attitudes and morality were overthrown and replaced by a new secular, scientific, relativistic outlook.[1] True, few Americans of the 1960s would deny that there is a vast difference between the intellectual attitudes of today and those of the days of Emerson and James Fenimore Cooper. But is this difference necessarily the result of a decisive intellectual revolution in American thinking during the Progressive age?

In those years secularism and materialism, long growing in power, became crucial. New scientific theories of evolution battered at Christian dogmas at the same time that urbanization and industrialization were presenting American churches with their most severe institutional problems. Traditional religions seemed to face the threat of mass revolution. Yet, it has been widely recognized that, while religion in its institutional form was playing a less important role in the daily lives of the people, popular opinion was still rooted in the tenets of nineteenth-century evangelical Christianity. It was the intellectuals, say the scholars, and not the men in the street who changed their basic orientation. Compelled by evolutionary theories and by the confusion of values engendered by industrialization, the intellectuals are usually pictured as having abandoned the religious heritage and the traditional value system, replacing it with a cult of science and matter-of-fact knowledge.[2]

How far is this true? It is my contention that, although these generalizations may emphasize the changes that were most significant in American thinking, they simplify to the point of distortion the multicolored intellectual atmosphere of those years. The real tension of the Progressive period, and perhaps of all periods of history, was created not by an about-face change in philosophic orientation, but rather by the conflict within the minds of individual intellectuals—the conflict between the values of the past and the scientific beliefs of the future. The significance of the Progressive era as a great transitional period lies precisely in this conflict. By suggesting that Americans lightly changed their commitments, deserting the traditional and seizing upon modern values, or by claiming that the Progressive generation divided into two groups, one accepting the new thought and the other clinging stubbornly to the old, students of Progressivism have failed to portray the emotional and intellectual excitement of the period.[3]

Nor were the contradictions in thought merely an example of cultural lag, of the glacierlike slowness of new ideas in passing from the creative minds of the few to the inert minds of the many. Most historians have been conscious of the problem which this phenomenon presents to any scholar who tries to establish the point at which one intellectual climate gives way to another. The real problem to be considered here is the divided commitment within the minds of the creative few themselves; the real task is to see the Progressive mind in its own terms rather than in those of succeeding generations. It is perfectly natural that modern scholars are interested in tracing the growth and development of the contemporary world view, but more care needs to be taken in analyzing the seminal ideas. No historian can completely separate himself from the ideas and problems of his own society, but current interests and concerns have been allowed to distort the historian's analysis of the Progressive generation to a greater extent than is necessary.

Part of the reason for this failure to appreciate the drama of transition is a result of the methods of analysis that have been used. Most American intellectual historians, like their European counterparts, have concentrated on presenting encyclopedic, narrative accounts of the course of American thought, emphasizing breadth of coverage rather than depth of analysis. As John C. Greene has pointed out, such narratives tend by their very nature to be relatively superficial. A closer examination of the general presuppositions that are widely held during a particular age or period, Greene suggests, would be of greater value than the encyclopedic approach.[4] Following this suggestion, I have tried to present a new perspective on Progressive thought by examining one crucial aspect of intellectual activity.

Progressive attitudes toward the nature and destiny of man provide one such key to the thought of the generation. It is a realm of thought in which the revolt against conventional attitudes supposedly took place and, as a basic aspect of all philosophies, it has important ramifications for an over-all climate of opinion. As one historian has suggested, "Once a philosopher has divulged what sort of creature he takes man to be, both in fact and in potentiality, his arguments in other fields of inquiry are often readily anticipated."[5] This statement would seem to hold true not only for a philosopher, but for a writer or any intellectually creative individual.

This is not to say that the average individual formulates a consistent theory of human nature for himself, or even consciously adopts such a theory from others. In any culture, all except the critical and creative minds tend automatically to accept the concept of man (along with other general presuppositions) that is currently dominant in their own society and age. Because their views of man seldom rise to the point of conscious reflection, most people would be unable to define their own beliefs with any precision. Yet their social attitudes and personal activities will continue to be influenced by the view to which they unconsciously subscribe.

Convinced that the only way to arrive at an accurate understanding of any age is through a careful analysis of the thought patterns of individuals, I have adopted this approach to the problem of Progressive attitudes concerning the nature of man. Historians have been forced to put forward educated guesses about general concepts in American intellectual development because they have had neither the time nor the resources to analyze with care even a fraction of the important writings of any age. This is the basic reason for the superficiality of the narrative histories noted by John C. Greene. This study itself should provide insights into the Progressive mind. In its design and execution, it may serve also as a building block which, added to similar studies, can form a substantial foundation for more accurate statements concerning American attitudes during the Progressive era.

It should be understood that my concern in this study is with the thought patterns of a generation which reached intellectual maturity during the 1890s, the Progressive generation. I am not concerned, except indirectly, with the political and social reform movements through which some members of this generation attempted to put their ideas into practice. The particular individuals whose ideas I have chosen to examine are all representative novelists of the period. There are two primary reasons for this use of literary subjects. In the first place, the literary community throughout history has been more successful than any other group in the continuing battle of the intellectual to transcend prevailing ideas and thought patterns. Literary figures have, consequently, both provided new insights into the actual conditions of their own society and illuminated the dominant thought patterns by their very critique of contemporary ideas and values. My attitude toward the value of the literary community for the historian does not, of course, conform to the older notion that the historian ought to be concerned with the arts only to the extent that the artist directly reflects the prevailing spirit of the age. But if the ideas of the novelist prove different from the accepted views of their own era—if they do provide a more accurate picture of past periods in history than is provided by some other observers—the intellectual and cultural historian may need to reexamine his own preconceptions on this point. This study will attempt to demonstrate that the literary community can be both a mirror of attitudes and opinions, and a reflector of the human condition. It can, in short, supply the historian with rich and diverse materials that have yet to be fully exploited.

Another reason for concentrating on literary men is that the only really adequate analytic study of a major segment of the Progressive generation is David W. Noble's *The Paradox of Progressive Thought,* a work which challenges the orthodox interpretation of such men as Charles H. Cooley, Richard T. Ely, and Thorstein Veblen.[6] It had been widely assumed that these men were complete converts to the new thought who rejected both the morality of the past and the deterministic metaphysics of Spencer and William Graham Sumner. They supposedly substituted for these outdated philosophies a relativistic approach to evolution which encouraged the Progressive generation to come to grips with the concrete problems of their age. The modern ideas and methodology of these social thinkers, who suggested that man could successfully grapple with the new world of industrial America, have impressed historians. The literary community, on the other hand, is said to have clung to pre-1890 theories of evolution. This fatalistic acceptance of cosmic determinism has frequently been contrasted in an unfavorable way to the activism of the social theorists.[7] Since Noble's study of men like Veblen and Cooley has revealed that there were errors in the standard interpretation of their ideas, it seems logical and proper to subject some of the novelists to a similar analysis. Such a study may well indicate that certain members of the literary community understood the conditions of their own day more clearly than did the more highly regarded social scientists.

With such an approach, the problem of selecting representative and significant authors becomes a matter of considerable importance. Three of the subjects chosen, Stephen Crane, Frank Norris, and Theodore Dreiser, are accepted by most historians as both giants of the age and examples of the literary revolt against the values of the past. It was obvious that they should be included in the study. Then, since all of these men were serious artists but none was particularly popular with the general public, it seemed essential to include a popular novelist if one could be found who approached his work seriously. The man who best fulfilled these qualifications was Winston Churchill, the most popular novelist of his day and a writer who was accepted by his contemporaries as a serious social critic. Finally, for purposes of contrast and comparison with these four, all of whom reached maturity at the beginning of the Progressive period, the writings of William Dean Howells have been included to represent the preceding generation which reached maturity before America was fully industrialized.

The choice of these particular writers is, of course, an arbitrary one. Others might have preferred to consider such iconoclasts as Henry and Brooks Adams in place of Howells, or David Graham Phillips instead of Churchill. Such a change in the figures to be examined would undoubtedly alter the conclusions, at least in some particulars. This danger arises whenever the historian decides to approach the spirit of an age by examining individuals in depth. But if the figures chosen are truly representative of various intellectual currents in a society, the general conclusions should still be valid. In any case, this method provides a starting point, an alternative to the broad and generally superficial survey of an entire generation.

In analyzing the writings of these novelists, my concern has not been with the truth or validity of their ideas in any absolute sense, but with the historical importance of the ideas, their connection or lack of connection with the past, and their place within the society in which they were expressed. In order to place the ideas of these men in proper perspective and, consequently, to gauge the extent of the literary revolt against traditional ideas, one must have some notion of what constituted the basic elements in conventional American concepts of man. Since there are no effective studies in this area of American intellectual history, it is impossible to make any definitive statements on the subject.[8] Certain beliefs, however, do seem to have been consistently present in American attitudes about human nature.

In order to establish a working hypothesis, I would suggest that the traditional concepts can be most clearly formulated by relating them to American attitudes concerning the nature of society and government. Considered in this way, it seems obvious that, as Louis Hartz has contended, Americans have shared the Lockean theory of the English middle class which stressed the primacy of the individual.[9] For nearly all American thinkers, the individual has been the basic reality; institutions have been artificial, man-made creations. In good mechanistic fashion, Americans accepted the notion of self-sufficient, isolated, atomistic individuals who create institutions, and especially the institution of government, to protect themselves from each other. They have further assumed that once this mechanistic society, this complex of institutions is created, man can still transcend the existing social order, come into contact with nature or natural law, and reform or remake society in the light of the knowledge thus derived.

Most Americans have worked within this dualistic framework, which corresponds to a Lockean version of the state of nature. On the one hand, man has within him elements of selfishness and irrationality which must be curbed by society—by government. On the other hand, he has elements of benevolence and rationality which, given his freedom to create, make him capable of forming and reforming his society. During certain periods of history one side of man's dual nature has been emphasized at the expense of the other, but few Americans in the eighteenth and nineteenth centuries dispensed altogether with the duality. For example, the philosophers and theorists of the Enlightenment placed less emphasis on the evil side of man, which they saw expressed primarily in social relations. They postulated a free, rational, benevolent natural man who could conform to nature and consequently had no need for government and social institutions. But man in society, man in history, man conforming to tradition still existed, and until he could be transformed into the "noble savage" he would still possess an evil, irrational side that must be restrained by institutions. Government might be an evil, but in historical society it was a very necessary evil. Thomas Jefferson would emphasize one side of this duality and John Adams another, but the dual concept of man was a vital part of the intellectual climate which influenced the Founding Fathers.

These views, however, were profoundly altered by the exuberant, expansive American of the mid-nineteenth century. Although the mid-nineteenth century democrat still believed that in society, where man finds himself plagued by institutions and traditions, the individual gives expression to the evil, irrational, selfish side of his dual nature, he had much more faith in the good natural man. The complex view of human nature held by the Founding Fathers, and even by earlier Americans, began to fade as this ever-increasing emphasis was placed on the natural side of man and especially on his almost complete freedom to will and act. This new emphasis found economic expression in the philosophy of laissez faire, theological expression in the doctrine of the individual's responsibility for his own salvation, and philosophical-academic expression in the doctrine of free will. By the time of the Civil War this new picture of man was implanted so strongly in the minds of Americans, and in their symbols and traditions, that it came to be accepted as a central part of the American ideology.[10]

But as the forces of a developing industrial society became

increasingly evident in the years after 1860, Americans found themselves facing challenges which might well have shaken the most firmly held convictions. Their rural, Anglo-Saxon, Protestant social order was challenged by the growth of the city and the flood of non-Anglo-Saxon, non-Protestant immigrants from eastern and southern Europe who congregated in the great metropolitan centers. As this new industrial society solidified in the last third of the nineteenth century the old leaders of the community were pushed aside by a new class of industrial giants, enterprising men whose trusts and monopolies were destroying the old idea of a free enterprise system in which creative and morally responsible individuals competed in an open market.[11] During the same period religious and moral absolutes were challenged by the doctrine of evolution and the growing secularization of society. The mid-nineteenth century concept of man, which had insisted above all on the freedom of man to control his own society and determine his own fate, found itself faced with growing institutional pressures and a deterministic evolutionary philosophy which seemed to explain these pressures.

Could the faith of this mid-century democrat survive in the new atmosphere of an industrializing America? Could the concepts which originated in an expansive rural society be stretched to explain the human condition in an equally expansive industrial world? The answer would seem to be an emphatic yes. And in the writings of the late nineteenth century one can see those beliefs, which in the Jacksonian period had been used as ideological weapons in the fight against social and economic privilege, degenerating into that defense of the status quo known as the Gospel of Wealth. This Gospel of Wealth was an attitude of mind, an approach to life, rather than a formulated social philosophy. In effect it contended that man was a free individual who competed in the race that was human existence. The race was most fairly run when the government remained a spectator, especially where economic matters were concerned. It rested on the Christian principle of the moral worth of the individual, the economic doctrine of laissez faire, and, increasingly, upon the prestige given to Spencer's struggle for existence by Darwin's scientific theories. "Genius thrives on adversity" became the motto, and those who had no jobs were told that there is "always room at the top." Poverty continued to be explained as a self-imposed mortification, the result of sin, laziness, and dissipation.[12] Horatio Alger expressed this attitude in fiction for youths, and Russell B. Conwell preached it to thousands of eager listeners of all ages. Nor, according to Ralph H. Gabriel, was this outlook on life simply the rationalizations of the rich converted into aphorisms for children. It was instead "a faith which determined the thinking of millions of citizens. . . ."[13] The concept of the free and creative individual which, through its various manifestations had helped to overthrow a privileged class that rested on government favors, had become a defense of a new privileged class that had risen out of the operation of the concept itself.[14]

The extreme individualism of the Gospel of Wealth was the most popular view of man and society when the revolt of the 1890s got under way. During that fertile decade, however, men appeared in every phase of life and thought who were to be hailed in later years as the philosophical founders of modern American thought. Most of the leaders of this revolt are so clearly within the American tradition of the free and creative individual that, for all their innovations in other areas, they can easily be dismissed as representatives of the revolt against the conventional view of human nature. A more difficult problem arises when one considers those Progressive social thinkers who are said to have rejected this traditional outlook. While it has already been suggested that these men did not accept Spencerian determinism, that they did not really deny the traditional role played by the free and creative individual, they did alter conventional concepts in an important way. The extent of their revolt against both traditional ideas and against the Spencerian version of evolution can best be understood against the background of ideas developed in the works of Louis Hartz, Henry Nash Smith, and David Noble. Hartz' contribution to an understanding of the American mind was his discovery that the predominance of middle-class Englishmen in early America, with an outlook similar to that of John Locke, permitted the tradition of atomistic, creative individuals to flourish without effective opposition. With Locke, Americans contended that the absence of institutional restraint was the key to the liberty of the self-sufficient individual.[15] Smith's contribution, an elaboration of the two agrarian myths found in American thinking, follows the same lines. He points out that, on the one hand, Americans embraced the "myth of the garden," whereby all men were saved by the frontier process of sloughing off their inherited traditions and institutions. On the other hand, they also embraced the idea of "manifest destiny," the belief that the continent would be conquered by Americans as they naturally extended their civilizations, their institutions and traditions.

Smith's "myth of the garden" and the Lockean individualism presented in Hartz' analysis are both manifestations of the concept of the free and creative individual. The problem arose from the growth of institutions and traditions implied in the idea of manifest destiny. The realization of this destiny would mean the loss of the innocence of the savage in the garden and an institutional infringement of the liberty of the self-sufficient individual. This was a problem which bothered men like Frederick Jackson Turner during the 1890s. Turner, himself, had no solution to the problems of the developing post-frontier industrial society. Filled with the sense of crisis that was common to many American intellectuals in the 1890s, he could pose only rhetorical questions concerning the future. But if the process of developing an industrial civilization could itself be interpreted as a mechanism which would free man from his burden of institutions and traditions, then the two concepts of the savage in the garden and manifest destiny would be combined, and the free individual of the American tradition could remain in the industrialized society of Progressive America.

Noble's analysis shows that the Progressive social theorists believed they had discovered the answer that had eluded Turner.[16] These men were part of a tradition of growing optimism regarding the ability of the free individual to create his own world, to be free of environmental or institutional influences. Yet they were faced with the fact of growing institutional pressures on the individual, of apparent class warfare, of gross exploitation of man by man. These social facts plainly contradicted the hope of the Gospel of Wealth that each man pursuing his own self-interest would automatically work for the benefit of the entire community.

When these social philosophers reacted against this contradiction and sought to find an answer in a new aspect of human freedom, they were faced with the dictates of the Gospel of Wealth. This doctrine insisted that man has to live free from institutions if he is going to be creative and avoid corruption; he must live by natural law, not governmental law. The Gospel of Wealth, in the tradition of dualism, conceded the need for a limited government to protect property, but the potentially dangerous government is, and must be, restricted in its powers by the Constitution. The Progressives, therefore, had to think of a way to operate through institutions and still save human freedom and creativity. To accomplish this, they had to alter the belief that man in society is corrupt whereas man apart from society is pure.

To the social theorists the answer seemed simple. They declared that man in the natural society of prehistory was a social animal. The mistake of the English political theorists had been their contention that the side of the individual which is inherently good and rational is self-sufficient and atomistic. Instead, Cooley and the others argued, man from birth is a member of society—the society of the family. Through the instincts and the emotions involved in being a part of the family group he acquires the values of social justice and the rights and responsibilities of creative individualism. Man in the natural society of the family is generous, cooperative, helpful, and loving. This innate goodness was the only aspect of human nature which was determined by natural, biological forces.

But what about human history as a record of evil? If man is naturally good, why is there evil? For the social philosophers the answer again was simple and it went back to the traditional belief that the individual within society is corrupt. Men were corrupted when they came to live in social groups larger than the family. There is a plastic side of human nature that is shaped by the institutional world, and throughout the history of man this malleable side of his nature was molded by a series of changing social environments. The history of social groups larger than the family was one of constant warfare. In direct contradiction to the natural qualities of love and cooperation, historical society had made the pliant side of human nature competitive and warlike. Life within the primary group was characterized by love and cooperation; life among the primary groups was characterized by a Hobbesian war of each against all.

When the Progressive theorists fought to persuade Americans to abandon the concept of pure laissez-faire competition, this was their major argument—laissez faire was not a natural law, but simply a cultural concept related to the industrial revolution. It was a disruption of natural conditions, not a universal norm. Indeed, according to these thinkers man is bound in no way by natural law, except that his gregarious, loving nature is a product of his biological background. Once biological evolution had brought man to the stage of development of the family group, for all practical purposes he had then achieved autonomy from further biological evolution—the social group of the family was natural and it was permanent. The more complex social groupings of history were the result of historical forces, not natural forces. Furthermore, man at this stage of biological evolution developed self-consciousness and reason, so that he was able to understand his real nature and shape his environment to meet these basic needs.

But, in the tradition of dualism, the Progressive social theorists argued that the new social environment had proven too strong for this rationalism. The plastic side of human nature is weak; it had been easily corrupted by the new institutional arrangements of exploitation, and the loving and rational side of man had been buried beneath cultural accretions. They agreed with the American tradition and the Gospel of Wealth that man in historical society is evil, irrational, and selfish. But this need not continue to be true. As they looked about their own society, they discovered an opportunity unique in the history of man, an opportunity to escape history itself. True, America was in crisis. The industrial revolution had transformed the very life of the country; it had removed the individual from any meaningful social relations. His traditions, his morality, even his established institutions had lost their meaning in this new world. Yet this same destruction of civilization endowed man with an opportunity to construct the new world without being handicapped by a connection with a past history of misdirected and corrupting institutions and traditions. The unique promise of the industrial revolution was that it provided man with the unfettered freedom to create a new society based on the family group, an opportunity for the loving and rational side of man to become truly autonomous for the first time.

Nor was this the end of their enthusiastic optimism. While they urged the individual to create an entire society on the moral model of the family group, they also promised vast help from the forces of industrialism itself. The factory and the city were bringing men into close-knit environments comparable to the smaller family group. The simultaneous revolution in communications and transportation was bringing these factory and city units into close proximity with one another. So, for the first time in history, the pliant and potentially corruptible aspect of human nature was being shaped to coincide with the goodness of the natural man of prehistory. These Progressive social scientists had stood the American concept on its head, but they came out in final support of the traditional notion of the free and creative individual. In their own opinion they had solved the problems of their age of crisis, and their optimism and confidence stand in dramatic contrast to the troubled hopes of the literary community.

In considering the academic thought of the Progressive period, then, many historians and commentators have tended to be somewhat extravagant in their claims that science, in either Spencerian or relativistic terms, replaced traditional values. Men like John Dewey and William James used the new science to explain and defend the major tenets of the traditional concept of human nature. Other Progressive social thinkers did alter the old ideas, and they brought about an important shift in the conventional dual concept of man. The result of this shift, however, was a renewed faith in human freedom and creativity. And this faith was based not upon scientific, matter-of-fact knowledge, but upon a traditional value structure with strong religious overtones.[17] Although they used evolutionary science and philosophical relativism to destroy the atomistic natural man of the Gospel of Wealth, here their revolt against formalism and natural law ended. They replaced the older version of the natural man, not with a relativistic belief that man is totally a product of his environment (which would have made social reform difficult, if not impossible), but with a value-laden natural man of their own creation. While science and relativism were useful as weapons to destroy the inhibiting doctrines of the Gospel of Wealth, their usefulness ended there. When the social theorists turned from destruction to construction they demonstrated the dual commitment of the Progressive generation by clinging to the value system of their own heritage.

So, despite the fact that this new generation of social thinkers felt the full impact of the social and institutional challenges to the American tradition, these challenges did not destroy their optimistic faith in human potential. If there was an intellectual revolution in the Progressive period, it must have been in the thinking of some other group of intellectuals. That group is, I would suggest, the literary community.

1

WILLIAM DEAN HOWELLS

The Mugwump Rebellion

THE RESPONSE of most Americans to the challenges that came in the post-Civil War period was a restatement of faith in the old way. There were those, of course, even among the older generation, who did recognize something of the challenge and who could not accept the sanguine rationalizations of the Gospel of Wealth. Some, like William Graham Sumner and Henry Adams, came to question much of the inherited view of man and society. But most of the thinkers of the older generation, in one way or another, came back to some form of belief in the free and creative individual of the American tradition.

One of the members of the older generation who during his long and productive life came face to face with many of the problems of an industrializing America was William Dean Howells. Howells was a modest example of the "rags to riches" theme in American history. Born in the small southern Ohio town of Martinsville, he received most of his education working in his father's print shop and from discussions with his father.[1] Young Howells felt deeply his abolitionist family's isolation in southern Ohio and he did not actually become a part of the local community even after his father moved to Ashtabula and became a minor leader in the newly formed Republican party.

Actual and imagined illnesses, as well as his intellectual tendencies, set him apart from his more active contemporaries, and this isolation turned him against the small-town life which he associated with it.

Although Howells thought of himself as a poet, it was a short period of service as city editor of the *Ohio State Journal* and a campaign biography of Abraham Lincoln which enabled him to escape from a distasteful environment. The biography provided funds for a trip to Boston, where he met and was encouraged by Hawthorne, Holmes, Lowell, and other members of the Boston-Cambridge literary circle. Then with the help again of his Lincoln biography and with the backing of a bevy of Ohio politicians, he secured a government position as Consul in Venice, where he remained during the Civil War.[2] After the war he returned to America and with his usual good fortune was given a position with E. L. Godkin and the *Nation*.

From this point on his rise to fame and respect was as rapid as anyone could desire. In 1866, as the newly appointed assistant editor of *The Atlantic*, he established his residence in Cambridge, where he became an intimate of the literary giants of the day. This association with the old, nonindustrial aristocracy proved to be an important factor in Howells' view of man and society. Then in 1871, at the age of thirty-four, he was named editor in chief of *The Atlantic*. To add to his prestige as editor of one of America's leading magazines, Howells had already become a successful author. His *Venetian Life* received praise from the critics and won popularity with the book-buying public. In about six years William Dean Howells had progressed from the status of an unsuccessful poet to that of a highly successful editor and author. Ten years later his increasing success as a novelist allowed him to leave the burdensome editorial job and devote his full time to fiction.

During these early years Howells was acutely conscious of the problems of the age and had accepted many socio-economic articles, including some by Richard T. Ely and Henry Demarest Lloyd, for publication in *The Atlantic.* Nonetheless, his social outlook was essentially conservative and he remained loyal to the Republican party. In all probability he continued to cast his ballots for Republican candidates until he demonstrated his changing social outlook by voting for Bryan in 1896.

This changing social outlook was the result of a concatenation of circumstances that pressed in upon the novelist during the decade of the 1880s. His move to New York, the "civic murder" of the Chicago anarchists following the Haymarket Affair, the death of his daughter, his discovery of the Tolstoyian ethic, and the invalidism of his wife all occurred during this short period, and each has been stressed by one or more of the biographers and commentators as the most significant factor influencing the change in Howells' attitude during the late 1880s. At approximately the same time, all of the challenges to American tradition were beginning to manifest themselves. One need not assume any cataclysmic revolution in Howells' mind, either from personal tragedy or from larger social and intellectual forces, but there was a change. Raised a Swedenborgian, utopian socialist, and abolitionist, Howells had become a social conservative in the 1860s and 1870s. But during the 1880s he developed a strong social consciousness and at the same time lost the buoyant, easy-going spirit of his earlier years.

In spite of Howells' change in residence and the chastening of his spirit, the novelist continued to fight for his beliefs. In 1886 he took over "The Editor's Study" column for *Harper's,* and for six years he used this column to expound his theories on realism in fiction. When his contract expired in 1892, he served a short time as editor of *Cosmopolitan* and then returned to *Harper's,* where he conducted the "Easy Chair" column in the years after 1900. The twentieth century was not kind to the aging realist; his popularity diminished rapidly and he spent the remaining years of his life, until 1920, searching for a spiritual home.

Howells was roughly a generation older than the other four writers included in this study, reaching maturity at about the time when Crane, Norris, Dreiser, and Churchill were born. The reason for his inclusion in this study is to see what differences there are in the concepts of man held by a sensitive man of letters born and raised in the social, physical, and intellectual climate of preindustrial America and the concepts of those born in an industrializing America. Since this study deals with the concepts of man held by the various authors during the 1890–1917 period, Howells' earliest, and admittedly less serious, novels are of no real concern. It is as a representative of an older generation who continued to write during the Progressive era that Howells' ideas are of importance here.

In this connection it is interesting that historians have generally been much more kind to Howells than have the literary commentators. The liberal outlook of the genial dean of American letters has impressed the historians who, in contrast with the literary critics, have been willing to overlook some of the more unrealistic elements in Howells' thought. The basic reason for the disapproval of the commentators would seem to be that most of them have identified the so-called naturalistic movement of the Progressive era as the dynamic element in the literature of that day and they cannot forgive Howells' lack of sympathy with that movement.

One of the central tenets of literary naturalism, as it has been formulated by the literary historians, was a new view of man and of his place in the scheme of things. Man for the naturalist was a prisoner of heredity and environment who was pushed and pulled by outward forces and inner passions. This view placed the naturalist outside the American tradition of the self-sufficient individual who could order his society in the light of his reason, and made these literary figures rebels against the middle-class society of their own day. Since these literary historians have tended to view the naturalistic movement as a positive good, they have denounced Howells' ideas about man and society as being old-fashioned, unrealistic, and unscientific. This analysis will attempt to demonstrate that these literary critics have both overestimated the extent of the so-called naturalistic rebellion and oversimplified the rather complex view of man which Howells presented in his writings.

One of the most important and least understood aspects of Howells' concept of man is the distinction he made between the natural man and the civilized man. In *A Modern Instance*, 1882, Howells presented his first real portrait of a natural man in Bartley Hubbard, and the plot of the novel concerns Bartley's marital problems and his rise in the newspaper world.[3] A self-made newspaperman who had fought his way from humble origins by his own brilliance and audacity, Bartley was lacking in what Howells considered the aristocratic sense of obligation, and he provides a prime example of the uncivilized natural man. Atherton, the Boston lawyer through whom Howells spoke his mind in this novel, made this identification of Bartley with the natural man whom he described as "a wild beast" whose "natural goodness is the amiability of a beast basking in the sun when his stomach is full. . . ."[4] For Howells it was what Atherton called "the implanted goodness," the flower of which he termed civilization, that was the saving aspect of man.[5] Bartley did not have this saving grace and consequently lacked any sense of obligation; he hadn't "the first idea of anything but selfishness."[6]

It is important for present considerations that Bartley was a very rational being who was a free agent in his own destruction, despite the large part accident played in this story. Toward the end of the novel Howells states that "nothing remained for him but the ruin he had chosen."[7] Bartley, then, as the natural man, would seem to be a self-centered, rational creature who determined his own destiny, and the natural man emerges from the pages of *A Modern Instance* as basically evil.

But in Silas Lapham, Howells presents another natural man

who is almost the antithesis of Bartley. The story of *The Rise Of Silas Lapham,* 1885, concerns the development of the title character as a moral man, not his economic success, which took place prior to the main events of the story.[8] At the opening of the novel Silas was a self-made man who had risen from lowly origins to a considerable fortune. Yet, partially through a series of personal mistakes and partially because of the rise of new competition, Silas was placed in a situation where he must either raise money through a dishonest business deal or sacrifice the last chance to recoup his shaky fortune. Here was a man in a dilemma. Would he surrender to what Howells was already beginning to consider the corrupt influence of the business world of contemporary society, or would he rise as a moral man? As the title of the novel indicates, he chose financial ruin. So, like Bartley, Silas made choices which determined his own destiny— he was free—but, unlike Bartley, he chose moral salvation at the cost of economic ruin.

At first glance it appears that Howells' picture of man, as presented in these two novels, is confused in the extreme. Silas and Bartley both come from the same background, both are self-made men, yet Silas had a highly developed moral sense and Bartley did not. What was the difference? One explanation of this confusion might well be that Howells at this point in his career did not have a developed philosophy of human nature at all; that the ideas presented here were simply unconscious assumptions of which he himself was unaware. But there is an emerging pattern. Bartley and Silas exhibit two sides of the natural man—both the good and the evil, selfish and unselfish. More specifically, Bartley was an example of the natural man who had accepted the morality, or what Howells viewed as the lack of morality, of the industrial society of his own day. Silas was the natural man who rejected "tooth and claw" morality and, like the natural man of the Progressive social theorists, he achieved salvation by rejecting contemporary morality for the civilizing spirit of community which the social scientists had postulated as part of the natural man of prehistory. While outside the civilizing tradition which Howells saw as the repository of the sense of community, Silas had unity with that tradition because he resisted the pressures of a society which encouraged selfish individualism. He, consequently, preserved his innate goodness which Howells, somewhat nebulously at this point, connected with a sense of social solidarity.[9]

Actually most of Howells' characters do not exemplify the natural man who lives apart from institutions and traditions. Institutions do not enter Howells' writings to any extent until *A Hazard of New Fortunes,* but many families, like the Corys in *Silas Lapham* and the Hallecks in *A Modern Instance,* are very much aware of another side of the inclusive society—the civilizing sense of obligation. Ben Halleck, a Boston blue blood of the best kind, is an excellent example of the civilized man. In *A Modern Instance* Ben displayed a strong sense of right and wrong which prevented him from revealing to Bartley's wife that he was deeply in love with her. Whenever he began to weaken in his resolution, Ben visited his friend Atherton, who gave him a lecture on the obligation of the social aristocracy. In a civilized state, according to the lawyer, each individual's actions affect the whole of the social structure. And, while the misconduct of such people as Bartley may have little effect on society, misconduct by a widely known and respected man like Ben would do irreparable harm. Ben's freedom of action is not circumscribed by society—a civilized society that made a human being of the natural man. It was Ben's realization of this obligation that caused him to suffer when he contemplated committing an act which would encourage social disintegration. He was, therefore, largely responsible for his own suffering.

This distinction between the natural man and the civilized man which was implicit in Howells' serious novels probably arose from his own experience and was, in all likelihood, not a clearly formulated concept. He had not been happy in Ohio and he was happy in Cambridge; he had not cared much for the natural men of his early days in Ohio, but he did like the associates of his Venetian and Bostonian days. And what was it that separated the typical Ohioan from a James Russell Lowell? Obviously one major factor was social training, a social tradition. Howells was too shrewd, however, to believe that this social tradition was always good, and in his early novels, and particularly in *Indian Summer*, 1886, he demonstrated that a slavish adherence to the traditions and patterns of conduct prescribed by polite society is absurd.[10] The rational man, like Theodore Colville in *Indian Summer*, understands the social tradition and is thus a civilized being, but he also knows when to break from it and thus is free.

The picture of man presented in Howells' novels to this point, that is until 1886, was a rather hazy one. On the one hand was the natural man whom Howells endowed with a dual nature, a capacity for both good and evil. The novelist did not really show what determines which of the two shall triumph and apparently felt that the natural man was relatively free to choose. On the other hand was the civilized man, like Ben Halleck, who was aware of an obligation to society and who could not choose evil without causing severe suffering to himself. The civilized man was consequently not as free as the natural man.

Howells' concept of man, to this point, was a relatively superficial one that largely ignored the institutional pressures of an industrializing society. Free from institutional restraint, his characters made moral decisions on the basis of a traditional value system and were responsible for their own material and spiritual destinies. But by the writing of his massive novel, *A Hazard of New Fortunes*, the changes which were taking place in Howells' approach to life are readily apparent. The story of this novel is very complex, but it revolved around the birth and growth of a literary magazine, *Every Other Week*, which Basil

Marsh came to New York to edit. Behind the magazine were the publicist, Fulkerson, and his financial angel, Jacob Dryfoos, a member of the new business class. Employed on the staff of the magazine were Lindau, a German "forty-eighter" and a socialist; Dryfoos' saintly son, Conrad, who was in charge of the counting room; and the egoistic Beaton as art editor.

The action of the novel, however, concerned not the fortunes of the magazine itself, but rather the conflicts among the various philosophies and personalities of the characters. These conflicts came to a head during a streetcar strike, when young Dryfoos was accidentally shot to death as he tried to save Lindau from being clubbed by a policeman. Dryfoos, stunned by the loss of his son, then sold the magazine to Marsh and Fulkerson.

The characters of this novel are a very mixed breed. Basil Marsh, who was rather obviously patterned after his creator, occupied the stage most frequently and served as the center of revelation. He was a man of artistic temperament and sound good sense but, unlike Howells' earlier heroes, he was not a man of pristine virtue. Beaton, the artist, was a typical Howells' villain, presented as innately selfish and egoistic, but with a conscience which plagued him even though he seldom followed its prompting. He was unemotional and considered both self-interest and, on rare occasions, duty in a more rational manner than any of the others. Like Howells' other villains, Bartley Hubbard before him and Jeff Durgin after him, Beaton rose from humble origins and was not guided by the traditions and obligations of civilized society.

Most of the other characters are representatives of some philosophy for social salvation. Lindau was a fanatic socialist, and while Howells presented the old German with affection, he repudiated the idea of reform through violence. Colonel Woodburn, an unregenerate southern gentleman of the ante-bellum type, was a dreamer. He agreed with Lindau that the capitalistic structure of society was an abomination, but his answer was a return to feudalism. Conrad Dryfoos and Margaret Vance were presented as saints—kind, loyal, and devoted. There was a marked resemblance between the death of the innocent Conrad as a result of social evil and the Christian doctrine of atonement that did not escape the all-seeing eye of Basil Marsh.

But while all these people were important in presenting the positions of Christian socialism, Marxian socialism, and feudalism, they were not the major personalities of the novel. That distinction was saved for the capitalist, Jacob Dryfoos, who encountered the hazards of a new fortune. Dryfoos was of Pennsylvania Dutch background, born and raised on his father's Midwestern farm. Old-fashioned but intelligent, Jacob made a good living from his large farm. When the natural gas boom hit the area, he fought it and waved the specter of the Standard Oil monopoly in an attempt to persuade his neighbors not to sell their farms. His wife agreed with him, but his daughters who had "been away to school" favored selling out. When Dryfoos received an offer of $100,000, his daughters finally talked him into selling all but eighty acres, and the family moved into town, where the old man became so ill and bored that he finally tried to buy back his farm. Up to this point Howells presented the old farmer as a moral man.

There had been a time in his life when other things besides his money seemed admirable to him. He had once respected himself for the hard-headed, practical common sense which first gave him standing among his country neighbors; which made him supervisor, school trustee, justice of the peace, county commissioner, secretary of the Moffitt County Agricultural Society. In those days he had served the public with disinterested zeal and proud ability. . . . He was a good citizen, and a good husband. . . . His moral decay began with his perception of the opportunity of making money quickly and abundantly, which offered itself to him after he sold his farm.[11]

Slowly he sloughed off his old moral nature as "the poison of that ambition to go somewhere and be somebody which the local speculators had instilled into him began to work in the vanity which had succeeded his somewhat scornful self respect. . . ."[12] Dryfoos took the eighty acres he had saved out of his farm and turned it into a housing development. The money began to pour in, and with his half-million dollars in hand he left for New York to launch his daughters into society. There he engaged in speculation and his fortune multiplied. Fulkerson was able to enlist him as financial backer for *Every Other Week* because Dryfoos wanted to see if, under this guise, he could interest his son in business.

To Mrs. Marsh, Dryfoos was "just a common, stupid, inarticulate country person. . . ."[13] But Marsh saw more to him than that.

Ah, I'm *not* so sure. I don't believe a man's any better for having made money so easily and rapidly as Dryfoos has done, and I doubt if he's any wiser. I don't know just the point he's reached in his evolution from grub to beetle, but I do know that so far as it's gone the process must have involved a bewildering change of ideals and criterions. I guess he's come to despise a great many things that he once respected. . . . He must have undergone a moral deterioration, an atrophy of the generous instincts, and I don't see why it shouldn't have reached his mental make-up. He has sharpened, but he has narrowed; his sagacity has turned into suspicion, his caution to meanness, his courage to ferocity.[14]

A trace of the old Dryfoos appeared in a discussion with his wife upon his return from a trip back home. She was upset about having to move the graves of their twin girls to make room for more gas wells. Their conversation and the attempts of Jacob to console her reveal a man once sensitive and just, who, to his wife, remained the soul of kindness.[15] Unable to adjust to a new life, she badgered her husband to go back to the farm, a return to the past which he sensed was impossible.

"We *can't* go back!" shouted the old man, fiercely. . . . "If I was to give all I'm worth this minute, we couldn't go back to the farm, any more than them girls in there could go back and be little children. I don't say we're any better off, for the money. I've got more of it now than I ever had; and there's no end to the luck; it pours in. But I feel like I was tied hand and foot. I don't know which way to move; I don't know what's best to do about anything. The money don't seem to buy anything but more and more care and trouble. . . . But it had to be. I couldn't help but sell the farm, and we can't go back to it, for it ain't there." [16]

It was Marsh, naturally enough, who supplied the author's interpretation of old Dryfoos. The editor, who understood the problem of the nouveau riche, contended that "such people as the Dryfooses are the raw material of good society. . . . All the fashionable people there tonight were like the Dryfooses a generation or two ago." [17] Marsh also saw beneath the bluster of the millionaire. At the banquet given at Dryfoos' home for the *Every Other Week* staff, he saw that Dryfoos "had an old rankling shame in his heart for not having gone into the war. . . . He felt sorry for him; the fact seemed pathetic; it suggested a dormant nobleness in the man." [18]

Following the death of his son, Dryfoos resumed his old nature of kindness and humanity, at least in part. Mrs. Marsh and the others were inclined to attribute this change, this softening in the nature of Dryfoos, to the sudden loss of his son. But Marsh did not agree.

I suppose I should have to say that we didn't change at all. We develop. There's the making of several characters in each of us; we *are* each several characters, and sometimes this character has the lead in us, and sometimes that. From what Fulkerson has told me of Dryfoos, I should say he had always the potentiality of better things in him than he has ever been yet; and perhaps the time has come for the good to have its chance.[19]

If man has within him several characters, the question again arises as to what it is that determines which of these shall gain ascendancy. Following a monologue against the capitalistic ordering of society, the "economic chance world," Marsh provided his answer.

We can't put it all on the conditions; we must put some of the blame on character. But conditions *make* character; and people are greedy and foolish, and wish to have and to shine, because having and shining are held up to them by civilization as the chief good of life. . . . We can't help it. If one were less greedy or less foolish, someone else would have and would shine at his expense. We don't moil and toil to ourselves alone; the palace or the poor-house is not merely for ourselves, but for our children, whom we've brought up in the superstition that having and shining is the chief good. We dare not teach them otherwise, for fear they may falter in the fight when it comes their turn, and the children of others will crowd them out of the palace into the poor-house.[20]

This, then, was Howells' reinterpretation of the nature of man, or perhaps more accurately his first real formulation of a concept of man in society. In the preface to the new edition written in 1909, he wrote that he considered *Hazard of New Fortunes* "the most vital" of his fictional work.[21] It certainly was the most monumental of his novels in both length and scope, and was probably the most significant.

It is particularly important then, to examine in greater detail the picture of man presented in this novel. This can best be accomplished through an analysis of the life of Jacob Dryfoos and of Marsh's comments upon Dryfoos and upon life in general. Dryfoos the farmer was the social scientist's natural man of prehistory. He had roots and a feeling of membership in the community. Then, again like the natural man of the social scientists, when he entered the chaotic contemporary society where "having and shining" was held to be the chief good, his old natural morality was corrupted. But when he entered this "economic chance world" which stressed the freedom of the individual to pursue rationally his own self-interest, Dryfoos felt trapped. Paradoxically, he was a prisoner in a society that promised freedom. It was as impossible for Dryfoos to go back to his farm as it was for the industrializing America of 1885 to go back to the agrarian society of 1830.

However, this was not presented solely as a black and white picture between the goodness of the natural man and the evil, competitive nature of man in society. Marsh explained that man has within him several natures, and conditions act upon the individual to bring forward one or another of these. That is to say, man has a dual or multiple nature and what he becomes is dependent largely upon the social order. Thus the man who is separated from the communal spirit and morality of the natural man, and who has not entered into the world of society as civilization, is doomed to moral destruction by the "economic chance world" of contemporary society.

Was there a way out? The various philosophies of society and social change were discussed and found wanting. The feudalism of Colonel Woodburn was dismissed as fantasy, and the reform-through-revolution of Lindau was repudiated as essentially evil.[22] But Howells did offer one implicit and one explicit solution. The implicit solution was shown in Marsh's comment that "such people as the Dryfooses are the raw material of good society. . . . All the fashionable people there tonight were like the Dryfooses a generation or two ago." [23] If all the people could be made aware of, and would accept, the society of the aristocratic tradition with its stress on obligation, then salvation might be possible. Howells did not specifically offer this solution in any of his novels, but it remained a somewhat nebulous possibility that intrigued him.

In a discussion with his father, Marsh's son asked, "What's the use of our ever fighting about anything in America? I always thought we could vote anything we wanted." [24] This was the explicit answer which Howells offered in *A Hazard of New Fortunes,* and the answer that continued to be present in his later works. As long as man retained the vote he could alter his society as he saw fit. This was something of a contradiction to his contention that the evil side of man's nature was brought out by contemporary society, but Howells retained his faith that man's natural goodness would surmount this obstacle. Man was still essentially free, and in his utopian romances (to be discussed later), he explained more clearly how this contemporary society could be supplanted. It is important to note here, however, that these two paths to social reform, the extension of the aristocratic sense of obligation to the whole society and the achievement of utopia through the democratic process, were not completely compatible, and the conflict between the two approaches created an uneasy tension in the mind of the novelist.

Howells' next fictional study, however, followed directly upon the premises established in *A Hazard of New Fortunes*. *The Quality of Mercy*, 1892, was the story of J. Milton Northwick, treasurer of a New England corporation, who had been using company funds for his private speculations.[25] His defalcations were soon discovered and he fled to Canada where the extradition laws could not reach him. Howells then discussed the result of Northwick's actions upon his two daughters, his associates, and himself.

Northwick had been raised to believe in a moral government in the universe, to believe that wrong would be punished, even if virtue was not always rewarded. He had learned in the business world that this was not necessarily so, but had held himself to the idea of moral responsibility, even if he did not act upon that idea. The example of others in the business world allowed him to violate his ideas in practice, but he retained the principles themselves.[26] Howells maintained that Northwick "had a conscience, that mechanical conscience, which becomes so active in times of great moral obliquity. . . ."[27] At another point the author referred to his "mechanical scruple" against lying.[28] The old nineteenth-century moral faculty concept, that each individual has within him a moral faculty which distinguishes right and wrong, was still part of Howells' thinking and would remain a part of his outlook throughout his life.

The personal wages for Northwick's sins were spiritual demoralization and inner suffering. But this was not the main concern of the novel. The central question was whether Northwick or society was basically at fault, and Howells' indictment of the existing society continued to be a damning one. His own interpretation of the matter would appear to be that presented by the intellectual Maxwell in a newspaper article concerning Northwick's disappearance. Maxwell contended that there must be something wrong with a society in which defalcation is an everyday occurrence. The only reason that Northwick's case stirred any interest was the possibility that he had been killed in a train accident on his flight to Canada. Otherwise his case was a typical one. According to Maxwell, most of the defaulters were not men who needed money, but men who were tempted by the chance of immediate wealth.[29]

On the one hand, you had men educated to business methods which permitted this form of dishonesty and condemned that; their moral fiber was strained, if not weakened, by the struggle for money going on all around us; on the other hand, you had opportunity, the fascination of chance, the uncertainty of punishment. . . . It behooved society to consider how far it was itself responsible, which it might well do without ignoring the responsibility of the criminal.[30]

Matt Hilary, the son of the president of the corporation, agreed that Northwick was not the disease but merely the symptom. It was the social body that was sick.[31] And lawyer Putnam's view, which Howells allowed to stand at the end of the novel, was similar.

He just seems to be a kind of—incident; and a pretty common kind. He was a mere creature of circumstances—like the rest of us! His environment made him rich, and his environment made him a rogue. Sometimes I think there *was* nothing to Northwick except what happened to him. He's a puzzle.[32]

The concept of man presented in *The Quality of Mercy* appears to be essentially that of *A Hazard of New Fortunes*. Northwick was a weak man who was incapable of withstanding the temptations of his capitalistic environment. Like Dryfoos, who was a much stronger individual, his character assumed its worst form because of the world in which he lived. It is difficult to ascertain whether or not Northwick was given any responsibility for his actions. Putney's speech seems to indicate that he was not—Maxwell's article that he was. Certainly the tenor of the book is that he had a choice, and that the weakness of his character, combined with the temptations offered him, did not wholly excuse him from moral responsibility.

Howells' idea that man in contemporary society was a product of his environment was less strongly felt in this novel than in *A Hazard of New Fortunes*. In the earlier work, all of the characters were shown to be somehow affected by the quest for the dollar. Fulkerson, Beaton, and even Basil Marsh were tainted. The saintly Conrad Dryfoos was affected in the sense that he was made to atone for the sins of society by his death. But in *The Quality of Mercy* the evidence is less strong. Howells did, however, speak of the newspaperman Pinney's "more delicate and generous self, which he was obliged to pocket so often in the course of business. . . ." [33] Here again was a man who had at least some good instincts—certainly the family ones—which were curbed by the society in which he lived.

But, in contrast to the moral destruction of Northwick and Pinney, Howells portrays the Hilary family as above the corrupting influence of contemporary society. Matt, the son, did not believe in the capitalistic order and tried to live on his farm apart from the business world. Here was the good man within society but trying to withdraw from it. He struggled with a conflict between his ideals, which placed him outside society, and his obligations to his family, which forced him to be a participant.

More important was his father, who, as president of the corporation, seemed to be an individual who could and did retain his
integrity as a moral man and was still successful in business.
Reliability, honesty, and good faith were his ideals and he
maintained them. Here was a good man, not only in society but
participating in the most sordid aspect of that society—the corporation. But during the course of the story he, too, found himself in an ambiguous position. Having urged that Northwick be
given time to repay what he had stolen, he felt responsible for
his escape and the losses to the company. As a moral man he
had no choice but to give Northwick the opportunity to make
recompense; as president of the corporation he had no right to
do so. As the story progressed and he found himself bound more
closely to Northwick, especially after the engagement of his
son and Northwick's daughter, his position became impossible
for a moral man and he retired. Perhaps even Hilary and the
tradition which he represented found that in the capitalistic
society his standard of conduct and good faith were incom-
patible with an active position.

But the fact remains that both Hilary and Northwick had
been participating in the same economic world which Howells
said was the essential part of the environment; indeed they had
worked in the same corporation. Yet Hilary could retain his
moral nature and Northwick could not. The difference, it would
seem, was again in the backgrounds of the two men. Northwick
was of humble origins which lay mainly outside civilized society.
Hilary was a product of the traditions of polite society. Northwick came from the same social background as Dryfoos, and
like Dryfoos he was corrupted by the "economic chance world."
Hilary came from the same tradition as a multitude of Howells'
characters, the Boston social aristocracy, and, like the rest of the
members of that class, he was not corrupted. This would seem
to indicate a continuation in Howells' thinking of the dichotomy
which was earlier pointed out between the essentially natural

man like Bartley Hubbard, Dryfoos, or Northwick, and the inheritor of the social traditions like the Hallecks, the Hilarys, or the Marshes. Apparently it was this tradition which implanted the seed of moral responsibility, allowing the individual to withstand the evil side of his dual nature and the temptations of the economic world which he experienced in contemporary society.

The author's next major novel was *Landlord at Lion's Head,* published in 1897.[34] Jeff Durgin, the leading character, was raised in the hill country of New England. The lion's head, a stone formation, was best seen from the Durgin farmhouse, and at the suggestion of Mr. Westover, an artist, the Durgins established a summer hotel which over the years provided them with a very comfortable living. This enabled Mrs. Durgin to send Jeff to Harvard, where he met with social rejection as an ill-bred country person. Meanwhile, various love interests arose in which Jeff showed his lack of character, shocking the noble Westover, who remained a family friend. When Jeff finished Harvard, he was rejected by his childhood sweetheart and fiancée, Cynthia Whitwell, because of his affair with a Boston girl. He finally married yet another girl and revamped Lion's Head into a fashionable and very successful resort. Concurrently, Westover finally proclaimed his love for Cynthia, and the book ended with the union of these two noble characters.

Jeff Durgin was another villain in the line of Bartley Hubbard and the artist Beaton. During the course of the novel he grew from a happy, mischievous boy into a strong, determined man. He was a tower of strength with no particular moral scruples, but, like the rest of Howells' villains, with a definite moral sense. For example, he had no particular qualms about wronging Cynthia, but he did realize he had done so and he even made a special trip from Boston to Lion's Head to explain things to her.

During the course of the novel, Jeff appeared to be master of his own fate. The sense of the inclusive society of institutions and traditions which Howells had developed in *A Hazard of New Fortunes* and *The Quality of Mercy* was gone. Jeff was not bound by the institutions and traditions of society, nor did he seem to have been affected to any degree by his environment. There was some discussion of hereditary influences, but this was vague and unclear, as was customary in Howells' comments on heredity. Jeff decided what he wanted, went after it, and achieved it.

Westover, a typically high-minded hero wedded to traditional morality, tried to convince Jeff that he was not wholly a free agent; when he did a wrong he must expect to suffer the consequences. But Jeff, embracing Howells' version of the business ethic, insisted that there were no necessary consequences and that strength and weakness, not goodness and badness, were the essential categories.[35] And in the course of the story it appeared as if he might be right, for he did achieve his goals. Cynthia's father, who had a philosophical turn of mind, was bothered by the manner in which the efforts of a man who was not essentially good had been crowned by success, and in order to hold fast to the idea of a moral government in the universe, he suggested that Jeff might have changed.[36] Westover, however, found a way to retain moral law without falling back upon the unsatisfactory expedient of a change of character. "That kind of tree bears Dead Sea apples, after all. He sowed evil and he must reap evil." [37] But even Westover had to admit that such retribution might have to be postponed to another life, "a world where there is room enough and time enough for all the beginnings of this to complete themselves. . . ." [38]

This did not mean that Howells had abandoned any notion of a causal relationship between goodness and happiness for a form of pie-in-the-sky, by-and-by philosophy. He knew enough of the world by 1890 not to believe that success came only from moral action, but he still retained his belief in personal morality. In

A Modern Instance, Bartley Hubbard had to die for his sins, but there were others in the same drama, notably Squire Gaylord, whose tragedy did not arise from their own actions. Howells had a strong tendency to grant a "live happily ever after" ending to those who lived the moral life, witness Silas Lapham, but this was by no means always the case. Yet there is in his novels a consistent notion that those who do evil must reap the rewards of that evil in personal unhappiness. Jacob Dryfoos was unhappy and the artist Beaton was unhappy, and the implications of this story were such that one can assume qualms of conscience would mar the personal happiness of Thomas Jefferson Durgin, landlord at Lion's Head. He achieved personal freedom through a rational exploitation of the "economic chance world" of contemporary society. But because he submerged the natural moral faculty and could not understand the aristocratic sense of obligation, Jeff was morally lost. Howells was by no means willing to accept the Gospel of Wealth notion that worldly success implied virtue.

In *Landlord at Lion's Head,* as in most of his early work, Howells tended to portray man as a rational creature who made choices between good and evil, two fairly distinct entities, and this choice revealed the man's true character. But in *The Son of Royal Langbrith,* 1904, he penetrated several layers beneath this traditional black and white, Sunday school morality to discover the good man caught in a moral dilemma. This novel relates the story of James Langbrith, proud son of an evil father, who, through ignorance of the facts, worshiped his father's memory. From Harvard, James came to visit his mother and while at home he fell in love with Hope Hawberk, whose father had been cheated and mentally destroyed by the elder Langbrith. James' mother was in love with Dr. Anther, one of the few men who knew the real history of the patriarch of Saxmills. She was too weak to reveal her dead husband's past to her worshipful son, and she refused to allow Anther to tell James the true story. Consequently, James' image of his father stood between the mature lovers and led to a scene with James when he discovered their love.

Earlier, James had considered placing a plaque commemorating his father on the village library, which the elder Langbrith had donated. Anther, horrified at the notion of honoring such a scoundrel, opposed this, and the major issue of the novel revolves around the problem of whether or not to tell James of his father's sins in order to prevent the celebration. Many developments culminated in the final revelation to James of his father's misdeeds after everyone had decided it would be better to keep the secret. James at once decided that the noble course of action was to reveal the truth to the community and suffer the infamy which would result. Hope opposed this, and with the help of the enlightened Reverend Enderby persuaded James to suffer the greater torments of silence.

This is an important novel for the consideration of Howells' concept of man, for the central problem is man caught in a moral dilemma. Anther, the central character in this drama, was the only one who could reveal to the community leaders the past history of Langbrith and prevent his public commemoration. At the start Anther seemed to act at least partially from self-interest (if the truth were revealed, James would presumably withdraw his objections to the marriage of Anther and Mrs. Langbrith), and in the belief that it would be an outrage to allow the marriage of James and Hope without revealing the fact that the elder Langbrith was responsible for the tragedy of Hawberk.[39] But the most important of Anther's arguments came from the realm of absolute morality and natural law. In his argument with Reverend Enderby, the doctor asked if "the truth itself, merely as truth, has no claim upon our recognition?"[40] And also he wondered if we have "no such a thing as a duty to justice?"[41]

Anther discovered, however, that his obligation to truth and justice was not the only obligation of the moral man in such a situation. He took the problem of revealing Royal's past to Judge Garley, who asserted that it was a "moral necessity" to let the matter rest. Royal's success was a light to guide the feet of youth only as long as it was felt to rest upon virtue; to destroy that illusion by revealing the man's corruption would destroy public morality.[42] Anther then asked Reverend Enderby whether silence or exposure would have the greatest "advantage of religion or morals." [43] Reverend Enderby, who said that he was not concerned primarily with the community but with interference in the "divine scheme," nonetheless agreed that "it could not help this community to know the truth about that wretched man. It would only render it cynical and deprave it." [44]

The importance of this situation for an understanding of Howells' concept of man lies in his presentation of men whose freedom of action or free will was severely circumscribed by the conditions in which they found themselves. On the one hand, as a moral man, Anther felt an obligation to truth and justice; on the other hand, and again as a moral man, he realized that he had a conflicting obligation to public morality. The doctor found himself a victim of circumstances not of his creation, and he cried out against it.

"Why," he asked himself, bitterly, "should *we* [he and Mrs. Langbrith] be doing things by stealth? We hide our affection, as if it were something to be ashamed of. We behave like guilty persons, but you are the most innocent of victims, and I am to blame only for not forcing you to right yourself." [45]

Later Anther decided that he had made a positive error by not forcing Mrs. Langbrith to "right" herself and that he was suffering for his sins of omission. Mrs. Langbrith was a moral weakling, and, since he had perceived this, he realized that the responsibility for telling James had been his. "Anther realized that the boy had been deeply injured, and he accepted his own share of the retribution as the just penalty of his share in the error." [46] He was, then, a victim, but a victim of circumstances which had arisen at least in part because of his own inaction. Howells had not forgone his conviction that man, in the final analysis, is a free agent.

Nor was Anther's dilemma solved by his decision that his actual duty lay in allowing Royal's past to remain hidden, for he then found that he was in danger of revealing that past through his cure of Hawberk, who was regaining his lost memory as Dr. Anther slowly broke him of opium addiction. For Anther, having relinquished all hope of marrying Mrs. Langbrith, "nothing but his duty remained, a duty that was barren of personal reward, and that if done successfully, as regarded Hawberk, must be done at the risk of fruitless suffering for others." [47]

But Anther was not the only moral man in this novel who was trapped by circumstances and circumscribed in his exercise of free will. Mr. Enderby found himself in the moral dilemma of either having to reveal Royal's past, which he felt would do no good and would tend to corrupt society, or of making a speech commemorating the good works of this evil man. He made the compromise that the moral man must make and gave the speech, but, separating the good deed from the doer, said nothing about Royal as a person.[48] As Dr. Anther said, he "did the best that any man could, in the circumstances." [49] And it was Enderby again, in his explanation of why James and Hope should not reveal Langbrith's true character, who explained why the moral man cannot act only in the name of abstract justice when he said, "To take upon ourselves any agency for supposed justice—for the discovery and the retribution implied by the concealment and the wrong in the case, would be in a manner forcing God's purposes. . . ." [50] Howells, himself, took the question out of the realm of theology and placed it in the realm of moral law. He wrote as direct interpolation:

Life is never the logical and consequent thing we argue from the moral and intellectual premises. There ought always to be evident reason in it; but such reason as it has is often crossed and obscured by perverse events, which, in our brief perspective, give it the aspect of a helpless craze. Obvious effect does not follow obvious cause; there is sometimes no perceptible cause for the effects we see. The law that we find at work in the material world is, apparently, absent from the moral world; not, imaginably, because it is without law, but because the law is of such cosmical vastness in its operation that it is only once or twice sensible to any man's experience.[51]

It is here that one can see the central point of the novel. Howells had reverted to making all of his characters good, moral, unselfish, and rational, although some of them did have defects. James Langbrith was trapped by his own delusions; no one ever told him his father was a saint. But James was essentially a good man and a rational one. Possessed of a strong personality, he was capable of moral action once that action was made clear to him. Mrs. Langbrith was a good, unselfish woman whose weakness had evil consequences. The others—Dr. Anther; Hope Hawberk, who was one of Howells' all-good and all-wise females; and the Enderbys—were essentially without defects of character. Royal Langbrith, who had been dead for some years when the story opened, was the exception.

But the important point was that these moral people were all caught in a dilemma which they as individuals had little part in creating. The dilemma arose from a complex pattern of actions and inactions, none of which were fundamentally of base motivation. Nor could these same individuals solve the problems arising from this dilemma. Not that the novel lacked a happy ending— Dr. Anther died a happy, though single, man; Hope and James lived happily ever after—but the problems were resolved largely by actions and events beyond the control of the principals.

The quoted interpolation by the author indicates his belief not only that man cannot understand the moral laws of the universe, that he cannot see justice, but also that such moral law does exist. Consequently, when all the characters were convinced that they had to maintain silence about the life of Royal Langbrith, when they were convinced that they must not tamper with the "divine scheme" of the moral government of the universe, then retribution began to work itself out. And, "from the moment of the dedication of the votive tablet by the son, the myth of the father suffered a kind of discoloration. . . ." [52] Not only did the myth of the public benefactor dissolve from the public mind, but it apparently took place without the decline in public morals which all agreed would have been the result of direct revelation of the fact that Langbrith's fortune was founded upon dishonesty. Howells even leads one to believe, through Reverend Enderby, that Royal himself did not wholly escape the consequences of his evil life. He first indicated that retribution might have to await the day of judgment, but more importantly he said:

Could there be fearfuller suffering than his consciousness in his sudden death that he could not undo here the evil he had done? Why should we suppose him to have been without that anguish, if men in the presence of mortal peril are tormented with the instantaneous vision of their whole lives? [53]

Thus Howells, in his last major work of fiction, presented man as capable of evil but basically good, rational, and unselfish. Yet man is not wholly free because he can be caught by circumstances, not essentially of his making, in which his freedom is circumscribed and his duty unclear. He is a moral being living in a moral universe whose method of achieving justice is sometimes beyond his comprehension. The crux of the novel would seem to be that in an imperfect society man cannot simply pursue his own self-interest and still be a moral man. For the moral man, like Anther, rational self-interest must be sacrificed to social obligation. The world was far more complex than it was pictured in the pronouncements of the Gospel of Wealth.

Some of these ideas on man and society which were left unclear in Howells' novels were given explicit formulation in his nonfictional writings and in the two romances, *A Traveler From Altruria,* 1894, and *Through The Eye Of The Needle,* 1907. These works, together with Howells' personal letters of the period, clarify many of the important points implied in the novels.

The story lines of the two romances are relatively simple. *A Traveler From Altruria* had its setting in a New Hampshire summer hotel where Mr. Twelvemough, a writer, was entertaining a guest from the little-known country of Altruria. Spending his time trying to understand American society, the Altrurian, Mr. Homos, embarrassed his host by helping the waitresses, bellboys, and other employees with their work. With his complete naïveté, Mr. Homos could not understand the social distinctions that existed in a land of political democracy, and although he had conversations with people from all walks of life, they failed to make him understand American society. In the first section of the second book Mr. Homos was in New York, in 1893, where he was patronized by the social set, especially a Mrs. Makely, and he fell in love with Eveleth Strange, a rich widow with an interest in social welfare. Later they were married and went to live in Altruria, and the letters which Eveleth wrote to Mrs. Makely from there constitute the second part of the book. The newly married couple toured Altruria, and Eveleth wrote of the customs, society, and institutions of her new home. Aside from this description, the chief interest of this section lies in the account of the parvenu Thralls, their daughter, her titled husband, and their entourage, who accidentally landed their yacht in Altruria. The assimilation of this hostile group was presented as one of the small country's greatest accomplishments.

The whole problem of equality was one of the problems which Howells had skirted in his novels, but in the romances he made the separation of political equality from social and economic equality the basis of American life.[54] Mr. Bullion, the most intelligent American in the romances, admitted that the notion of social equality in America was a myth and had never existed except in the "most primitive communities." [55] By unfavorably contrasting the American notion of the separation of political equality from social and economic equality, in the name of freedom, with the Altrurian practice of full equality, Howells proclaimed his faith in the basic equality of all men.

This was not a new idea for the genial author, but the concept of basic equality was sometimes obscured in his novels by his obvious personal preference for the social aristocracy. In one of his essays he wrote that while the victims of society "are ugly and vicious, cruel, filthy," they are "not altogether loathsome because the divine can never wholly die out of the human." [56] The rich are as bad, or as good, as the poor; the poor as bad, or as good, as the rich. In a letter to John Hay about his novel, *The Breadwinners,* Howells accepted the fact "that the workingmen *as* workingmen are no better or wiser than the rich *as* the rich, and are quite as likely to be false and foolish." [57] Writing of his own experience in the third person, Howells said, "As nearly as he could make out, his liberation . . . took place through his gradual perception that human nature was of a vast equality in the important things, and had its difference only in trifles." [58]

A much more complex problem than that of equality is the problem of the fixity of human nature. Is man a product of his society? Is there such a thing as human nature apart from society? And most important of all, can man transcend his society? All of these are questions with which Howells flirted in his novels and with which he dealt at length in the two romances and in his private writings.

Throughout the story of *A Traveler from Altruria,* various

Americans called upon the theory of the fixity of human nature as a justification for the egoistic, competitive society. They assumed that conditions cannot be altered because human nature is constant. Speaking with regard to the inequality of American social and economic conditions, Mr. Twelvemough said, "We regard them as final, and as indestructibly based in human nature itself." [59] He called upon this principle whenever he wanted to defend some piece of "everyday selfishness." [60] Mrs. Makely presented the same view of human nature as essentially selfish and always the same. On this basis she contended that the Altrurian system of cooperation was impossible. [61]

All this was an expression of the prevalent Gospel of Wealth philosophy that society was composed of atomistic, competitive individuals, a contention with which Howells, at least after the middle 1880s, was in basic disagreement. The very fact that he could portray a society in which the egoistic basis was gone is proof that he did not believe that human nature is entirely fixed. The over-all impression one gets from the two romances is that any great or sudden alterations in human nature within the context of the existing American society would be impossible. But man can be changed to some extent, even within that unpromising context. Howells writes that in Altruria they studied the history of the outside world to show that conditions beyond Altruria remained essentially the same, although

with some slight changes through the changes of human nature for the better in its slow approaches to the Altrurian ideal. In noting these changes the writers get some sad amusement out of the fact that the capitalistic world believes human nature cannot be changed, though cannibalism and slavery and polygamy have all been extirpated in the so-called Christian countries, and these things were once human nature, which is always changing, while brute nature remains the same. [62]

Mr. Homos said that the old conditions—that is, the old capitalistic system which Altruria had also had at one time—

"compelled" man to be egoistic, but that under the new system human nature had changed.[63] Conditions in Altruria had so changed man that crime, illness, and insanity were no longer problems,[64] and belief in an afterlife seemed natural as a continuation of the present existence.[65] Heaven on earth could become an actuality if men were properly conditioned.[66] The unstated implication of Howells' development of this environmentalist approach is that human nature is frustrated and hedged about in the capitalistic, competitive system of contemporary American society. In Altruria, human nature was not so much changed as it was simply freed, thus allowing man to burst forth in all his goodness. The goodness seems to be innate and the evil conditioned. Man, Howells was saying, is basically ⁃ocial and it was contemporary society which led man to view himself as egoistic.

The force of environment as it brings out the good that is in people can be seen in the changes which took place in the Thrall party after they had been in Altruria for a while.[67] They were cast ashore in Altruria as examples of the egoistic outside world, and their conduct compared quite unfavorably with that of the more civilized Altrurians. Mrs. Thrall, by far the worst of the lot, was of the Dryfoos wing of the moneyed class rather than from the civilized wing of the Hallecks. But the Altrurian conditions worked wonders, and before long even this horrible example of the capitalistic world was participating in the work which was required of everyone in Altruria and she was slowly assimilated into Altrurian society.

A continuation of this belief in the force of the environment can be seen in Howells' concern about the proper social setting for his utopia. George Arms has written that after 1894 "Howells was increasingly inclined to regard agrarian America as the ideal to which the new commonwealth must return. . . ."[68] And in *A Traveler from Altruria* he does seem to have been of the typical American mind about the evils of the city and the virtue of rural life. He had the Altrurians break up all the large cities and form a society based upon a combination of rural life and the small city.[69] Mr. Homos said, "We had . . . a great many large cities under the old egoistic conditions, which increased and fattened upon the country, and fed their cancerous life with fresh infusions of its blood." [70]

Homos also stated that farming was the most honored occupation in Altruria. "We believe that this, when not followed slavishly, or for gain, brings man into the closest relations to the deity . . . and that it . . . awakens a natural piety in him. . . . " [71] Eveleth wrote that her mother, who accompanied the couple to Altruria, felt that her new home was like the America of her girlhood.[72] She felt she had abandoned the artificialities of industrial American life for the simple life which she had formerly known. But, although Altruria was much like the agrarian America of the pre-Civil War period, it should be noted that there is an important difference. In Altruria all of the people lived in small cities which were but a short trip from the great cultural centers. These were not self-sufficient individuals carving out a niche for themselves in the wilderness, nor were they the simple uncultivated barbarians which Howells tended to see as the natural product of isolated rural life in America. He had not forgotten his own sense of isolation in rural Ohio. What he did was to combine the supposed virtues of the rural, natural man with the broadening influences of life in civilized society.[73]

But Howells, with his fear of the corrupting influence of contemporary society, did not feel that molding character was always a hopeful doctrine, even in America. Writing of the man of letters as a man of business, he spoke of "human nature, as competition has deformed human nature. . . ." [74] He frequently felt "limp and helpless in the presence of the injustice which underlies society. . . ." [75] He had developed a sense of what Altha Leah Bass has called "the inevitableness of life," a "sense of the larger social values and of the importance of social movements. . . ." [76] The plasticity of human nature could bring forth optimistic declarations like the formulation of a utopia, but it could also bring forth a sense of impotence, as illustrated in this quotation from a letter to S. Weir Mitchell, written in 1890.

You speak of deepening convictions, but I have none except of absolute helplessness. . . . But I am not unhappy, and I do believe that as far as I am responsible for myself, I am as well used as I deserve, and better. I doubt if anyone, however, is really accountable; we are not really given into our own keeping.[77]

Howells' continued belief in the possibility of reform depended upon his belief that man is never wholly a product of his environment. Writing of Mrs. Makely, frequently his hostess during the New York sojourn, Mr. Homos said that she was "perfectly selfish by tradition, as the American women must be, and wildly generous by nature as they nearly always are. . . ." [78] The same thing could be said for the whole plutocratic-capitalistic system which was much better than it logically should have been, "for the personal equation constantly modifies it, and renders it far less dreadful than you would reasonably expect. That is, the potentialities of goodness implanted in the human heart by the Creater forbid the plutocratic man to be what the plutocratic scheme of life implies." [79] In one of his letters back to Altruria, Mr. Homos stated, "We must remember that men have always been better than their conditions, and that otherwise they would have remained savages without the instinct or the wish to advance." [80] He also used the phrase "inherent good of human nature," [81] and it was this "inherent good" which would enable man to transcend contemporary society and achieve the utopian society of Altruria. Howells said essentially the same thing in his own essays. In an article arguing against people who say that human nature is bad, he wrote:

It seems to me we are always mistaking our conditions for our natures, and saying that human nature is greedy and mean and false and cruel, when only its conditions are so. We say you must change human nature if you wish to have human brotherhood, but we really mean that we must change human conditions, and this is quite feasible. It [human nature] has always been better than its conditions and ready for new and fitter conditions.[82]

But while Howells considered man to be better than his conditions and, apart from his conditions, essentially good, he knew that man was not wholly good. As Daniel Aaron suggests, "He was too highly trained in the art of ferreting out human frailties not to suspect in his more cynical moments . . . that men individually and collectively, were the most unreliable of animals and capable of the basest as well as the noblest actions." [83]

An example of this more pessimistic side of Howells' thought can be seen in his personal writings in the period of the late 1880s and the early 1890s, a time of personal trial and deep despair for the author. The most important of these was a small volume of poetry called *Stops of Various Quills*. The whole mood of this collection of poems was one of melancholy, brooding, and even despair. The primary themes were death and the question of an afterlife. These poems constitute a dramatic contrast with *A Traveler from Altruria*, which was written in the same general period.

In a poem entitled "From Generation to Generation," Howells brooded over the fact that men are born and die—they know not where or why.

> We have not to consent or to refuse;
> It is not ours to choose:
> We come because we must,
> We know not by what law, if unjust or if just.[84]

Life itself was not a very pleasant experience, at least not for all. In his poem, "Society," Howells first described the beauty and splendor of social pageantry, and then wrote the following second stanza.

I looked again and saw that flowery space
Stirring, as if alive, beneath the thread
That rested now upon an old man's head
And now upon a baby's gasping face,
Or mother's bosom, or the rounded grace
Of a girl's throat; and what had seemed the red
Of flowers was blood, in spouts and gushes shed
From hearts that broke under that frolic pace.
And now and then from out the dreadful floor
An arm or brow was lifted from the rest,
As if to strike in madness, or implore
For mercy; and anon some suffering breast
Heaved from the mass and sank; and as before
The revellers above them thronged and prest.[85]

And the novelist who in the utopian romances had presented
a picture of man molded by his environment, had this to say
about "Heredity."

That swollen paunch you are doomed to bear
Your gluttonous grandsire used to wear;
That tongue, at once so light and dull,
Wagged in your grandam's empty skull;
That leering of the sensual eye
Your father, when he came to die
Left yours alone; and that cheap flirt,
Your mother, gave you from the dirt
The simper which she used upon
So many men ere he was won.

.   .   .   .   .

Your vanity and greed and lust
Are each your portion from the dust
Of those who died, and from the tomb
Made you what you must needs become.
I do not hold you aught to blame
For sin at second hand, and shame;
Evil could from evil spring;
And yet, away, you charnel thing! [86]

Nor was Howells always proud of what he knew to be the weaknesses of his own nature. In the poem, "Company," he seems to be presenting the fundamentally evil nature of all men.

> I thought, "How terrible, if I were seen
> Just as in will and deed I have always been!
> And if this were the fate that I must face
> At the last day, and all else were God's grace,
> How must I shrink and cower before them there,
> Stripped naked to the soul and beggared bare
> Of every rag of seeming!" Then, "Why, no,"
> I thought, "Why should I, if the rest are so?" [87]

One can see in these poems some of Howells' most sober and pessimistic thoughts on man and the world in which he lived. There was, he said, not only evil in the social order, but in man as well. And in the most important aspects of life man is unfree, ruled by a fate whose actions seem to be governed by no rules known to man. It was Howells' most complete departure from "the smiling aspects of life."

Taking Howells' writing as a whole, man is basically good and rational, but his conditions bring out the evil side of his nature by encouraging egoism. Is it, then, possible for man to transcend his environment and, through his reason, reform his society? An individual answer to this question can be seen in a letter from Howells to the young poet Madison Cawein, who was worried because he supported his literary activities by working in a "betting house." Howells agreed that this was an unfortunate way of making a living, but assured the poet that his soul was in his own keeping. He wrote, "A life of success is before you, and it is for you to make it beautiful and beneficent or not." [88] Man is essentially in charge of his own destiny. This opinion was expressed on a broader scale by Howells in an "Easy Chair" study for *Harper's* on historical inevitability. Here he again affirmed that men continually make choices that affect the course of history.[89]

Howells was convinced that man can transcend his society

and bring about the utopian goodness of Altruria, but he realized that making basic changes in his own society would not be an easy task. Nor was simple reform an easy matter. In a collection of reportorial essays called *Impressions and Experiences,* he gave a good account of his awareness of poverty and the impossibility of alleviating it under the existing conditions of capitalistic society.[90]

But reform and change can be brought about. The question is how. He agreed with Hamlin Garland concerning the eventual good that would result from a redistribution of land, but he did not feel that it was the first step to take. "I can't yet bring myself to look upon confiscation in any direction as a good thing. The new commonwealth must be founded in justice even to the unjust, in generosity to the unjust rather than anything less than justice." [91] Howells was somewhat ambiguous as to what constituted this just means of over-all social change. In writing of Tolstoy, he said that the Russian taught him to see the brotherhood of man as one knows it before he comes to understand "the evil wisdom of the world." [92] It was a way which convinced his conscience but was beyond his will. He objected to Tolstoy's belief in the ability of the individual to walk the path alone. For Howells it was "as comrades and brothers that men must save the world from itself. . . ." [93] He never really solved the problem of how men are to become comrades and brothers in a society which teaches them that they are atoms of self-interest.

In a letter to Edward Everett Hale, Howells expressed appreciation for Hale's work which, he said, made him realize that, while the world was out of joint, men must bear with these conditions until they can be changed. And they cannot be changed "except through the unselfishness you enjoin, the immediate altruism dealing with what now is." [94] That letter was written in 1888, and in 1896 he expressed this idea more fully in an article for *Century* magazine called, "Who Are Our Brethren." Here he expressed his belief that the unselfish family relationships can be extended to society at large, an idea that is very close to that being formulated by the Progressive social scientists at almost the same time.

The millennium, the reign of Christliness on earth, will be nothing mystical or strange. It will be the application of a very simple rule to life, which we find in no wise difficult or surprising when the economic conditions do not hinder its operation. The members of a family live for one another as unconsciously as they live upon all others. There is no effort, no friction, in their perpetual surrender of their several interests to the common good; and in the state there need really be none, if once the means of livelihood were assured to each citizen.[95]

Man, in other words, can establish a society in which his selfish, his animal side, is completely subordinated to the good of the community; but this apparently can come about only when man no longer engages in egoistic, capitalistic competition. This change from a capitalistic order can come about, but for Howells it must not come through violence. He deplored the whole notion of violence, and of such labor efforts as the Homestead Affair he said:

I come back to my old conviction, that every drop of blood shed for a good cause helps to make a bad cause. How much better if the Homesteaders could have suffered the Pinkertons to shoot them down unarmed. Then they would have had the power of martyrs in the world.[96]

Consequently his path to social reform was not violence but the vote. The banker in *A Traveler from Altruria* presented Howells' view when he said that strikes for higher wages and shorter hours which end in the destruction of property and interference with the life of the community are not the answer. But since the workers did have the franchise they could vote in all their demands.[97] Howells had said the same thing in a letter to his father, written in 1892. "In one thing the labor side *is* wrong. It has the majority of votes, and can *vote* the laws it wants, and it won't, but prefers to break the laws we share." [98] Man is capable of altering his society, but he must join with others and do so by the democratic process.

Man can and will transcend his society in order to alter that society in the light of reason. This was Howells' belief, and he clung to it in the face of a changing order, and in spite of personal heartache and disillusion. H. C. Belcher, in an article on Howells and religion, put it this way. Howells had first placed his faith in a benevolent God "who ordered this world for man's ultimate good. . . ." [99] As his faith in orthodox religion diminished, he turned to a secular religion "which aimed to apply the Christian ethic in such a manner that life in this world would approach the ideal, regardless of the validity or falsity of traditional beliefs." [100] He never lost his faith in the moral nature of man, and when his religion was gone, he still had his faith in man to sustain him. With Mr. Homos he could say, "Indeed, our own state is testimony of a potential civility in all states. . . ." [101] Recognizing man's inhumanity to man, Howells still felt that a society could be established which would allow men to live as brothers.

In 1890 he felt that the day of deliverance was not far in the future. "By and by labor will be so pinched that the politicians will have to put a socialistic plank into a platform, and then the party that stands on it will win." [102] The old parties may be in decay, but "my faith in the grand and absolute change, sooner or later, is so great that I don't grieve over their success." [103] This faith remained with him, and in 1909, in an author's preface to a new edition of *A Hazard of New Fortunes*, he could still write as follows:

Certain hopes of truer and better conditions on which my heart was fixed twenty years ago are not less dear, and they are by no means touched with despair, though they have not yet found the fulfillment which I would then have prophesied for them. Events have not wholly played them false; events have not halted, though they have marched with a slowness that might affect a younger observer as marking time.[104]

Perhaps his faith can be summarized in a sentence which he wrote to his sister in 1895. The men of the Brooklyn trolley strike of that year, Howells felt, were definitely in the right, but they had lost. Still Howells proclaimed, "But I believe the right will win in the end." [105]

From this analysis what statements can one make about Howells' concept of man; how does his concept compare with that of the American tradition and with the general response to the industrializing of America, as expressed in the Gospel of Wealth? It has been postulated that the American view of man, like the English, was predicated upon the notion that man has within himself a dual nature—a capacity for both good and evil. Up until the late nineteenth century it was generally held that man, if he were unhindered by institutions, if he were free of the burden of tradition, would give expression to the good side of his nature. William Dean Howells worked within this tradition, but, as he would put it, the "personal equation" was in his case operative. For Howells the natural man contains within himself innate evil as presented in Bartley Hubbard and Jeff Durgin, and innate good as presented in Silas Lapham. This dual nature finds an expression of its manifold complexity in a man like Jacob Dryfoos. In Dryfoos, Howells presented a picture of the multiple character of the natural man and showed how at one time one side of that nature will gain predominance, at another time another side. Man does not change, said Howells, he simply gives expression to different sides of his nature at different times.

But most of the characters in Howells' novels were not natural men, that is, they were not apart from both institutions and social traditions. The majority of his characters were touched by one side of the inclusive society, the side of social tradition. In people like the Hallecks and the Corys, the passionate, evil side of man was curbed by the inherited tradition of civilized society. They were not bound by it, but they lived within its framework and were guided by its direction.

This tradition can be learned by the natural man, but such a learning process would probably take several generations, and until this civilizing tradition makes itself felt the natural man is very likely to be corrupted by contemporary society. Once a man becomes aware of social tradition and gains a sense of obligation for the continuation of that tradition, his freedom of action is restricted. He can no longer choose to express the evil, passionate side of his nature without suffering the pangs of conscience, as experienced by Ben Halleck. He has gained, however, what was infinitely more important to Howells, a standard of conduct.

In this sense of inherited tradition, society is a civilizing element. It contains the dual nature of man and brings forth and develops his good side. But this is not the whole of the matter. Howells also used the term society to mean the inclusive society, society as institutions and customs, as well as a civilizing tradition. This society can bring out either the good in man or the bad, depending upon its structure. Contemporary America brought out the worst; Altruria brought out the best.

Historical society has always brought out the worst in man— man is always better than his conditions. He is better than his conditions because he has a dual nature, and while the good side of that dual nature can be stunted and hedged about, it cannot be destroyed. All historical society had been bad because it had encouraged the worst side of man—the egoistic, competitive side. But man can transcend this historical society and give expression to his inherent goodness in the formation of a just society which can be created by man through his own efforts— that is, by man collectively, not by man individually. When created, the just society encourages the good side of man's dual nature by removing the necessity for egoistic competition, and once this restriction is removed, the good side of man will blossom forth and utopia will be achieved. Like the Progressive social thinkers, Howells maintained that the basic unchanging core of man is good. But he laid far more stress than did most of his contemporaries, or the social scientists, on the evil that is in man himself. For this reason he was not quite as certain as others, including the social theorists, that man would transcend contemporary society and achieve utopia. Perhaps for this reason, among others, he laid more emphasis on the importance of maintaining the civilizing tradition already in existence in contemporary society. The conflict between the necessity of maintaining this tradition of aristocratic obligation and the desire to achieve utopia produces a sense of tension in Howells' work which has frequently been overlooked.

Yet, despite what seems to be a considerable amount of realism in Howells' thought, it has frequently been contended that the reason for his loss of popularity after 1900 was that he was too Victorian, too traditional, too unrealistic for the scientific-minded Progressive generation. This is an important question in any attempt to picture the Progressive climate of opinion, but its validity can be judged only after an examination has been made of the writers who were part of that generation.

2

STEPHEN CRANE

The Promethean Protest

STEPHEN CRANE was certainly the most exciting and probably the most talented member of the new generation of writers who arrived on the American scene in the 1890s. During his short lifetime he was part of that generation which, under the pressure of the new, chaotic industrialism and guided by the evolutionary philosophies of Darwin and Spencer, are often said to have rejected the traditional American notion that man is the free and creative center of a moral universe, embracing in its stead an amoral philosophy of biological determinism. The general and monographic studies give the impression that the "watershed" period of the 1890s was peopled with a totally new breed of writers called naturalists, men who rejected the traditional values and assumptions of the past for the new cult of science.

Critics and literary historians have disagreed rather violently about the exact nature of this new philosophy of naturalism, but Ernest Marchand has given a good working description of the naturalistic view of man which indicates most of the basic ideas.

It was but logical that naturalism, with its theory of the determining influence of heredity on human life and its reduction of psychology to physiology, should focus its attention on the physical man. That man was seen to be a complex of instincts, desires, hungers, toward the satisfaction of which all his energies were bent. All the elaborate machinery of law and custom developed by civilization is scarcely sufficient to hold in check the self-assertive impulses, the hard-driving force of the ego. Hence the continual aggressions, unscrupulous acts, crimes of all sorts, which trouble society. It was readily imagined that man in his primitive state would admit no restraints to the fulfillment of his desires but superior force, whether of things, of beasts, or of other men. . . . Concentration on the animal in man and on instinct tended to diminish the importance of reason and of ethics in human life and to magnify brute strength and energy.[1]

Here, then, is a philosophy which not only rejected the traditional assumptions about morals, ethics, and human nature, but which also was in complete revolt against the Victorianism of the "Genteel Tradition" of William Dean Howells. The young writers of the 1890s would not tolerate what they considered to be the overfastidious, prudish character of contemporary writing. The notion that sex was evil and a subject to be avoided at all costs was one that they repudiated as unnatural. The grip of the "Genteel Tradition," where all was sweetness and light, where love was platonic, and sexual intercourse was a degradation of noble womanhood, was to be broken.

It has been contended that an analysis of basic presuppositions has shown that in the field of academic thought, in the writings of the social scientists, the picture of the Progressive era has been distorted by an overemphasis on change. It is the purpose of this and the following chapters to subject some of the literary giants of the age to the same kind of analysis of their basic assumptions. Were these writers in rebellion against the intellectual and moral world of their own day? If so, to what extent did they manage to free themselves from traditional assumptions and value judgments? The first author whose writings will be examined with these questions in mind is a man who is considered by most literary historians to be the foremost rebel of his day—Stephen Crane.

Among the writers who came of age in the 1890s, William Dean Howells considered Crane to be one of the most promising; yet this young genius' approach to man and society was fundamentally at odds with the view held by the genial dean of American letters. Howells' view, while in many ways more sophisticated than that of the social scientists of the day, yet was comparable with theirs in its emphasis on the basic goodness and rationality of the natural man—a natural man capable of sloughing off the debilitating teachings of a corrupt contemporary society, capable of achieving the true society of unselfish devotion to the common good. With Howells and the social theorists, Crane rejected the teachings of the Gospel of Wealth, but he also rejected the easy optimism of the Progressive era. The tension in his writings arose from two basic conflicts in his own mind. The first of these is a tension resulting from his belief in the essential weakness of man as opposed to his insistence on the importance of the human struggle. The second arises from his conviction that man is alone in a neutral universe coupled with his nostalgia for the loving God of his father. Partially because of these tensions, Crane's own life was one of the most tragic in the history of American letters.

Stephen entered the world in 1871 as the fourteenth child of Reverend Jonathan and Mary Peck Crane.[2] Reverend Crane was a humble, sensitive man who worked hard all his life in small New York and New Jersey parishes, and Stephen described his father as being "so simple and good that I often think he didn't know much of anything about humanity."[3] When Reverend Crane died in 1880, Mrs. Crane, an ambitious and dogmatic woman who was descended from a long line of prominent Methodist clergymen, engaged in newspaper work to help support the family.

As a youth Crane seems to have been interested in little but baseball, and when he went to the Hudson River Institute in 1887 he added only poker to his former interests.[4] In September,

1890, he went from the military school to Lafayette College, where he was to prepare for a career as a mining engineer. Here, again, he played baseball, boxed, and smoked endlessly but seldom attended classes, and on the recommendation of the school officials he departed at the end of the first term. From Lafayette he went to Syracuse University, where he added newspaper reporting to his extracurricular activities. Concerning his lack of application in college, Crane later wrote, "Not that I disliked books, but . . . humanity was a much more interesting study. When I ought to have been at recitations I was studying faces on the streets. . . ." [5] Perhaps more important is John Berryman's comment, "It is not easy to think of another important prose-writer or poet so ignorant of traditional literature in English as Stephen Crane was and remained." [6]

After his one year in college, Crane spent the next two years as a struggling writer in New York City, where he explored the slums, lounged in saloons, and reported for the New York *Times* and the New York *Tribune*. His earnings barely paid for food and lodging and frequently not even that. During this period he did meet and become acquainted with Hamlin Garland, and he found time for several one-sided love affairs, all with ladies older, more experienced, and considerably higher in the social scale than he.

Corwin E. Linson, an artist friend of Crane's during his early New York days, gives an interesting description of the author as he appeared during the 1890–91 period.

Crane shed a long rain ulster and was surprisingly reduced in bulk by the process, showing a comparatively slight figure, of medium height but with the good proportions and poise of an athlete. His face, lean but not thin, was topped by rumpled blondish hair that neither convention nor vanity had yet trained. The barely discernible shading of a mustache had just begun to fringe a mouth that smiled with engaging frankness. [7]

Linson also records that Crane disliked the fiction of most of the authors then in vogue, including that of Dickens, Scott, and Mark Twain. He had no use for Ambrose Bierce's work and considered the writings of Robert Louis Stevenson suitable for children but not for adults. The young author apparently spoke highly only of Olive Schreiner's *Story of an African Farm*.[8]

Crane wrote very little about his theories of art and literature, and the only expression of his "creed" is the one he stated in a letter to Lily Branden Munroe on February 29, 1896.

You know, when I left you [1892], I renounced the clever school in literature. It seemed to me that there must be something more in life than to sit and cudgel one's brains for clever and witty expedients. So I developed all alone a little creed of art which I thought was a good one. Later I discovered that my creed was identical with the one of Howells and Garland and in this way I became involved in the beautiful war between those who say that art is man's substitute for nature and we are the most successful in art when we approach the nearest to nature and truth, and those who say—well, I don't know what they say. Then [sic] that they can't say much but they fight villainously and keep Garland and I out of the big magazines.[9]

Crane was a young man of very decided opinions and could be bitingly sarcastic about those who incurred his displeasure, as witnessed by the following tirade against an old keeper of the social code whom he encountered.

There is a feminine mule up here who has roused all the bloodthirst in me and I don't know where it will end. She has no more brains than a pig and all she does is sit in her kitchen and grunt. But every when she grunts something dies howling. It may be a girl's reputation or a political party or the Baptist church but it stops in its tracks and dies. . . . Sunday I took a 13 year old child out driving in a buggy. Monday this mule addresses me in front of the barber's and says, "You was drivin' Frances out yesterday" and grunted. At once all present knew that Frances and I should be hanged on twin gallows for red sins. No man is strong enough to attack this mummy because she is a nice woman. She looks like a dried bean and she has no sense, but she is a nice woman. Right now she is aiming all her artillery at Cornelia's new hat. I have been deprived by heaven of all knowledge of hats but it seems to be a very kindly hat. . . . But we rustle in terror because this maggot goes to and fro grunting about it. . . . Now, my friend, there is a big joke in all this. This lady in her righteousness is just the grave of a stale lust and every boy in town knows it. She accepted ruin at the hands of a farmer when we were all 10 or 11. But she is a nice woman and all her views of all things belong on the table of Moses. No man has power to contradict her. We are all cowards anyhow.[10]

By the middle 1890s Crane was working on his first literary adventures. *Maggie* was approved by Howells, who had many words of encouragement for the young author, but the story was not a success. In 1894, he was also working on the verses which would one day be *The Black Riders*. It was, however, *The Red Badge of Courage* that launched him on his literary career. Americans flocked to read the short Civil War novel and in the first ten months of 1896 thirteen editions were issued.[11] Success, however, did not bring happiness to the brooding young writer. Concerning his success following the public acceptance of *The Red Badge*, Crane wrote:

Now that it is published and the people seem to like it I suppose I ought to be satisfied, but somehow I am not as happy as I was in the uncertain, happy-go-lucky newspaper writing days. I used to dream continually of success then. Now that I have achieved it in some measure it seems like mere flimsy paper.[12]

In New York, the "Crane Myth" was already developing and he was falsely accused of using drugs, of alcoholism, and of general depravity. At least in part, this myth grew out of the mutual dislike existing between Crane and the New York City police department. He was involved in a considerable amount of trouble over defense of several girls (probably prostitutes), at least one of whom he protected from a police charge of soliciting. Crane's concern for these semioutlawed women has become legendary. A friend of the young author told of an experience when he was walking with Crane one night in New York. A young prostitute passed them and Crane bowed to her, asking if she were a stranger in town. She replied that she was, and asked if he could show her anything. "Yes," replied Crane, "I can show you the way out, but if you prefer to remain. . . ." He shrugged. When she had gone by he remarked to his friend, "I wonder if there is a way out." [13]

Following the success of *The Red Badge of Courage,* Crane was thrust into the mold established by his first success and spent most of the remainder of his life seeing and writing about war. In December, 1896, he sailed for Cuba aboard a filibustering vessel which sank off the Florida coast, and with four others he endured the fifty-hour struggle with the sea which he described in his most famous short story, *The Open Boat.* The next year he went to Greece as a war correspondent in the Greco-Turkish War, and shortly after his return he left the United States for England.

His reasons for leaving the United States are unclear. Part of the reason may have been the early and enthusiastic response to his work on the part of the English critics. Then, too, he was interested in the more intellectual climate of the old country where, he said, "you can have an idea . . . without being sent to court for it." [14] But the main reason for his expatriation was probably Cora Taylor Stewart. Crane had met her in 1896, at a time when she had left her English husband and was mistress of a brothel in Jacksonville, Florida. She was a capable, attractive woman and again was somewhat older than Crane. Recently, letters from Sir Norman Stewart, an older brother of Cora's husband, have been discovered and these reveal that she and Donald Stewart were never divorced, thus adding the final conclusive proof that she and Crane could never have been legally married.[15]

In England, Crane formed close friendships with H. G. Wells,

Joseph Conrad, and Harold Frederic, another expatriate who was not married to the woman with whom he lived. Crane was also on amiable terms with Henry James. This friendship, however, appears to have been on a personal rather than an artistic basis, for although James liked Crane's work the admiration was not reciprocal.

When war broke out in April, 1898, between the United States and Spain, Crane departed immediately for Cuba, where he served as a war correspondent for *The World.* Despite the fact that he wrote few dispatches and missed nearly all the real engagements, he did win official recognition for coolness under fire in the skirmish at Guantanamo and was described by Richard Harding Davis as the best correspondent in Cuba. All accounts of Crane in Cuba reveal a man with little fear for his life. Berryman feels that "it is almost certain that Crane tried to be killed, and it is probable that he consciously tried to." [16] Whether or not Crane desired death, he did emerge from the war with his health broken. Dazed by quinine and worn physically beyond his strength, the young expatriate paid his last visit to America, where the charges of drug addiction, alcoholism, and depravity, supplemented by police harassment, caused him to leave New York permanently.

Back in England, he and Cora spent his last year in a dilapidated, medieval manor in Sussex. Here they entertained H. G. Wells and the Conrads, and despite a host of uninvited and unwelcome guests Crane managed to do a great deal of writing until he once again became ill. After a hurried journey to Badenweiler in the Black Forest to improve his health, he died of tuberculosis at the age of twenty-eight years and seven months.

In his short working lifetime (only about eight productive years), this intense young author produced twelve volumes of prose and verse, and carved for himself a definite niche in the history of American letters. A sensitive, intelligent writer, he obviously rejected the easy optimism both of the Gospel of

Wealth and of the Progressive social theorists. Here was a cross-current to the prevailing climate of opinion, an alternative answer to the crisis of the 1890s. It will be the purpose of this chapter to elaborate in some detail Crane's opinions about man and society and to see to what extent he was able to free himself from the traditional concepts.

Crane is usually included among the school of emerging writers in the America of 1890–1917 who, influenced by the naturalism of Zola, wrote of man as the product of natural forces and as devoid of free will. In the first place this conclusion must be qualified by the fact that many of Crane's minor works show no evidence of determinism at all.[17] More importantly, Crane did not accept the notion, entertained by both Spencer and Zola, that the deterministic scheme of nature would lead to ultimate progress. Both God and nature, he felt, were totally indifferent to man and his aspirations. In *The Black Riders,* for example, he pictured the world as slipping away while God's back was turned to make meaningless voyages upon the sea of the universe.[18] A similar sentiment is expressed in the following poem from *War is Kind.*

> A man said to the universe:
> "Sir, I exist!"
> "However," replied the universe,
> "The fact has not created in me
> A sense of obligation." [19]

The indifference of nature to human struggle in this meaningless world is also an important aspect of the short story *Death and the Child.*[20] This story, set in Greece during the war which Crane witnessed there, portrayed the people in a panic, fleeing from the scene of battle. They seemed to be tumbled forward as if caught in a torrent, one couple even forgetting their young son in their haste to reach safety. But the mountains, the bay, and the sky were serene. "The sea, the sky, and the hills combined in their grandeur to term this misery inconsequent." [21] As he went toward the battle, Peza, the main character, "wondered if the universe took cognizance of him to an important degree," and he finally concluded "that the accidental destruction of an individual, Peza by name, would perhaps be nothing at all." [22] To the universe it was all very unimportant; nature is indifferent, both to the death of an individual and to the misery of the mass.

Life itself is tragic, meaningless, inscrutable. In another short story a sheepherder named Bill, a man who had had many jobs, one who had been hardened to life, was warned by some Mexicans that they were either going to drive him off the range or kill him. A stranger rode into Bill's camp during the battle which took place. Bill was killed, as were several Mexicans, and the stranger rode off again.[23] Where is the meaning, where the moral? There is none. The world is

> A reptile-swarming place,
> Peopled, otherwise, with grimaces,
> Shrouded above in black inpenetrableness.[24]

The incompatibility of Crane's indifferent universe with the progressive determinism of Spencer and Zola is quite obvious.

No doubt much of Crane's apparent sense of the futility of life arose from the young writer's sense of conflict between the religious orthodoxy of his early training and the realities of life as he saw them. This conflict received its most direct expression in a collection of poems entitled *The Black Riders*. Crane was extremely fond of this collection and stated that in it he had tried to set forth his ideas about life in general.[25] He was insistent that when the volume appeared in print it should contain all of the poems on religion, even if it meant that the scheduled publishers would refuse to handle the collection at all. He wrote:

I should absolutely refuse to have my poems printed without many of those which you just as absolutely mark "No." It seems to me that you cut all the ethical sense out of the book. . . . The ones which refer to God, I believe you condemn altogether. I am obliged to have them in when my book is printed.[26]

It is important for understanding the mind of the young poet that he felt his poems contained "ethical sense," and despite the fact that he was, as usual, almost penniless, he was willing to forego publication rather than have the "ethical sense" deleted.

Granville Hicks and Amy Lowell have both noted that one of the main themes of *The Black Riders* is the rejection of the wrathful God of orthodox, Old Testament theology who intervenes in the affairs of men. Their assertion that the God pictured in *The Black Riders* is the vindictive deity of the Old Testament is supported by a number of the poems. In one poem, Crane, after quoting the verse that the sins of the father shall be visited on the children, wrote:

> Well, then, I hate Thee, unrighteous picture;
> Wicked image, I hate Thee;
> So, strike with Thy vengeance
> The heads of those little men
> Who come blindly.
> It will be a brave thing.[27]

In another poem Crane rejects both the God who persecutes men and the people who cry out when one man strikes back.

> A god in wrath
> Was beating a man;
> He cuffed him loudly
> With thunderous blows
> That rang and rolled over the earth.
> All people came running.
> The man screamed and struggled,
> And bit madly at the feet of the god.
> The people cried,
> "Ah, what a wicked man!"
> And —
> "Ah, what a redoubtable god!" [28]

Similar sentiments are expressed in less violent form in the other volume of Crane's poetry, *War is Kind,* where God is asked if he has ever made a just man. He says yes, He has made three. Two are dead, and, as for the third, if one listens one will hear the thud of his defeat.[29]

This poem, like many other works of the young rebel, pictures God as a cold being, indifferent to man rather than an actual oppressor. Crane's most complete rejection of the idea that God intervenes in human affairs was presented in "Man Adrift on a Slim Spar," an uncollected poem which was discovered in 1928. In this poem a man was floating in the ocean on the spar of a wrecked ship while wave after wave washed over him—and God did nothing. Crane was not denying God the power to act, for he wrote:

> The seas are in the hollow of Thy hand;
> Oceans may be turned to a spray
> Raining down through the stars
> Because of a gesture of pity toward a babe.[30]

Yet God did not help the man whose pale hand was sliding from the polished spar. Why? Because "God is cold." [31]

If this were the extent of Crane's poetic statements on religion, the critics who portray him as a rebel against religion would be guilty of no more than literary exaggeration. But this is not all, for Crane's rejection of the Old Testament God of the Mountain did not mean that he was able to separate himself from his religious heritage. Van Wyck Brooks was perhaps the first to make a clear distinction between the two Gods that appear in *The Black Riders,*[32] an insight that was developed by Daniel Hoffman. Hoffman correctly contends that Crane knew little, if anything, of scientific determinism; that on the contrary he was of an essentially religious nature, inheriting from his father the belief in a merciful, indwelling God.[33]

This personal, indwelling deity of Crane's is the God who rises from his throne to embrace the little blade of grass that can think of no noble deeds it has accomplished. He is the God who "whispers in the heart so softly that the soul pauses, making no noise. . . ."[34] Crane wrote of strange peddlers holding forth their little images of the gods they prefer, but he says, "Hence! Leave me with mine own,/ And take yours away. . . ."[35] His own God, as opposed to the wrathful God of orthodoxy, is clearly seen in this poem from *The Black Riders.*

> A man went before a strange God—
> The God of many men, sadly wise.
> And the Deity thundered loudly,
> Fat with rage, and puffing,
> "Kneel, mortal, and cringe
> And grovel and do homage
> To My Particularly Sublime Majesty."
>
> The man fled.
>
> Then the man went to another God—
> The God of his inner thoughts.
> And this one looked at him
> With soft eyes
> Lit with infinite comprehension,
> And said, "My poor child!" [36]

Similarly, Crane presented a "blustering God" who stomps arcoss the sky and casts spears at men's hearts. "I fear You not, puffing braggart," he wrote, "So threaten not, Thou, with Thy bloody spears,/ Else Thy sublime ears shall hear curses." But then he continued:

> Withal, there is One whom I fear;
> I fear to see grief upon that face.
> Perchance, friend, He is not your God;
> If so, spit upon Him.
> By it you will do no profanity.
> But I—
> Ah, sooner would I die
> Than see tears in those eyes of my soul.[37]

Among other unpublished poems by Crane, Hoffman's book contains one called "The Battle Hymn," which was later found in the saddlebags Stephen had used during the Spanish-American War. It seems to contradict the notion that God does not interfere in the affairs of men, which Crane had expressed in "Man Adrift on a Slim Spar."

> All-feeling God, hear in the war-night
> The rolling voice of a nation:
> . . . . .
> Bend and see a people, O, God,
> A people rebuked, accursed,
> By him of the many lungs
> And by him of the bruised weary war-drum
> . . . . .
> Suffer us to grope and bleed apace
> For the wisdom is Thine.
> . . . . .
> —And if the path, the new path, leads straight—
> Then—O, God—then bare the great bronze arm;
> Swing high the blaze of the chained stars
> And let them look and heed
> For we go, we go in a lunge of a long blue corps
> And—to Thee we commit our lifeless sons
> . . . . .
> For the seas shall not bar us;
> The capped mountains shall not hold us back
> We shall sweep and swarm through jungle and pool,
> Then let the savage one bend his high chin
> To see on his breast, the sullen glow of death-metals
> For we know and we say our gift.
> His price is death, deep doom.
> (He shall be white amid the smoking cane.) [38]

This is very strange talk for a man who was supposed to have rejected God!

From these examples one can see the tremendous emotional

strain that existed in the mind of this young writer, a tension that arose from his dual commitment to the past and to the future. He was aware that he could not accept the dogmas of orthodox Christianity, but he could not forget the personal, benevolent, God of his childhood. Here was no simple rejection of the old for the new, no neat change from a religious to a scientific orientation, but a crisis of the mind, the individual mind, that could not be solved by an intellectual acceptance of new ideas.

In the light of Crane's views on man in relation to God and nature, it is interesting to examine the extent of his cosmic determinism as it is expressed in some of his stories. One of the places in which Crane dealt allegorically with the question of free will was in the collection of brief stories, *The Sullivan County Sketches.* The central character in these stories was "the little man," a rather insignificant being who, through fear, greatly exaggerated the problems that confronted him, only to strut and brag when he emerged victorious. Actually, in only two sketches was his success or failure dependent solely upon his own freedom to will and act: *The Cry of a Huckleberry Pudding,*[39] in which he becomes ill from his own cooking; and *Killing His Bear,*[40] in which he successfully shot the animal. In the remainder of the sketches, his success or failure was dependent largely upon chance. In *Tent in Agony,*[41] he was saved from a bear because the bear became entangled in a tent, rolled down a hill, and ran away. Here, as in most of the other stories where the little man triumphed, his success was dependent upon the workings of chance-accident-fate.

A more familiar story in which Crane dealt with the problems of fate and free will is *The Blue Hotel.*[42] In this story a Swede, an Easterner, and a cowboy were at the Blue Hotel with Scully, the owner, and his son, Johnnie. The Swede, who had just arrived, insisted that one of the others was going to kill him and was prevented from leaving only when Scully plied him with whiskey. Later he accused Johnnie of cheating at cards. By this time the others were completely irritated by the Swede, and in the ensuing fight they cheered loudly for Johnnie. But the Swede finally won the fight, left the hotel, and went to a bar where he demanded that people drink with him. When he became too insistent, a gambler stabbed him.

If Crane had ended the story at this point one would assume that the petulant Swede got what was coming to him—that he was the agent of his own destruction. This would seem to be the implication of the following paragraph, which concludes the story proper.

The corpse of the Swede, alone in the saloon, had its eyes fixed upon a dreadful legend that dwelt atop of the cash-machine: "This registers the amount of your purchase." [43]

But Crane did not stop there. In a two-page epilogue, the cowboy and the Easterner again met to rehash the events of the story. When the cowboy insisted that the Swede got what he was asking for, the Easterner disagreed. Johnnie had been cheating and he, the Easterner, had seen him but had "refused to stand up and be a man." He blamed them all for what happened.

This poor gambler isn't even a noun. He is a kind of an adverb. Every sin is the result of a collaboration. We, five of us, have collaborated in the murder of this Swede. Usually there are from a dozen to forty women really involved in every murder, but in this case it seems to be only five men—you, I, Johnnie, old Scully; and that fool of an unfortunate gambler came merely as a culmination, the apex of a human movement, and gets all the punishment. [44]

Crane's conclusion, then, would seem to be that the death of the Swede was a combination of human action or, on the part of the Easterner, failure to act, and circumstances. But human action—free will—was certainly a positive factor in the tale.[45]

One final example of the stories in which Crane dealt most

explicitly with the question of man's place in the cosmos is *The Open Boat*.[46] At the opening of the story, four men—the cook, the captain, an oiler, and a correspondent—were afloat in a small boat after the sinking of their ship. Crane did not say what had happened to the ship, so one must assume that they were thrown into the sea because of an accident—the work of fate. Once they were in the sea Crane made it very clear that nature was flatly indifferent to them as they rowed their small boat toward the mainland. When they came within sight of land it was impossible for them to get through the surf, and they had to turn the boat back out to sea to keep from being swamped. After all hope of rescue from shore faded away, they were forced to run the boat into the surf and swim for shore. All of them finally arrived safely except the oiler, whose outstretched hand lay touching the shore. He alone was dead.

Several important aspects of Crane's philosophy are dramatized in this story, but the central question here is whether these men had free will or were simply the victims of fate and an indifferent universe. As in the poems and stories cited earlier, Crane left little room for doubt about the indifference of nature. To the correspondent, the tower on the shore represented "the serenity of nature amid the struggle of the individual. . . . She did not seem cruel to him then, nor beneficent, nor treacherous, nor wise. But she was indifferent, flatly indifferent." [47]

What is man's reaction to all this? Crane wrote:

When it occurs to a man that nature does not regard him as important, and that she feels she would not maim the universe by disposing of him, he at first wishes to throw bricks at the temple, and he hates deeply the fact that there are no bricks and no temples.[48]

In other words, his reactions are defiance and frustration.

This is particularly true when he is faced with the caprice of fate as well as with the neutrality of nature. In this story Crane makes a distinction, which is implicit in his other works, between nature, which is stable and indifferent, and fate, which seems to be utterly arbitrary and impulsive. When it looked to the men in the boat as if, after incredible struggle, they might be drowned within sight of shore, Crane speculated on their thoughts in this fashion.

"If I am going to be drowned . . . why, in the name of the seven mad gods who rule the sea, was I allowed to come thus far and contemplate sand and trees? Was I brought here merely to have my nose dragged away as I was about to nibble the sacred cheese of life? It is preposterous. If this old ninny-woman, Fate, cannot do better than this, she should be deprived of the management of men's fortunes. She is an old hen who knows not her intention. If she has decided to drown me, why did she not do it in the beginning and save me all this trouble? The whole affair is absurd.—But no; she cannot drown me. Not after all this work." Afterward the man might have had an impulse to shake his fist at the clouds. "Just you drown me, now, and then hear what I call you!" [49]

Again, man seems to be helpless in his rage. But what about the action and logic of the story? Fate undoubtedly landed the first blow by casting these men adrift upon the sea. There, faced with the indifference of nature, their first reaction was frustration. But their next response was action. The captain, using his nautical knowledge, calmly and intelligently took command and directed his miniature crew to the brink of safety. All of the men acted rationally and effectively to make the best of the given conditions. So men can make decisions, and act according to those decisions, in a crisis situation.

But willing and acting in the face of a neutral cosmos does not preclude frustration by inscrutable fate. While the others were saved largely by the joint action of the group, the oiler, who had worked hardest and had been the least excitable member of the crew, died on the very brim of safety. Here, then, is Crane's view of man in his relations with the Cosmos. Given the neutrality of nature, man can express his relative freedom in action, but the success or failure of that action is not totally dependent upon the extent of his efforts or his moral worth, but also upon the decision of fate. In spite of his freedom to will and act within a context, man in his relations with the universe faces ultimate frustration. Life is essentially tragic, but tragedy is possible only when there is not absolute determinism. The essential indifference of God and nature means that man has relative free will and freedom of choice as far as cosmic forces are involved. To this extent Crane remained within the American tradition, and the path to progress through the faith of the Progressive social thinkers in human creativity remains open.

But what about the force of the social environment? Does man for Crane escape cosmic determinism only to be bound by the institutions, traditions, and socioeconomic conditions of his own society? Actually, man in his relationship to society was not one of Crane's major themes and, as Hoffman has pointed out, "one feels the presence of society as a complex inter-relationship of persons and classes only in *Maggie* and *The Monster*. . . ."[50] Still there has been much discussion of whether or not Crane was a social critic, and this problem must be considered if one is to arrive at an over-all view of his concept of man and society. If one accepts the position that Crane was in active revolt against his society and had hopes of substantially improving man's condition, then one must concede that Crane did not disagree with traditional interpretations of man as much as the preceding part of this chapter would lead one to believe. Both sides in the argument have substantial evidence for their position.

The main evidence cited by those who consider Crane a social critic is contained in his first short novel, *Maggie*.[51] Maggie was a child of the Bowery. Her mother and her father were both alcoholics, and her brother was a young tough. Maggie left her miserable home with Pete, a bartender and ladies' man. When he tired of her she tried to return home but was repulsed, and consequently was forced to try the life of a streetwalker. She proved a miserable failure in this role and ended her life in the East River. Russel B. Nye and the others who have interpreted Crane as a social reformer have argued that the underlying causes of Maggie's fall—poverty, tenement life, and all the rest—are things remediable by intelligent social reform.[52] In this they agree with Berryman's contention that *Maggie* showed "the determinant power of the environment." [53] This argument is given strong support by the inscription which Crane wrote in a copy of *Maggie* which he sent to Dr. Lucius L. Burton in 1893.

It is inevitable that you will be greatly shocked by the book but continue, please, with all possible courage, to the end. For it tries to show that environment is a tremendous thing in the world and frequently shapes lives regardless. If one proves that theory one makes room in Heaven for all sorts of souls, notably an occasional street girl, who are not confidently expected to be there by many excellent people.[54]

This letter would seem to imply not only that the environment exerts a strong influence, but also, since one is affected by the environment, that moral responsibility—at least in the traditional form—is gone.

These arguments which picture Crane as a reformer are considerably strengthened by the report of his friend, Linson, on the author's reaction to the lack of a receptive audience for *Maggie*. He quotes Crane as follows:

I sent copies to some preachers who were maniacs for reform—not a word from one of 'em.

I wrote across the cover so that they couldn't miss it, that if they read it, they would see its sense. I knew they'd jump at first, but I hoped they were intelligent. You'd think the book came straight from hell and they smelled the smoke. Not one of them gave me a word! Icebergs, OK, flints! [55]

Linson also tells of Crane's indignation at the sights they witnessed when they went through a Pennsylvania coal mine together. "Here at the mines were children who moved Steve

profoundly. He regarded the presence of these little 'slate-pick-
ers' as a crime against nature." [56] *McClure's Magazine* deleted
from Crane's article the passages where he waxed eloquent
about the conditions in the mines and attacked the mine owners.
His reaction when he read the censored article shows his social
concern. "The birds didn't want the truth after all. Why the hell
did they send me up there then? Do they want the public to
think the coal mines gilded ball-rooms with the miners eating
ice cream in boiled shirt-fronts?" [57]

And in 1892 Crane reported a parade of the Junior Order of
United American Mechanics in which he pictured them as dull
but honest laborers confronting the unprincipled Asbury Park
money-changers. Somehow this article slipped by the editor,
and at its appearance in the New York *Tribune* attacks came
from all sides. The laborers resented having their parade referred to as "the most awkward, ungainly, uncut and uncarved
procession that ever raised clouds of dust on sun-beaten streets,"
and the average Asbury Park colonist took exception to the
comment that he was a man "to whom a dollar, when held close
to his eye, often shuts out any impression he may have had that
other people possess rights." [58] Garland said Crane showed him
the article after he was fired, and Garland asked him what he
expected. Crane's reply again showed a strong social consciousness.

I guess I didn't stop to consider that. I was so hot at the sight of those
poor, misshapen fools shouting for monopoly that I gave no thought
to its effect on my own fortunes. I don't know that it would have made
much difference if I had. I wanted to say those things anyway.[59]

One need not accept Schoberlin's contention that in the Asbury
Park article Crane launched "the first attack of his personal war,
pursued relentlessly and fearlessly so long as he lived, against
social and moral injustice," to admit that the article, and the
statement to Garland, do show strong feelings.[60]

Crane's treatment of poverty, while it was certainly not one of his major themes, did differ greatly from the traditional treatment of that subject in American literature. In his study of American attitudes toward poverty, Robert Bremner showed that the subject was generally handled in the late nineteenth century as a temporary condition out of which the hero or heroine might rise.

Most popular writers continued to portray the poor with pity strongly tinged with condescension. They portrayed the victims of poverty indulgently, delighting in their childlike simplicity, ignorance, and uncouthness—in all the outward signs of their inferiority. There was something humorous about the usually ill-fated efforts of the poor to become like other people; that is, to obtain education, respectability, and security.[61]

But the younger writers, among them Crane, did not find the slums a place where the nobility of human nature would find nourishing fruit and the individual could develop his innate goodness. They found it offensive. They rejected the "light touch, the specious felicity, and optimism of the fabricators of popular fiction." [62] Bremner's analysis supports those who interpret Crane as a social critic devoted to changing the environment that he might improve man.

Some of Crane's stories of the slums definitely do show that he had sympathy for the people who lived there. In *An Eloquence of Grief,* he related a courtroom scene in which a young woman was arraigned by the judge for stealing silk clothes from her employers.[63] Though the story was told in a very straightforward manner, Crane's sympathy for the girl was obvious. The same was true of *Men in the Storm,* a story about a group of men seeking shelter from a raging storm in a five-cents-a-night, charitable house.[64] Similarly, his sympathy was evident in *An Ominous Baby,* where a very small, very dirty boy of the slums wandered into a better district.[65] There he took a toy fire engine from another boy and ran away with it, "weeping with the air of a wronged one who has at last succeeded in achieving his rights." [66] The revolutionary social implications of this story, however, are unusual in Crane's writings. Much more characteristic is the simple note of a class oppressed, which was heard by the youth of *Experiment in Misery,* in the moan of a man sleeping in a flophouse.[67] Crane wrote that the moan was "the protest of the wretch who feels the touch of the imperturbable granite wheels, and who then cries with an impersonal eloquence, with a strength not from him, giving voice to the wail of a whole section, a class, a people." [68]

Crane could also express extreme bitterness against the men who made their financial success at the expense of others.

> The successful man has thrust himself
> Through the water of the years,
> Reeking wet with mistakes—
> Bloody mistakes;
> Slimed with victories over the lesser,
> A figure thankful on the shore of money.
> Then, with the bones of fools
> He buys silken banners
> Limned with his triumphant face;
> With the skins of wise men
> He buys the trivial bows of all.
> Flesh painted with marrow
> Contributes a coverlet,
> A coverlet for his contented slumber.
> · · · · ·
> Complacent, smiling,
> He stands heavily on the dead.
> Erect on a pillar of skulls
> He declaims his trampling of babes.[69]

One of his poems is also a satirical commentary on the Gospel of Wealth itself. The trees rained flowers in the garden and these were gathered in great heaps by those with opportunity and skill, so that there were none left for the feeble. The children's tutor went to the father complaining that this was unjust. But the father replied:

> "Not so, small sage!
> This thing is just.
> For, look you,
> Are not they who possess the flowers
> Stronger, bolder, shrewder
> Than they who have none?
> Why should the strong—
> The beautiful strong—
> Why should they not have the flowers?"

After reflecting, the tutor had to admit, "The stars are displaced/ By this towering wisdom." [70]

Those who argue that Crane was at heart a social reformer have some evidence and some distinguished scholars on their side. So, too, do those who deny this assertion. Lars Ahnebrink contends that Crane was not a reformer. "Nor did he give any indication of faith in a change of the existing conditions, for he was suspicious of social programs, and he refused to believe in the doctrine of progress." [71] Along the same line Alfred Kazin has suggested:

The surest thing one can say about Crane is that he did not care which way the world went. No one was ever less the reforming mind; revolutions were something foreigners attempted that Hearst would pay good money to report. He accepted the world always, hating it always, plotting his way through it alone with a contempt that was close to pain.[72]

Crane was never fond of reformers. If his opinion of Frances Willard, a famous reformer of the period, is any indication, this suspicion of reformers had very early beginnings. While at Syracuse, Crane refused to meet her for the simple reason that "he thought Miss Willard a fool." [73] Nor did he change his mind, for he later said of her, "Frances Willard is one of those wonderful people who can tell right from wrong for everybody from the polar cap to the equator. Perhaps it never struck her that people differ from her. I have loved myself passionately now and then but Miss Willard's affair with Miss Willard should be stopped by the police." [74]

Just as he considered reformers to be busybodies, so he considered charity to be a balm with which the rich eased their consciences.

> Charity, thou art a lie,
> A toy of women,
> A pleasure of certain men.
> In the presence of justice,
> Lo, the walls of the temple
> Are visible
> Through thy form of sudden shadows.[75]

If reformers were busybodies and charity was useless, what did Crane feel was at the core of the slum problem? What was at the heart of Bowery life? Crane answered this question directly in a letter to Catherine Harris on November 12, 1896. This letter is so central to Crane's thought on the subject and to his view of man that it must be quoted at length.

Mrs. Howells was right in telling you that I have spent a great deal of time on the East Side and that I have no opinion of missions. That —to you—may not be a valid answer since perhaps you have been informed that I am not very friendly to Christianity as seen around town. I do not think that much can be done with the Bowery as long as the . . . [blurred] . . . are in their present state of conceit. A person who thinks himself superior to the rest of us because he has no job and no pride and no clean clothes is as badly conceited as Lillian Russell. In a story of mine called "An Experiment in Misery" I tried to make plain that the root of Bowery life is a sort of cowardice. Perhaps I mean a lack of ambition or to willingly be knocked flat and accept the licking. The missions for children are another thing and if you will have Mr. Rockefeller give me a hundred street cars and some money I will load all the babes off to some pink world where cows can lick their noses and they will never see their families any more. . . . I had no other purpose in writing "Maggie" than to show people to people as they seem to me. If that be evil, make the most of it.[76]

The only environmentalism that occurs in this explicit statement is the part about the children, and it is difficult to tell if Crane was being satirical about the whole notion of saving the children by removing them from the slum environment or if he simply felt it would be impossible to accomplish. It certainly leaves little hope for any kind of social progress. The root of Bowery life is cowardice, or the lack of ability to withstand the knocks of fortune. This means that the essence of the problem is personal; it is contained in the men themselves; it is a flaw in the nature of some men. The same idea is presented by Crane in a number of his stories.

In the letter quoted above, Crane referred to *An Experiment in Misery* as containing these ideas. This is the story of a youth who decided to see what it felt like to be a bum. He dressed accordingly and spent the night in a cheap flophouse, observed, and listened. It was here that he heard the "wail of a whole section, a class, a people," which was mentioned before. The following morning, seated on a park bench with one of the men of the Bowery, he saw the classic skyline of New York—

to him emblematic of a nation forcing its regal head into the clouds, throwing no downward glances; in the sublimity of its aspirations ignoring the wretches who may flounder at its feet. The roar of the city in his ear was to him the confusion of strange tongues, babbling heedlessly; it was the clink of coin, the voice of the city's hopes, which were to him no hopes.[77]

Crane did not say that it is right for society to pursue its material goals, forgetting those who fall in the race. It is not right, but it *is*. What he wanted to stress, however, is the acceptance of their lives by those who are left behind; their refusal to look to the future.

This attitude can be seen more clearly in *Maggie* than in the example Crane himself mentioned, and it seems to rest fundamentally on two points. First, there is the feeling of superiority manifested by Maggie's brother, Jim, by Pete, and by the other toughs of the neighborhood who thought they knew what life is all about. Crane's portrait of the bartender is a particularly bitter caricature.

His mannerisms stamped him as a man who had a correct sense of his personal superiority. There were valour and contempt for circumstances in the glance of his eye. He waved his hands like a man of the world who dismisses religion and philosophy, and says "Rats!" He had certainly seen everything and with each curl of his lip he declared that it amounted to nothing.[78]

. . . . .

When he said, "Ah, what d' hell!" his voice was burdened with disdain for the inevitable and contempt for anything that fate might compel him to endure. Maggie perceived that here was the ideal man.[79]

Yet, simultaneously, these same people felt that the world was taking advantage of them, and the irony of this dichotomy was obvious to Crane. The second point, which can be seen clearly in the last part of the above quotation, is an attitude of submission, or perhaps more accurately, the acceptance of what Crane considered to be false standards. They were content with almost anything. They had no vision and no ambition to strive for more than enough to eat and drink. Maggie, for instance, was overwhelmed by the false grandeur of Pete, the archposeur.

The same ideas are to be found in Crane's other short novel of the East Side, *George's Mother*. George showed the trait of self-pity which Crane found characteristic of Bowery life. And the characteristics of bravado, ability to avoid work, contempt for their contemporaries in life, are revealed in his satirical treatment of the corner gang, whose fatalism and supposedly worldly wisdom attracted George, at least for a time.[80] Since these are the attitudes Crane found in the people of the Bowery, it is not strange that one of his biographers can quote him as defining pity as "a virtue almost useless in ninety-nine cases out of a hundred. . . ."[81]

Crane's rejection of environment as a determinative power can be further seen in some of his letters. Beer reports that although Crane disliked most of Zola's work, he was pleased by the Frenchman's portrait of Nana. Beer quotes him as saying, "This girl in Zola is a real streetwalker. I mean, she does not fool around making excuses for her career. You must pardon me if I cannot agree that every painted woman on the streets of New York was brought there by some evil man."[82] Why were they on the street in Crane's opinion? They were there because "most streetwalkers would be demimondianes [sic] if they had money. Lots of women are just naturally unchaste and all you jays know it. . . ."[83]

Further evidence against the hypothesis that Crane was an environmentalist is a statement in a letter he wrote to Nellie Crouse in 1896.

I swear by the real aristocrat. The man whose forefathers were men of courage, sympathy and wisdom, is usually one who will stand the strain whatever it may be. He is like a thoroughbred horse. His nerves may be high and he will do a lot of jumping often but in the crises he settles down and becomes the most reliable and enduring of created things. [84]

On the basis of the foregoing arguments it is impossible to accept Nye's contention that Crane believed in free will with regard to the social world. Nye has contended that Crane felt that "the forces of society, those which lead to the social evil seen in Maggie and other of his stories, are man-made forces, and can be controlled by man, who set them in motion. The world of nature we can only face with stoicism; the world of society, however, can be reshaped—progress is possible on the human and social level." [85] But it has been argued here that Crane did not believe the basic problem was economic dislocation and tenement life—environmental influences. Does this mean that man in society is unbound? Has Crane, by another route than Nye's, saved man's traditional free will in society?

As usual, Crane's answer is not direct and must be pieced together from a variety of sources. The force which binds these people, when they are bound, is not the environment as environment is generally understood, but the moral code and the clash between that idealized code and the reality of the society in which they live. This is what restricts the operation of man's will in society, and perhaps this is what Crane meant when he said "environment is a tremendous thing," not economic dislocation and sweatshops as such. In regard to Crane's slum stories, C. C. Walcutt notes the fact that "these people are victimized by their ideals of moral propriety which are so utterly inapplicable to their lives that they constitute a social insanity. . . . Their freedom is limited as much by their conventional beliefs as by their poverty. . . ." [86]

Maggie, Crane wrote, "blossomed in a mud-puddle," yet "none of the dirt of Rum Alley seemed to be in her veins." [87] She was essentially untouched by the environment, and there was no degeneration by natural laws because Maggie remained an innocent to the end. Although living her life amid poverty and squalor, she thought nothing about it until she met Pete. He seemed to offer security, or at least a haven in the storm of life that was her lot at home. Her sexual awakening, if she ever had one, was not mentioned. With Pete she "imagined a future rose-tinted. . . ." [88] But Maggie lived in society and she had broken the moral code of that society, a code which might not be applicable to the situation but one that operated with crushing force nonetheless. Here is the real force in *Maggie* that determines conduct and cannot be opposed without disaster. Maggie could exercise freedom of the will by violating the code, but once she did so the motors of social convention were put into action and her defeat was certain.

The breadth of this code which gives man a choice only between conformity or destruction is shown in Crane's treatment of Maggie's brother, Jimmy. As both boy and man he adhered to a code of conduct which determined his actions. By this code he stood and fought the children from Devil's Row and was degraded when dragged home by his father. He never backed down from a fight, he had loyalty to his kind, and he looked down on all "well dressed men." [89] Jimmy did not worry about the girls he had seduced, but Pete was his friend and "Jimmy had an idea it wasn't common courtesy for a friend to come to one's home and ruin one's sister." [90] Though he publicly damned his sister "that he might appear on a higher social plane," [91] he was not convinced that she had, of her own free will, chosen the wrong path. The code determined his actions, not his inner thoughts.

The two themes which were operative in *Maggie*—the dreamer versus reality and the force of the social code—were handled separately in two of Crane's other major works. George Kelsey, in *George's Mother,* was the dreamer, and Dr. Trescott, in *The Monster,* was the violator of the social code.[92]

George Kelsey was a young, healthy lad who lived in an apartment with his mother, an old woman, gnarled by work but with a strong personality. At one time they had lived in the country, and George was essentially apart from the environment of the Bowery. When the story opens, George is working and all is well. But he was a dreamer, and the facts of his life failed to measure up to the dreams which society had led him to expect as the rewards of the hard-working and virtuous life. George met an old acquaintance and his companions, and with them he began to drink. When these men failed to appreciate him sufficiently, he fell in with the Bowery toughs. At the conclusion there appeared to be a way out for George, precipitated by alienation from the gang and the death of his mother, but over the transom sounded the voice of young Johnnie, the typical Bowery boy, who apparently would follow the same route.

It would seem that George had a great deal of free will. Neither instincts, forces, fate, nor institutions seemed to be pushing him unduly. More than anything else, his dreams of grandeur led him astray. He emerged somewhat battered, but since he had not essentially violated the code of the society in which he lived, he was not destroyed. Visions of wooing his dream girl and of impressing the world with his wit and genius were, however, shattered on the rocks of reality.

Dr. Trescott, in Crane's major study of society, *The Monster*, was not so fortunate as George. The doctor had a Negro groom named Henry Johnson, who was a good-looking, dapper, young fellow and popular with the rest of the Negroes in town. Henry was also devoted to the Trescotts' young son, and when a fire broke out in the Trescott home while the doctor was out on a call, Henry rushed into the blazing house after the boy. He managed to get him to a side door, where he was pulled to safety by his returning father. Henry, however, had fallen in the doctor's laboratory, and an exploding bottle of acid destroyed his face and much of his mind. While the townspeople expected Henry to die, he was a hero, but when he recovered, horribly disfigured, and people heard of his appearance, their attitude changed. Dr. Trescott boarded Henry, who was perfectly harmless, with a Negro family that was terrified of him, until one night he got out and frightened the townspeople out of their wits. Despite the urgings of the pillars of the community, the doctor refused to send the harmless creature to an institution and made a place for him above the stable behind his own home. When this occurred, the town turned against the physician; he lost his patients and found his wife socially ostracized.

Did the doctor in this story have free will in the social situation? It would seem that he had limited free will, for he could either follow the dictates of his own conscience or he could succumb to popular pressure. He had been driven by accident or fate into a position where he had to make a decision which he would have preferred not to make. He, too, faced a critical choice. But, unlike Maggie and George Kelsey, the doctor was not a dreamer; there seemed to be nothing directly determining his choice and he did recognize that a choice existed. Tragedy entered the life of the Trescotts, but it did so, not because of the accident, but because of the doctor's choice to save Henry and later to become his protector. When the doctor exercised his will, he was destroyed by the operation of the social code. But he became a man in Crane's conception of that term.

The heart of Crane's viewpoint seems to be that man in society is subject to illusions that are at variance with reality, and that human conduct is sometimes directed by a moral code which has little applicability to the lives of the participants. Man can break the code, he can depart from the social norm, and to this extent he has free will; but if he does so he must expect defeat at the hands of social prejudices. This Crane had certainly learned from his own experience!

Still, man can exert his free will in defiance of society and Crane's position here was in line with the old American tradition that the individual is essentially free from the control of institutions and traditions. So, while it is true that Crane expressed indignation over social and economic injustice, it is not true that he felt these were the cause of the human dilemma. Crane made this quite clear in the letter to Catherine Harris where he stated that the root of Bowery life is cowardice, a lack of the ability to take the knocks of fortune and rise from them. This means that the root of the problem is personal; it is contained in the men themselves. This conclusion is supported by Crane's stories and by the fact that few of his plots deal with the problem of social evils—a fact that is in line with his basically religious orientation with its emphasis on the "inner-directed man." Hoffman has explained this as follows:

His religious training had led him to consider most important the moral fortitude of the individual man, whatever his temporal circumstances. Crane consequently considered secondary the sort of social problems which the radical young Garland and the older socialistic Howells made the subjects of their fiction.[93]

Crane, in other words, was more interested in the inner struggle of man alone in the universe than with man against, or even in, society. This is clearly shown in another of Crane's letters to Nellie Crouse.

From this moment to that deathbed may be a short time or a long one but at any rate it means a life of labor and sorrow. I do not confront it [life] blithely. I confront it with desperate resolution. There is not even much hope in my attitude. I do not even expect to do good. But I expect to make a sincere, desperate, lonely battle to remain true to my conception of my life and the way it should be lived, and if this plan can accomplish anything, it shall be accomplished. It is not a fine prospect. . . .
   When I speak of a battle I do not mean want, and those similar spectres. I mean myself and the inherent indolence and cowardice which is the lot of all men.[94]

Crane continued, saying that he feared "applause"; feared that he would become self-satisfied now that some of his work was being accepted. He concluded:

For the first time I saw the majestic forces which are arrayed against man's true success—not the world—the world is silly, changeable, any of its decisions can be reversed—but man's own colossal impulses more strong than chains, and I perceived that the fight was not going to be with the world but with myself.[95]

From this letter it becomes obvious that Crane was not a fatalist in the sense that he felt it is useless to make an attempt to reform society. Man must try, but he must be aware that in all probability he will fail. What is it specifically that Crane felt man should do? Can man do the things he should? The answers to these questions are crucial in understanding Crane's concepts of man and society.

One of the things which Crane felt that man cannot do is to discover truth. Like most of Crane's themes dealing with ideas, the question of truth finds expression in his poetry. In *The Black Riders* he wrote:

> For truth was to me
> A breath, a wind,
> A shadow, a phantom,
> And never had I touched
> The hem of its garment.[96]

Just as man can never discover truth in this world neither can he find justice.

> Friend, your white beard sweeps the ground.
> Why do you stand, expectant?
> Do you hope to see it
> In one of your withered days?
> With your old eyes
> Do you hope to see
> The triumphal march of justice?
> Do not wait, friend!
> Take your white beard
> And your old eyes
> To more tender lands.[97]

With his conviction that these things cannot be discovered in this life, Crane had no faith in those who feel themselves wise or holy.

> A learned man came to me once.
> And I was overjoyed at this.
> He said, "I know the way—come."
> Together we hastened.
> Soon, too soon, were we

> Where my eyes were useless,
> And I knew not the ways of my feet.
> I clung to the hand of my friend;
> But at last he cried, "I am lost." [98]

Because Crane insisted that man can never find truth or justice, because he held that the end of life is frustration and that life itself is tragedy, he is many times dismissed as a fatalist. Many liberal historians and writers have not been kind to him for this reason. But those who dismiss Crane as a simple fatalist are as mistaken as those who want to enlist him in the ranks of the social critics and progressives. It was the attitude of cynical fatalism that so irritated him in the people of the Bowery, and it has been pointed out that he treated the Bowery gangs in *Maggie* and *George's Mother* with satiric scorn. The "indolent and cynical young men" in the small-town setting of *The Monster* were treated in the same manner,[99] and *The Black Riders* pillories the cynic in verse.

> Once there was a man—
> Oh, so wise!
> In all drink
> He detected the bitter,
> And in all touch
> He found the sting.
> At last he cried thus:
> "There is nothing—
> No life,
> No joy,
> No pain—
> There is nothing save opinion,
> And opinion be damned." [100]

Crane specifically repudiated the cynic and pointed out some of the positive aspects of his own philosophy in this letter to Nellie Crouse.

The final wall of the wise man's thought however is Human Kindness of course. If the road of disappointment, grief, pessimism, is followed far enough, it will arrive there. Pessimism itself is only a little little way, and moreover it is ridiculously cheap. The cynical mind is an uneducated thing. Therefore do I strive to be as kind and as just as may be to those about me and in my meagre success at it, I find the solitary pleasure of life.[101]

In addition to his repudiation of the cynic, here is a glimpse of his belief in a code of conduct. This code is one of the most important, yet least appreciated, aspects of Crane's philosophy, for it illustrates in striking fashion his adherence to the central core of his father's religious code and the tradition of free will. He never elaborated the details of this code of conduct in one place, so its content must be pieced together from various writings. In the letter above, he stated that man can never achieve complete kindness and justice, but he can have limited success in striving toward them. The same is true of honesty, as can be seen in the following letter to Joseph O'Connor in which Crane also definitely embraced the Promethean struggle.

For I understand that a man is born into the world with his own pair of eyes, and he is not at all responsible for his vision—he is merely responsible for his quality of personal honesty. To keep close to this personal honesty is my supreme ambition. There is a sublime egotism in talking of honesty. I, however, do not say that I am honest. I merely say that I am as nearly honest as a weak mental machinery will allow. This aim in life struck me as being the only thing worth while. A man is sure to fail at it, but there is something in the failure.[102]

The most misunderstood aspect of Crane's code of conduct is his espousal of the heroic ideal. This ideal does not mean, as Hartwick has taken it to mean, that Crane, like Norris and London, particularly admired "men with the bark on." [103] Nor can it be added to his denunciation of the lack of ambition in the Bowery to link Crane "in a curious way with contemporary purveyors of uplift and success literature," as Stow Persons has suggested.[104] Crane's heroes were not big, brawling giants who triumphed over the universe as well as their human foes. Indeed, they usually did not triumph at all. They could not be classed with the heroes of literature because they seldom, if ever, succeeded. The individual simply proved himself on the battlefield by his heroism—by his adherence to a code which all know and none can express. Similarly, in civilian life one became a man by striving after truth, honesty, and kindness. The chances are that the man in war would no more succeed in his attempt than the man in peace, but success was not the important factor. Rather, success in such pursuits is beyond human grasp; the important thing is the attempt. In Crane's writings the result of heroic action, the result of almost every attempt to live up to this code, was death for the actor. Nor was this death usually of any significance from the viewpoint of military strategy or social improvement. The only significance was the development of the individual through willed involvement and adherence to the code. Crane, in one way, demanded more of man than did the purveyors of success literature, or even the orthodox clergy, for he asked man to strive with no hope of ultimate success or reward.

Crane's admiration for the fighting men who lived up to the code by doing their duty on the field of battle is shown in many of his writings. This quotation is from his *War Memoirs* of the Spanish-American War.

They stood out in simple, majestic commonplace. It was the behaviour of men on the street. It was the behaviour of men. In one way, each man was just pegging along at the heels of the man before him, who was pegging along at the heels of still another man, who was pegging along at the heels of still another man who—
It was that in the flat and obvious way. In another way it was pageantry, the pageantry of the accomplishment of naked duty. One cannot speak of it—the spectacle of the common man serenely doing his work, his appointed work. It is the one thing in the universe which makes one fling expression to the winds and be satisfied to simply feel.[105]

The "excellence of human conduct" was what Crane admired, and he admired it in the individual no matter which side he was on. Anyone who can conquer the animal instinct to flee, who will cling to the code of conduct and do his duty, is a man.

These men who stand and fight are not boasting, strutting heroes, but common, everyday men who know that adherence to the code may well mean their death. The qualities of doing one's duty and accepting death are perhaps best shown by Crane's group of battle veterans in *The Little Regiment*. In this regiment were two brothers, Dan and Billie Dempster, both hardened veterans who treated each other as if they were the worst of enemies. But when one was away in battle the other was uneasy. During this story Billie was lost in action, and Dan sat and stared at the fire until his brother returned. When Billie walked into camp, Dan started to rise and rush to him; but he checked himself and they exchanged a simple greeting.[106] Here one sees Crane's admiration for quiet self-restraint, with an acceptance of the almost inevitable death. He celebrated the same kind of quiet hero in a poem, recently published, of a young hero who received the "flower of duty" upon his lifeless breast.[107]

In many of his stories Crane showed what he believed man not only should, but could, do. Not all men, however, measured up to his standards, and light is shed upon the code by a look at one man who could not make the grade. Such a man was Peza, the main character in the short story *Death and the Child*, mentioned previously. Peza, an Italian-educated Greek, went back to Greece as a war correspondent during the Greek War. There he became emotionally involved in the scene of his father's homeland under invasion and the people in flight. He decided, therefore, to enter the conflict and joined the battle with dreams of grandeur. Then, frightened more by the dead men around him than by the enemy, Peza bolted and fled. He managed to crawl to the top of a hill where he was confronted by an abandoned child. When Peza emerged over the hill crest, the child looked up from his play and asked, "Are you a man?" The reader is left with no doubt that, in Crane's mind, Peza was not a true man. He could not assume the sacrificial role that brings death, but brings also dignity.

Crane spoke more directly of the code in his short story *Clan of No-Name.*[108] This is a series of connected sketches at the opening of which Crane portrayed a young girl who was deceiving her wealthy suitor to write to an unknown lover. Then the scene changed to a field in Cuba where an insurgent force was trying to get a supply of ammunition through Spanish lines. Among the insurgents was a new man, a young American lieutenant. When this group was attacked by the Spanish, the American, although new to the fight, realized instinctively that he was bound by a code of honor to fight a delaying action so that the supplies would not be captured. When he was killed, Crane revealed that the lieutenant had been the young girl's lover. Finally the scene switched back to the girl who had agreed to marry her wealthy suitor. Crane concluded with this description of the code.

For the word is clear only to the kind who on peak or plain, from dark northern ice-fields to the hot jungles, through all wine and want, through lies and unfamiliar truth, dark or light, are governed by the unknown gods; and, though each man knows the law, no man may give tongue to it.[109]

The young lieutenant who knew and obeyed the code lost his life but achieved tragic dignity. The girl, who either did not know or would not follow the code, achieved material success but lost dignity as a human being.

For the men in *The Open Boat* there was also a code of conduct, just as there was for the men in battle. Crane wrote:

To express any particular optimism at this time they felt to be childish and stupid. . . . On the other hand the ethics of their condition was decidedly against any open suggestion of hopelessness. So they were silent.[110]

Throughout the ordeal there seems to have been complete agreement on everything, as each man followed the same unspoken code of conduct. It would also seem that through adherence to this code of conduct in a crisis situation, man can achieve a sense of brotherhood and lose the sense of isolation that is so prevalent in Crane's writings.

It would be difficult to describe the subtle brotherhood that was here established on the seas. No one said that it was so. No one mentioned it. But it dwelt in the boat, and each man felt it warm him.[111]

The correspondent, "who had been taught to be cynical of men," knew that this feeling of comradeship was "the best experience of his life." [112]

This bond of fellowship that developed in the boat was not limited to the members of the small crew, but rather it involved a fellowship with mankind. As they were coasting along, the half-forgotten verse of "A Soldier of the Legion Lay Dying in Algiers" crept into the head of the correspondent. He had had to learn the poem as a child, and he

had been made acquainted with the fact that a soldier lay dying in Algiers, but he had never regarded the fact as important. . . . Now, however, it quaintly came to him as a human living thing . . . it was an actuality—stern, mournful and fine. . . . He was sorry for the soldier of the Legion who lay dying in Algiers.[113]

This sense of the discovery of comradeship and fellowship, not only with those who share the crisis situation but with the struggles of mankind, can also be found in Crane's war stories.

Man can and should seek truth, justice, honesty, and kindness. He can and should seek involvement with mankind through the doing of duty and obedience to the code. These things he should seek, though the personal qualities he can never truly find and involvement with mankind may very well mean death. This in itself is a great deal to ask of man, but there is still another facet to Crane's requirements, one which in many ways is the most difficult to explain. That loyalty to one's fellows in a crisis situation is part of the code has already been shown, but Crane also dealt with another kind of loyalty, which might be called love-loyalty, or loyalty of one individual to another.

Love, in Crane's writings, is a very difficult concept to handle. He almost never concerned himself directly with sexual feelings. Even in *Maggie,* where the pivotal incident was the seduction of the heroine, the seduction itself was not discussed and Maggie's sexual feelings, if any, were not mentioned. Love themes occur most frequently in his poetry, and here love is generally linked with pain, despair, and violence. The whole of *Intrigue* expresses the themes of love as a sacrifice, love as momentary joy and ceaseless remorse, and love as violence.[114]

This connection between love and suffering which is evident in so much of Crane's poetry is important in connection with the idea of loyalty. To love truly is to suffer. But if one can scale the heights of devotion to a love that surpasses devotion, he can find life. Thomas Beer reported an incident which Crane witnessed on the Bowery, where a young prostitute was protecting with her own body the head of her drunken procurer from the kicks of his assailants. Daniel Hoffman has connected this incident with Crane's poem *God Lay Dead in Heaven.* The last lines of this poem read as follows.

> Then from the far caverns
> Of dead sins
> Came monsters, livid with desire.
> They fought,
> Wrangled over the world,
> A morsel.
> But of all sadness this was sad—
> A woman's arms tried to shield
> The head of a sleeping man
> From the jaws of the final beast.[115]

Here is Crane's idea of love-loyalty. The relationship of two lowly individuals is universalized as "the streetwalker and her drunken pimp are become Man and Woman." [116] Love-loyalty, like so many other aspects of Crane's code, demands involvement which will in all probability lead to sacrificial death.

Crane has set a very high standard of human conduct in his code, but he admitted that man can never achieve these things totally. They can, as he showed in his stories, achieve partial success but, in success or failure, human dignity arises from the attempt itself. Why is it that man cannot succeed? One reason is, of course, that he is a rather insignificant *isolato* in a universe that does not recognize him as important. But if this were the whole story, the mere attempt to fulfill the code would hardly bring dignity. If man were essentially good he would experience little difficulty in attempting to fulfill the code, despite an indifferent universe and a vagarious fate. With regard to this question of Crane's conception of man's basic nature, Nye contends that

man is not innately evil; he rather learns and adopts. This, I think, is the real social significance of *The Whilomville Stories*, that in them Crane is searching in the child's society for the answers to the questions of an adult society. They seem to show that the origin of social evil is without rather than within mankind, and thus may be escaped.[117]

This is a possible interpretation of these stories, but the general lack of environmentalism in Crane's writings suggests that it is an incorrect one. The people made the Bowery, not the Bowery the people. The rather strict limitations of Crane's environmentalism have been pointed out earlier and need not be repeated here. What does need emphasis is that in *The Black Riders*, where Crane said he wrote about life as a whole, man is represented as essentially sinful and weak. For example:

I stood upon a high place,
And saw, below, many devils

> Running, leaping,
> And carousing in sin.
> One looked up, grinning,
> And said, "Comrade! Brother!" [118]

Nor did he exempt the seemingly holy from the ranks of fallible man.

> You say you are holy,
> And that
> Because I have not seen you sin.
> Ay, but there are those
> Who see you sin, my friend.[119]

There is evil within all men, for that is the way they are made. It is for this reason, and not because of a universe that disregards him, that man can never find truth, nor do complete justice, nor be wholly unselfish. In a poem recently published, Crane gave his own version of the first chapters of Genesis. Here he showed God placing "a glorious apple" within the reach of man and then forbidding him to touch it. But the man rebelled.

> The man answered in this wise:
> "Oh, most interesting God
> What folly is this?
> Behold, thou hast moulded my desires
> Even as thou hast moulded the apple.
>
> How then?
> Can I conquer my life
> Which is thou?
> My desires?
> Look you, foolish god
> If I thrust behind me
> Sixty white years
> I am a greater god than god
> And then, complacent splendor,

Thou wilt see that the golden angels
That sing pink hymns
Around thy throne-top
Will be lower than my feet.[120]

A similar sentiment is to be found in *The Black Riders*. Here again the implication is that man has evil within him that cannot be completely overcome.

"It was wrong to do this," said the angel.
"You should live like a flower
Holding malice like a puppy
Waging war like a lambkin."

"Not so," quoth the man
Who had no fear of spirits;
"It is only wrong for angels
Who can live like the flowers,
Holding malice like the puppies,
Waging war like the lambkins." [121]

In these poems and in his other writings Crane indicated his belief that man has evil within. In his code he suggests that man also has good in him, good which will find expression in the Promethean struggle. So here again one finds a duality, but a duality which differs from the more optimistic pronouncements of both the Gospel of Wealth and the Progressive social thinkers in that Crane insists that man can never wholly repudiate the evil side of his nature. He sometimes seemed to speak of this evil side of man as human nature, but in his stories he indicated that man can achieve human dignity by involvement in the struggles of mankind.

No mention has so far been made of Crane's only best-seller, *The Red Badge of Courage*. This work contains so many of the elements of Crane's thoughts about the problems which have been discussed that its analysis as a whole will provide a summary of these ideas. Lars Ahnebrink describes *The Red Badge of Courage* as "a sample of naturalism because of its candor, its treatment of man as dominated by instincts, its pictures of masses, and its pessimistic outlook." [122] He pictured Henry Fleming as a pawn, guided by instinct and moved by forces beyond his control. According to Ahnebrink, Henry was boxed in by law and tradition and had no free will. Joseph Hergesheimer also wrote of the meaning of the novel as pointing up the insigificance of the individual.

A tranquil countryside is torn for a little by human strife, the stillness is broken by a hideous clamour of explosions and cries, and then the quiet comes back with evening. The dead are removed, the trees are healed, the brooks are again softly audible. Wars are unimportant; individuals are unimportant—actually there are no individuals, but only connected and momentary activities, one fading into the other in a march from dark to dark. That is the burden of *The Red Badge of Courage*.[123]

If either Ahnebrink or Hergesheimer are correct in their statements, then my analysis of Crane's concept of man must be seriously questioned, for they have excluded the possibility of the attainment of human dignity through willed involvement with other men in a crisis situation. A careful analysis of this work, which Crane himself called a "psychological portrayal of fear," [124] is therefore in order.

Henry Fleming, like so many of Crane's characters, was a dreamer. He dreamed of battles and titanic struggles but he doubted that the modern world could be the scene of such activities. Still, he had his hopes and he was disappointed when his mother said nothing about "returning with his shield or on it." [125] But his mother, like George Kelsey's mother, was the practical member of the family, and she threw a damper on his enthusiasm. Nonetheless, she expected him to be a man, and if the time came "when yeh have to be kilt or do a mean thing, why, Henry don't think of anything 'cept what's right. . . ." [126]

This is what it means to be a man, but Henry was not concerned about such realities. His own dreams of glory and the normal public adulation of the enlistee built up his esteem of himself and his dream of the glories of war, but like all of Crane's characters he was brought back to earth by the realities of life, in this case by an army that did nothing.[127]

When the eve of battle finally came, Henry began to doubt whether he actually had the courage to face it. His life before had been smooth, and "he felt that in this crisis his laws of life were useless. Whatever he had learned of himself was here of no avail. He was an unknown quality." [128] When he tried to find out if the other men felt as he did, they convinced him they did not. Again, like George Kelsey, he felt a sense of isolation which turned to self-pity.[129]

As they marched to battle Henry saw that he would have to face a situation which he did not feel he could handle. "But he instantly saw that it would be impossible for him to escape from the regiment. It enclosed him. And there were iron laws of tradition and law on four sides. He was in a moving box." [130] In his feeling of isolation and self-pity, he wondered how he had ever gotten into such a predicament. He decided that "he had not enlisted of his free will. He had been dragged by the merciless government. And now they were taking him out to be slaughtered." [131] This, of course, was blatantly false; Henry had enlisted in the hope of gaining glory. Again there is the attitude of the Bowery boys. When they are involved in a crisis situation they try to put the blame on anything or anybody except themselves.

Henry's thoughts and actions in this situation were contrasted with those of "the tall soldier," Jim Conklin, who took everything like a man. When they marched, Conklin objected neither to the distance nor to the speed. Three times he was ordered away from protective mounds he had built; but he said not a word.

As they approached the battle, Henry's sense of isolation

became so acute that even death seemed preferable. "He would die; he would go to some place where he would be understood. It was useless to expect appreciation of his profound and fine senses from such men as the lieutenant." [132] And then, when the attack came, he experienced a momentary sense of unity.

He suddenly lost concern for himself, and forgot to look at a menacing fate. He became not a man but a member. He felt that something of which he was a part—a regiment, an army, a cause, or a country— was in a crisis. He was welded into a common personality. . . . He felt the subtle battle brotherhood more potent even than the cause for which they were fighting. It was a mysterious fraternity born of the smoke and danger of death.[133]

After the first attack had been repulsed Henry felt great self-satisfaction, but when the rebels reattacked he was awe-struck. He began to see them as machines of steel with incredible skill, valor, and endurance. As the enemy swept down on them, a man near Henry broke ranks and fled from the firing line. This apparently broke the communal spirit, and Henry "ran like a rabbit." [134] This was an instinctive act, but as soon as he was out of immediate danger he began to rationalize his actions. The situation, he decided, was hopeless, and he was the superior man because he had had sense enough to get out in time. Here again is the Bowery boys' attitude of superiority. When it appeared as if the Union line would hold, Henry wallowed in self-pity.

He was ill used. He was trodden beneath the feet of an iron injustice. He had proceeded with wisdom and from the most righteous motives under heaven's blue only to be frustrated by hateful circumstances.[135]

When he stopped to rest he casually threw a pine cone at a squirrel, and the squirrel rapidly fled. In this he felt "nature had given him a sign." [136] The squirrel had not waited to be bombarded but had taken to its heels. Here was a sign from nature that he had made the right move. This highly satirical treatment of Henry's rationalizations would certainly seem to indicate that

Crane held Henry morally responsible for his actions. He had allowed the animal side of his nature to carry him away—he had refused to be a man.

After a while Henry joined the line of wounded marching back to camp. But he obviously didn't belong and "he wished that he, too, had a wound, a red badge of courage." [137] In this line Henry encountered the tall soldier and perceived that he, too, was afraid. But he had remained at his post. Like Henry he had feared, but he had conquered his fear, at least during the crisis. All men are afraid, Crane seems to say, but some run like rabbits and squirrels and some stand like men. Instinct need not predominate.[138] By this time Henry had reached the point where he would welcome the defeat of his own army. This would be unfortunate, but at least he would be vindicated. He did not want to face the other men because he was sure he could not hide his guilt from them.[139] And suddenly the Northern line broke; his fellow soldiers joined him in retreat.

The youth was horror-stricken. He stared in agony and amazement. He forget that he was engaged in combating the universe. He threw aside his mental pamphlets on the philosophy of the retreated and rules for the guidance of the damned.[140]

Henry was once again part of the whole (though uneasily), and a swat on the head from the rifle of a retreating soldier gave him the outward symbol of belonging—a wound. Finding that many men had wandered around and fought with other outfits, Henry told them this was what he had done. No one had seen him flee; he was still a man (outwardly), and he began to feel himself quite a good fellow after all.

The next day Henry went out to battle with a new feeling of belonging. The opposing army became a machine which was persecuting him and his fellows, and it must be destroyed. He fought unconsciously, and when a pause came in the battle he found himself a hero. "He had slept and, awakening, found himself a knight." [141] When Henry and a friend went for water, they heard an officer order their regiment into a charge from which most would probably not return. They were but a unit in a whole.

New eyes were given to him. And the most startling thing was to learn suddenly that he was very insignificant. The officer spoke of the regiment as if he referred to a broom. Some part of the woods needed sweeping, perhaps, and he merely indicated a broom in a tone properly indifferent to its fate.[142]

Returning to the regiment, Henry and his friend told about the attack but not about the chances for survival. They knew they would meet death and they accepted this. When the attack started, the men rushed forward with mad enthusiasm. "There was the delirium that encounters despair and death, and is heedless and blind to the odds. It is temporary but sublime absence of selfishness." [143] Here Crane showed that man can act without selfishness. Bound up in a feeling of brotherhood he can transcend self. But when the emotional charge ran out the men began to falter; having ceased to be a unit, they became selfish individuals once again. Then they felt driven and resentful as the whole advance again became incomprehensible to them.[144] When the series of charges and counter-charges were over, the regiment was back at its old position; they had botched the job and the colonel was raving mad. But Henry and his friend were singled out for praise.

Nevertheless, Henry was bitter about the lack of appreciation the officers showed for his regiment, and he resolved to accept death rather than retreat. The bullets now became only obstacles between him and his goal. He had reached the state of mind of the veteran mentioned previously. With his friend, he struck for a fence held by the rebels, and together they captured the enemy's flag—their sign of unity. After the battle Henry felt pride in his work and now he had time to think about his actions of the previous two days. He found that he not only despised his flight but, even more, his rationalizations for it.

With the conviction came a store of assurance. He felt a quiet manhood, non-assertive but of sturdy and strong blood. He knew that he would no more quail before his guides wherever they should point. . . . He was a man.[145]

The heart of *The Red Badge of Courage* is again the heart of Crane's concept of man. Man is an insignificant creature in the universe, and Henry was an insignificant pawn in the totality of the war. But this insignificance does not deprive man totally of free will or relieve him of moral responsibility. He has the instinct to flee from danger, and the evil, selfish side of him can rationalize this flight. But he also possesses the capacity to fulfill his essential humanness by conquering his instinctive fears and, through a feeling of involvement with his fellows, to achieve manhood. The immediate occasion of this feeling of unity and consequent loss of selfishness may not be, indeed probably will not be, a willed rational act. But once it comes, the individual still must deliberately involve himself to achieve full manhood. Henry became a full man after the battle when he rejected his old rationalizations, accepted the realities of life, and became involved in the human struggle. *The Red Badge of Courage* is a particular instance in which a particular individual achieves human dignity in a particular way. But it is also a symbol of what man can achieve.

From the foregoing analysis it appears obvious that Stephen Crane was out of sympathy with the society of which he found himself a part, just as his contemporaries, the social scientists, were at odds with that society. It is equally obvious that, had he been aware of the teachings of those social scientists, he would have been in rebellion against them also, and the key to this alienation would have been his distrust of their adherence to the traditional American concept of the natural man as essentially good, unselfish, and creative. The central factor in Crane's concept of man is his conviction that man is an insignificant *isolato* in a universe that does not regard him as important. Alone in this neutral universe man can act freely, but the success or failure of that action is dependent upon the operation of fate.

Man in the social situation is within, not apart from, this cosmic drama, a drama where man's fate tends heavily toward the tragic. For Crane, man in the social situation is bound not by his environment but by the evil side of his own nature. Too weak to reform himself, man is unable to reform society or even to attain sustained social solidarity. This position places Crane in essential opposition to two of the social scientists' fundamental concepts—the social nature of man and the doctrine of progress.

Yet Crane embraced one aspect of the Progressive code in his insistence that to be a man means willed involvement in the human struggle. This activist spirit finds expression in the fulfillment of duty in war and in the quest for truth, justice, and kindness in civil society. Perhaps nowhere else did Crane more clearly show his nostalgia for the faith of his father than by this retention of the basic elements of New Testament Christianity as the core of his ethical code. Although he placed his emphasis on human frailty, Crane actually demanded more of man than any other writer of his period, for he insisted that to be a man means to engage in the Promethean struggle without hope of either victory or reward. And, by his writings, Crane indicated his belief that some men can achieve this true manhood through willed involvement in the human struggle, an involvement that will probably mean suffering and death, but which also means the achievement of the only goal open to him—the attainment of tragic dignity.

From this discussion it becomes obvious that, while Crane was in rebellion against the intellectual and moral world of his own day, his philosophy was not the result of a simple conversion to the determinism of Spencer and Zola. Rather, it was a modification of basically religious orientation brought about through his perception of the realities of life in fin-de-siècle America. Like many others of his generation, Crane could not totally reject the ideas and values of his tradition. His mind tried to accept the conclusions of scientific, matter-of-fact knowledge and the realities of the world around him, but he could not rid himself of his intellectual and emotional inheritance. Historians, aided and abetted by literary critics, have tended to lose sight of this continuity in their rush to demonstrate the change in ideas and ideals that ushered in the twentieth century, but to ignore this conflict within the minds of the men of this period is to miss the absorbing intellectual drama of their generation.

3

FRANK NORRIS

The Romantic Rebel

FRANK NORRIS and Stephen Crane are frequently discussed in the same chapter or section of literary histories, and with some justification; but it would be difficult to find two individuals more unlike. Crane walked through life like a shadow, alone, apart from his fellows, saddened by the world he saw about him. He lived his life on the fringe of society, rejecting many of its mandates and suspected of rejecting those he did not—an enigma to his own age. Norris was just the opposite kind of man. As Ernest Marchand has suggested:

If Norris was not the son of the Gilded Age he was its grandson, and hence never able to sever himself completely from its notions and prejudices. His family was almost fabulously representative of the American middle class in its ideal of success and of the appropriate roles of huband and wife.[1]

Norris' mother, Gertrude Doggett, was a successful actress when she married Benjamin Franklin Norris, a rising young jewelry salesman, in 1867.[2] Benjamin Franklin, Jr. was born in March, 1870, and by the time he was twelve years old his father had made a modest fortune and moved the family into a Michigan Avenue mansion in Chicago. Then in 1885 the family moved to San Francisco, where Frank attended a private school until he broke his arm playing football. While convalescing at home, he displayed considerable ability at both illustration and story-telling, and this precipitated a battle when it was time to return to school. Mrs. Norris was eager to have him study art, but Mr. Norris, with his more practical turn of mind, held out for a business training. His father won the first round and Frank was sent to a boys' school. The budding artist soon rebelled, however, and with his mother as a staunch ally he entered the San Francisco Art Association.

But Frank soon decided that he needed European training and, after a long family battle, the seventeen-year-old artist sailed for Paris to pursue his studies. The literary life of Paris, where Zola had just published *La Terre*, seems to have passed him by entirely, but his interest did tend more and more toward French literature and the history of the Middle Ages. Consequently, most of his time in Paris was spent studying medieval armor and participating in a claque at the opera. And it was while he was making a study of medieval armor for an epic picture on the Battle of Crecy that he wrote an article on the development of armor which appeared unsigned in the San Francisco *Chronicle* as his first published work. A further attempt at writing resulted in a very bad novel, *Robert d'Artois*, which he sent serially to his brother Charles in his letters. Mr. Norris soon discovered this and, considering it a complete waste of time, ordered Frank home.

Mr. Norris was losing patience with his son's lack of diligence and decided to prepare him for the jewelry business by sending him to the University of California at Berkeley. Frank, busily working on a three-canto narrative poem that was later published (largely at his mother's expense) as "Yvernelle," was not interested in preparing himself for the entrance exams, and when he entered the university in 1890 he was not a fully accredited student. His lack of interest in formal education continued through the four years he spent as a student at Berkeley, and he never received a degree.

The fact that he failed to receive encouragement from the English Department of the university undoubtedly increased his anti-intellectual attitude, an attitude he maintained all his life. The boys in the fraternity house were much more congenial to him and most of his lifetime friendships were made during those years. While at Berkeley he did contribute quite a few stories, sketches, and poems to student magazines and to two San Francisco newspapers.

Frank left the university in 1894, the same year in which his parents were divorced. It may be, as his biographer suggests, that this divorce had a sobering effect on the young writer, who for the first time dropped his sophomoric attitude and took a serious look at life. Among other things, he lost out on a fortune, for his father left his million-dollar estate to his second wife, and though Frank was never actually hard pressed for money, that possibility now existed.[3] On the positive side, the departure of his father removed the threat of a forced career in the jewelry business and allowed the young writer to follow his literary bent. His mother encouraged him, and when he felt the need of formal literary training she moved the remainder of her family to Cambridge so that he could study in Harvard's famous course in creative writing.

There, away from the diversions of the fraternity, Norris applied his energy to the project at hand. Though he was still publishing stories in the *Overland Monthly,* Norris spent most of the year working on *McTeague* and *Vandover and the Brute.* Professor Lewis E. Gates, director of the composition course, recognized Norris' talent and encouraged the budding novelist, but Frank was convinced that experience was a much better teacher than was formal study. He decided to obtain this experience, after the manner of Richard Harding Davis, as a newspaper correspondent. This close connection between the men of letters and the newspapermen of the 1890–1917 period was a common phenomenon and has caused much comment. According to Van Wyck Brooks, it was Davis who popularized the combination.

The notion of the novelist and war-correspondent which prevailed so long in American writing began in the early nineties undoubtedly with him. It was the result of a personality that brought back in a humdrum business world the adventurous swashbuckling life of another time, and it was he who convinced Frank Norris that the journalist came in closer touch with the raw material of life than other people. When Norris went to Africa he was emulating Davis.[4]

Norris chose South Africa as his topic, and having made arrangements with the San Francisco *Chronicle* to publish his letters, he arrived in Johannesburg in December, 1895.

This was the period of the developing conflict between Paul Kruger's Boer government and the English Uitlanders, and Norris' sympathies lay with the latter. He secured a horse and gun and was ready to join the fight when news was received that the famous Jameson Raid had failed. He was actually involved in one little skirmish, however, and was fired on by the Boers. When order was restored, Norris was given twenty-four hours to leave the Transvaal, but an acute attack of African fever delayed his departure for some time.

In April, 1896, when he had recuperated sufficiently from the fever, Norris joined *The Wave* as assistant editor. He worked as he pleased, writing everything from sports to art criticism. Frequently he and the editor, John O'Hara Cosgrave, wrote almost the entire paper, sharing between them the pseudonym "Justin Sturgis." After a year, the period described in the semi-autobiographical *Blix*, Norris was heartily tired of newspaper work. Franklin Walker indicates that Norris was still plagued with lack of determination and was taking refuge in the role of playboy, though his own private life was apparently as devoid of pagan sex as most of his novels.[5] Twenty-seven and living at home, Norris was still very much influenced by his mother's strong personality and conventional tastes.[6]

In the summer of 1897, stimulated by his newly discovered love for the seventeen-year-old Jeannette Black, Norris produced a barrage of short stories and sketches for *The Wave*. He went to the Sierra Mountains, where he studied mountains and mines for the conclusion of *McTeague*, and then, like many other young writers of the period, he was introduced to the literary world by S. S. McClure, who had read *Moran of the Lady Letty* in *The Wave*. He published that novel and gave Norris a job on *McClure's Magazine*. Going to New York early in 1898, Norris met William Dean Howells, who read and approved of *McTeague* and urged further efforts to publish it. But then the Spanish-American War broke out, and Norris went to Cuba as a correspondent for *McClure's*. There he met Stephen Crane, whom he apparently disliked on sight.[7] Returning from Cuba, ill and utterly disillusioned with the war, Norris spent two months recuperating, during which time he put the finishing touches on *Blix* and started *A Man's Woman*.

Moran was published in the summer of 1898 and was largely ignored. Howells gave it a good review, as did Isaac Marcosson of the Louisville *Times,* who started his correspondence with Norris at that time. *McClure's* was publishing very little of Norris' own work, so money was a scarce commodity. Then in the spring of the following year, *McTeague* and *A Man's Woman* were published, *Blix* was serialized, and *Moran*, which was published in England under the title *Shanghaied,* was noticed by the English reviewers. *McTeague* received some attention, but even those who recognized Norris' talent urged him to turn his hand to more suitable subjects. At that time there was some indication that Norris might become a reformer. He had the topic in *The Octopus,* and he had the proper associates at *McClure's* in Ray Stannard Baker, Ida Tarbell, and Lincoln

Steffens. But, Walker contends, there was never any real chance of this. Norris, he suggests,

was interested in stories, not reforms. He was comparatively untouched by suffering and misery, and his sense of the dramatic outweighed his sympathies. . . . He was much more a story-teller than a social philosopher.[8]

Late in 1899 Doubleday and McClure separated, and Norris was given a job as special reader for the newly formed Doubleday, Page, and Company. The increase in salary meant that he could abandon journalism completely, and, with his royalties, put him in a position to marry Jeannette Black. Norris' main contribution as a reader for Doubleday was his famous discovery of Dreiser's *Sister Carrie*. He finished *The Octopus* in December of 1900, and in the spring of the following year he went to Chicago to study the operation of the grain exchange. There he learned of the spectacular attempt of Joseph Leiter to corner the wheat market which he utilized in the climax of *The Pit*. This novel was completed in June, 1902, and serialized in *The Saturday Evening Post*.

Neither of the Norrises seems to have liked New York. Although Frank knew most of the literary people there, he developed friendships only with Howells and Garland, and he much preferred the company of friends from his old fraternity at Berkeley. Walker suggests that he feared the influence of style upon his work, read few novels of other writers, and preferred businessmen or men of action to literary people. The "Bohemians" of Washington Square, like Crane, he detested.[9]

The Norrises left New York in the summer of 1902. Following a visit to San Francisco, they planned a world tour in a tramp steamer to view the effect of the holding up of the nation's wheat by the Chicago speculators and to find a suitable locale for *The Wolf*, the projected third volume of his Wheat Series. The trip was postponed when Frank was laid up by attacks which were dismissed as indigestion. When surgery was finally performed, Norris was found to have an advanced state of peritonitis resulting from a perforation of the appendix. He died almost immediately, in October, 1902, at the age of thirty-two years, six months.

The similarities in the lives of Frank Norris and Stephen Crane are obvious. They were born within a year of each other and died only two years apart. Both served a journalistic apprenticeship, acted as war correspondents, and wrote books that were shocking to their contemporaries. Both were from Anglo-Saxon, Protestant families that traced their lineage back to colonial times. But the differences, a few of which have been pointed out, were perhaps even more important. Charles Norris says of his brother, "At no time in his life did Frank take either himself or his work too seriously. . . . He was as much pleased, even toward the very end of his life, at a critic's praise as a school boy over an unexpected prize." [10] Stephen Crane took himself very seriously, and he scorned both the critics' praise and their blame. Isaac Marcosson has written of the "boyishness that was one of the most fascinating traits in Norris," and added that "like Peter Pan, Frank Norris was a wonder-child who never grew up." [11] Stephen Crane, in a sense, was never a child; Frank Norris never left his childhood behind. Besides, Norris was linked through his father with the newer America of big business, a connection that may have stimulated his interest in the captains of industry and finance, an interest Crane did not share. Indeed, once one moves beyond the surface similarities between Crane and Norris, he finds that the latter was more closely connected with the conventional attitudes of the period than with those of his brilliant, but erratic, fellow author.

Norris' collected works fill ten volumes, and from those volumes, with the addition of the small amount of his personal correspondence which was not destroyed in the San Francisco fire of 1906 and his numerous uncollected stories and sketches, an attempt will be made to derive an understanding of his ideas about man and society. Did Norris accept, modify, or reject the optimistic picture of man accepted by most of his contemporaries? To find the answer to this question, Norris' writings have been divided into several sections roughly following chronology. His short stories, dialogues, and sketches will be considered first, although most of them followed the actual composition of the second section, *Vandover* and *McTeague*. The third section will be composed of the less serious adventure stories, *Moran* and *A Man's Woman*, and the autobiographical romance *Blix*. This will be followed by an analysis of the two volumes of the Wheat Series, and the last section will deal with Norris' nonfictional writing.

Norris is considered by most literary historians to be a prime example of American prewar naturalism. Most of the critics have agreed that Norris did not completely follow this philosophy, although they have insisted that he tried to adhere to the canons of naturalism as formulated and demonstrated by Zola. Walker, however, feels that Norris was deterministic only when it appealed to his dramatic sense, and that he followed Zola because this approach made possible the use of the panoramic canvas that Norris loved.[12] On the other hand, William F. Taylor, in *The Economic Novel in America*, contends that Norris went far toward materialistic determinism, but not all the way.[13] Granville Hicks took the middle position, maintaining that Norris wavered between ethics and determinism and that the result of this wavering was ethical and intellectual confusion in his work.[14] For Frederic T. Cooper, Norris "adopted the creed of naturalism ardently, refashioning it to suit the needs of a younger, cleaner civilization, a world of wider expanses, purer air, freer life."[15] These diverse views of the literary historians will become clearer in the analysis of Norris' novels with which they were almost exclusively concerned. For the present they will serve as guides to understanding how far Norris went toward the deterministic, amoral position in his short stories and sketches. To what extent did these writings emphasize the forces of heredity and environment and show man as a low, vile creature living in an amoral world?

Norris depicted violence in a great many stories and in a variety of ways. An interesting example is *A Salvation Boom in Matabeleland*.[16] In this story, Otto Marks, a sergeant in the Salvation Army, was making a trek to Matabeleland with his guide when he encountered a party of drunken natives. He broke open one of the organs and started to play. As long as he continued playing the natives danced, but when, seized with fear and hysteria, he stopped playing, they bashed in his head and crucified the guide. In this, as in many other stories, there seems to be no moral, indeed no raison d'être whatever except the depiction of violence. In this case the man died when he lost his courage, but in *A Memorandum of Sudden Death* a young soldier remained brave and calm to the end.[17] The result in both cases was the same—sudden and violent death.

Perhaps a corollary of Norris' interest in violence was his interest in the superman, and all students of Norris almost immediately become aware of his interest in this type of individual. To Alfred Kazin, Norris "was the counterpart in literature of the tough and muscular new men of the new century—Roosevelt and Big Bill Haywood, Borah and Darrow." [18] Many other writers, like Henry Steele Commager, have noted the obvious connection between this interest in the superman and the Darwinian survival theories.[19] This doctrine of the survival of the fittest may be an optimistic or a pessimistic doctrine, depending upon the viewpoint of the interpreter. It may lead to the survival of the race or to the destruction of all commonly accepted ideas of justice and humanity. But in two of Norris' stories it appears that he simply gloried in the hero without worrying about the ultimate implications. In *Travis Hallett's Half Back*, Norris told, with seeming approval, of the rescue of a young lady from a burning theater by a football hero who used his gridiron experience to escape by trampling over and through everyone else. The girl's family, previously opposed to the boy, now saw that he was really a fine fellow.[20] *In the Heat of Battle* was another story in which the football hero won the girl, this time edging out a young English nobleman by winning a football game.[21] Both of these stories quite simply celebrate the virtues of the strongman.

Were these heroes whom Norris loved free individuals combating other free individuals, or were their lives and actions determined by heredity, environment, and fate? His story *Thoroughbred* is reminiscent of Crane's letter to Nellie Crouse on the dependability of the true aristocrat in time of crisis. In this story two men were in love with a beautiful girl of good family named Barry Vance.[22] One of the men, Jack Brunt, was a glib, burly, self-made man of humble origins. The other, Wesley Shotwell, was a rather quiet young aristocrat who lived on his inherited income. One day when both were at the Vance home, Brunt argued with the others that Barry's pure-bred dog couldn't really be worth much money, because he was only a dog, after all. Then a Chinese, all in tatters, ran across the lawn pursued by about fifty other knife-wielding Chinese from a different tong. Shotwell, dog whip in hand, took a stand in front of them and coolly refused passage to the vicious mob. When the crisis had passed Brunt emerged from under the bed upstairs and Barry, needless to say, married the aristocrat. Blood will tell, the story seems to say, and in this case the strongman emerged less than triumphant.[23] Similarly, in an article called "New Year's at San Quentin," Norris commented upon the "hatred of manual labor among certain of the criminal classes," and indicated that "it develops in the children of criminal families, like homicidal manias and the like." [24] Later he called this aversion to work "hereditary mental obliquity, taking the form of a horror of work." [25] In these two cases Norris was certainly stating a belief in the determining influence of heredity.

Norris does not seem to have placed much emphasis on the

determining influence of environment in these stories, but he did point up the rather antinaturalistic idea of man trapped by capricious fate. For example, in *Man Proposes, No. V,* Norris presents a couple on a sinking ship.[26] The girl loved another, but the man on the ship was in love with her and said he would die happy if he thought she cared for him. This, of course, placed the girl in a moral dilemma where she either had to lie or hurt the man uselessly. As they were about to sink anyway, she took the humane course and told him that she loved him, and at that moment the rescue ship came into view. Norris was very fond of this theme and used it on at least two other occasions. In each case the individual involved chose the humane course, only to be frustrated by fate.

Thus far in Norris' writings, heredity and circumstances or fate were shown to be strong determining factors in the lives of individuals, but the individuals themselves were mainly moral, rational creatures with some degree of free will. Norris also, however, wrote about the low, the brutish, and the evil. Many of the stories in his collection called *The Third Circle* fall into this category,[27] but the typical Norris brute is best described in a very short sketch entitled simply *Brute*.[28] This creature had been working all day in a squalid neighborhood among huge machines, crude, colossal in power. "By long association with such things he had become like them, huge, hard, brutal, strong with a crude, blind strength, stupid, unreasoning." [29] One day as he was returning home from work, he found a white violet whose beauty penetrated the clogged and muddy mechanism of his mind. How could he acknowledge his appreciation of this flower?

He looked at it stupidly, perplexed, not knowing what to do; then instinctively his hand carried it to his mouth; he ground it between his huge teeth and slowly ate it. It was the only way he knew.[30]

Here was a man who would have been at home in the coal fields

of Zola's *Germinal.* Crude and stupid, formed by his environment, he was not so much evil as below any moral judgment.

Norris' use of the brute as a type paralleled his development
of the theme of atavism. This theme has two different patterns,
both of which were utilized by the young author. The first of
these is the recurrence in a descendant of the characteristics of
a remote ancestor, and the second is the reversion of the individual to the behavior pattern of his primitive ancestors.[31] In
these cases of reversion, the individual, at least for a time, is
deprived of all free will as he obeys the call of some dormant,
inherited tendency within him.

But by no means all of Norris' short stories dealt with the
brute in man, or with man caught up in forces which he couldn't
control. Many examples could be cited in which Norris portrayed free and morally responsible individuals, but the basic
pattern can be seen in *The Wife of Chino.*[32] Young Lockwood,
the hero of the tale, was an engineer at a western mine. Felice
Zavalla, young, tall, and graceful, was the Mexican-Spanish wife
of Chino, the camp cook. Felice enticed Lockwood to fall in love
with her, though this was contrary to all his convictions, beliefs,
and ideals. The young engineer tried to stop his meetings with
the flirtatious Felice, but with little success. At this point he was
not free but was a prisoner of his instincts.

One day Lockwood was hurt in the mine and had to send the
trusted Chino alone to town with the gold shipment. After Chino
had gone, Lockwood received a message informing him that the
Reno Kid, a notorious outlaw who always killed his victims, was
planning to hold up the gold shipment on the trail. The situation was ideal for the young lover—Chino would be killed and
he would have Felice. All he had to do was sit and wait, but he
couldn't do it. Grabbing a gun, he managed to drag himself
onto a horse and started out to warn Chino, but on the trail he
mistook the cook for the Reno Kid and shot him. When they returned to the camp, Felice, thinking Lockwood had purposely

shot her husband to get her, was overjoyed. This killed Lock-wood's love for her, and, since Chino was not badly injured, the engineer was now free from the chains of his instincts.

Lockwood was obviously a man who had within him moral values, and supported by those values he could, by exercise of his will, eventually free himself. On the other hand, Norris portrayed Felice as essentially base and a slave to her instincts. Here, as in so many of Norris' writings, determinism and free will, goodness and evil, were inseparably scrambled and the ethical sense confused. In this case, however, Lockwood was the main character and it was his struggle that Norris emphasized.

The final example to be taken from Norris' short stories is one that he wrote when he was only twenty-two, but which includes some of his clearest statements on the nature of man. The title of the story was *Lauth*, and the character who lent his name to the title was a young, medieval scholar.[33] At the opening of the story he was taking part in a battle, and when he killed his first man Norris gave a classic statement of the reversion theme.

In an instant a mighty flame of blood lust thrilled up through all Lauth's body and mind. At the sight of blood shed by his own hands all the animal savagery latent in every human being woke within him—no more merciful scruples now. *He could kill.* In the twinkling of an eye the pale, highly cultivated scholar, whose life had been passed in the study of science and abstruse questions of philosophy, sank back to the level of his savage Celtic ancestors.[34]

Soon after this Lauth was killed, but was restored to life by his friends Anselm and Chavannes through the use of strong stimulants and a transfusion of sheep blood. The friends made this experiment to see if the difference between life and death were simply some life force or if it were the soul. Slowly Lauth came around until finally he seemed to be his old self again. But then he slowly regressed, going through the animal stage in which he went about naked on all fours (like the later

Vandover), to the stage of a protozoan, the border between the animal and vegetable world, and finally dying as a round, formless mass. Explaining the meaning of their experiment to Chavannes, Anselm contended that man is composed of body, life force, and soul.

Chavannes, there is no such thing as *man* existing as a type by himself. No: that which we call man is half animal, half God, a being on one hand capable of rising to the sublimest heights of intellectual grandeur, equal almost to his Maker; on the other hand, sinking at times to the last level of ignominy and moral degradation. Take life away from this being and at once the soul mounts upward to the God that first gave it. Take from him his soul—that part of him that is God—and straightaway he sinks down to the level of the lowest animal—we have just seen it.[35]

This story, and the explanation with which Norris concluded it, show him explicitly embracing the traditional Christian dualism of man as part God and part animal. There is no need to assume that Norris retained a dualistic belief in this form, but most of his stories make more sense if they are read in the light of some form of dualistic thinking where man is conceived of as capable of both good and evil, selfishness and unselfishness, rational and irrational acts, and as partially free and partially controlled by outside forces. This would seem to be the view of man expressed in his short stories in general. In some of them he emphasized the brutish, the violent, the instinctive, and the determined (by forces of some kind) to such an extent that for all practical purposes they excluded the good, the rational, and the free. But in others he did just the opposite. This would seem to indicate that Norris, perhaps in spite of his intellectual convictions, still embraced some kind of traditional dualism. His intellectual convictions were in conflict with the assumptions of his age and his tradition. But most of these stories were products of his youth, so perhaps the conflicts were simply the result of immaturity. Perhaps his "scientific realism" came forth in the context of his novels.

Although it was not published until 1914, *Vandover and the Brute* was the first novel Frank Norris completed and the theme—the degeneration of an upper middle-class youth—would seem to be a perfect one for a naturalistic novel. In the beginning Vandover is a complete innocent; when he learned about sex he could not believe that people were so "vile." Yet, even as he was shocked, "the innate vice stirred in him, the brute began to make itself felt." [36] Norris suggests that this side of Vandover's nature might have corrupted the boy in his early teens, had it not been that the other side of his nature began to develop at the same time. This was his artistic side. Here, as later, Norris, like a good Victorian, seemed to see evil epitomized in the sex act and good represented by art.

At college Van spent most of his time studying art and trying to be collegiate. When he returned to San Francisco the budding young artist found that his father had suffered economic reverses which would prevent the anticipated period of study in Paris, so he established a studio and entered into the life around him. In the social whirl, Van again found that his purity and clean habits made him an exception, and again his pliable character gave way as he entered into the night life of the city.

Finding that his respect for women stood in the way of desired sensual pleasures, Van set out to destroy that respect, knowing as he did so that "it was the wilful and deliberate corruption of part of that which was best in him." [37] He permitted the beast to satisfy its demands, "feeding its abominable hunger from that part of him which he knew to be the purest, the cleanest, and the best." [38] Norris continually emphasized that this was an act of will on Vandover's part—a willed action taken with knowledge of the consequences.

Three years passed during which Van engaged in occasional debauches and, at the same time, carried on a courtship of the pure and lovely Turner Ravis who, Norris wrote, "influenced him upon his best side, calling out in him all that was cleanest, finest, and most delicate." [39] Meanwhile Van struck up an acquaintance with a "gay" girl named Ida Wade, who committed suicide when she discovered she was pregnant with Van's child. This was the beginning of, and a causal factor in, a series of disasters that resulted in the death of Van's father and his own exile from the social circle of his friends. Van was upset by the exile, "yet he took his punishment in the right spirit. He did not blame anyone but himself; it was only a just retribution for the thing he had done." [40]

Now, beyond the restraining bonds of society, Van entered upon a year-long period of dissipation during which he lost contact with all his old friends. Then one night he found himself at the opera where, for the moment, his love of beauty saved him and he came to understand himself. In this rather extended passage Norris reveals many of the ethical and moral presuppositions upon which the novel is based.

There came over him a vague sense of those things which are too beautiful to be comprehended. . . . To be better, to be true and right and pure, these were the only things that were worth while, these were the things that he seemed to feel in the music. . . . The appeal had been made directly to what was best and strongest in Vandover, and the answer was quick and overpowering. . . . He had not yet destroyed all that was good in him; now it had turned in one more revolt, crying out against him, protesting for the last time against its own perversion and destruction. . . . He had been lured into a mood where he was himself at his very best, where the other Vandover, the better Vandover, drew apart with eyes turned askance, looking inward and downward into the depths of his own character, shuddering, terrified. Far down there in the darkest, lowest places he had seen the brute, squat, deformed, hideous. . . . And with the eyes of this better self he saw again, little by little, the course of his whole life, and witnessed again the eternal struggle between good and evil that had been going on within him since his earliest years. He was sure that at the first the good had been the strongest. Little by little the brute had grown, and he . . . self-indulgent, shrinking with the shrinking of a sensuous artist-nature from all that was irksome and disagreeable, had shut his ears to the voices that shouted warnings of the danger, and had allowed the brute to thrive and grow.[41]

Norris makes it quite evident that Vandover's problem was his own dual nature and his failure to curb the evil, sensual side of that nature. It was his surrender to the animal in him that was the basic cause of the young artist's decline. One by one he had separated himself from, or caused to be separated from him, all of the influences that had cultivated the better part of him— his father, Turner Ravis, and society itself.[42] Even his ability as an artist had slipped away through neglect. "It was gone—his art was gone, the one thing that could save him. That, too, like all the other good things of his life, he had destroyed." [43]

A final reverse came when Van lost the remainder of his money through a lawsuit instituted by the father of Ida Wade. Van was now a prisoner of his unreasoned fear. "It was the punishment that he had brought upon himself, some fearful nervous disease, the result of his long indulgence of vice, his vile submission to the brute that was to destroy his reason." [44] The disease, a nervous condition called *"Lycanthropy-Mathesis,"* was, in Norris' mind, a result of Vandover's dissipated life and not, as many critics have suggested, a primary causal factor in his destruction. Van's decline was not the result of amoral, scientific forces that moved along a predetermined path; it was a decline for which Van himself was responsible. "Great God!" Norris wrote, "his whole life had been one long suicide." [45] Heredity, environment, and amoral forces were all incidental to the major motif, which was the destruction of a young man who had willfully allowed the evil side of his dual nature to triumph over the good. The whole book is the kind of lesson in morals and ethics to which the Victorians were addicted.

Although *Vandover and the Brute* was the first novel Norris completed, he had probably done considerable work on *Mc-Teague* even earlier. In all probability, he started *McTeague* while he was still at Berkeley, worked on it at Harvard, then, unable to find a satisfactory ending, laid it aside until 1897. The novel was not published until 1899. Since the plot of this novel is rather well known, a brief sketch will suffice to set the stage for the analysis.

McTeague was a hard-working and relatively successful dentist on Polk Street in San Francisco. He knew no particular sexual desires until his friend, Marcus, introduced him to a cousin, Trina Sieppe, who awakened the sex instinct in the giant dentist. The progress of the Trina-McTeague affair was crossed by that of two old people, Miss Baker and old Grannis, who carried on their affair by sitting close to the partition that separated their rooms. They seem to have represented pure love as opposed to the sexual love of Trina and McTeague.

One day McTeague had to give Trina ether and was sexually aroused by her helplessness. When she awakened, he asked her to marry him and was naturally refused. But he had sighted his goal—Trina—and was in misery over his inability to obtain it. Marcus, who had been keeping company with Trina himself, sensed that something was upsetting his friend, and finally pried an admission from McTeague. Marcus was willing to step aside until Trina won $5,000 in a lottery. The old friendship broke up over Marcus' desire for the newly endowed Trina, but she and Mac were married and during the first three years were quite happy.

Then Mac received word from the city that he had to give up his practice because his formal training did not meet the city's requirements. This was obviously the work of the alienated Marcus. The idea of losing Mac's income terrified Trina, who made him move with her into a one-room apartment, selling their furniture and all of his office equipment. At first Mac suffered from the deprivation of his little luxuries, for she had taught him to like things she now said they couldn't afford, but then he slowly slipped back into his old slovenly ways. He got a job as an instrument maker, and his wife whittled out wooden animals, which she sold, and also received the interest on the $5,000, which she refused to spend. One day Mac lost his job and stopped in a saloon where a friend bought him whiskey. This always made him vicious rather than drunk, and he returned home to shout Trina into silence. From this point on he began to drink and to find pleasure in hurting and abusing his wife. He lost all interest in finding a job and Trina, ever on the lookout to save a nickel, moved them into even cheaper quarters. There she degenerated further, losing her figure and caring nothing about her appearance.

Then one day Mac picked up his beloved canary and $400 which his wife had hoarded and walked out. Though the interest on her intact lottery money would have supported Trina, she took a job as a scrubwoman and lived in a room over the schoolhouse where she worked. She again saved with a frenzy and played with her money as a child with toys. More and more she felt the need of her money around her and gradually drew the entire $5,000 out of her uncle's business, taking it home in $20 gold pieces in which she wallowed naked on her bed.

Mac, to whom money meant nothing, had spent the $400 and had no food or lodging. Finding Trina, he pleaded with her for money, which she refused him, and he then got a job in a music store, where he spotted his concertina, which Trina had sold. This was the final blow. He filled up with whiskey, went to the school, and demanded money. When Trina again refused he killed her, took the gold, and returned to his childhood home— the Big Dipper Mine. There he fell back into his old way of life and was happy until his sixth sense warned him that he was being pursued, and he left for Mexico two days before the arrival of the sheriff. At a site near Death Valley, he and a partner struck a rich vein of gold, but again his animal instinct warned him and he started out across the valley, fleeing from he knew not what.

Meanwhile, Marcus had heard of the affair, and with the lawmen had traced Mac to the valley. A six-foot three-inch giant, carrying a gilded bird cage, was not hard to follow! Marcus caught up with Mac in the desert; there the mule carrying the water bolted and, when Marcus shot it, rolled on the canteen, spilling the last of the water. They realized they were doomed but still fought over the gold. Mac killed his former friend, but with his last strength Marcus snapped them together with handcuffs. At the conclusion Mac found himself in the middle of Death Valley with no water—strapped to a corpse.

Most literary historians are in agreement that Trina and McTeague were not free individuals in charge of their own destinies. But if one is to understand Norris' view of man as presented in this novel, he must go further and inquire just why they were not free. What was it that bound these two individuals—heredity, environment, or their own natures? Most of the commentators have stressed the combined forces of heredity and environment. Carvel Collins, in an introduction to *McTeague*, has written, "The novel records the destruction of an innocent." [46] But does it?

Mac was born and raised in the northern mountain mining country. His father was a good steady fellow except when drinking, which was every other Sunday. Then he was an irresponsible brute, and Mac undoubtedly inherited, in Norris' opinion, this vicious tendency when drunk. His mother appears to have been relatively unimportant, except that it was she who apprenticed Mac to the half-charlatan dentist, and it was her meager savings that set him up in business on Polk Street.

Physically, Mac was a giant. He had the same heavily muscled limbs of Norris' other giants; the same large, red, powerful hands; the same square, angular features, with the salient jaw. His mind, like his body, was heavy and slow, but he was a fairly good dentist and he was happy in his little world. Then the snake entered the Garden of Eden as Trina awakened his sex instincts. As long as the affair continued on a rather platonic plane Norris treated it with quiet amusement. "This poor crude dentist . . . was living through his first romance, his first idyll. It was delightful." [47]

But McTeague's sex instinct rose to the flood when Trina was helpless under the ether, and Norris' tone changed accordingly. "Suddenly the animal in the man stirred and woke; the evil instincts that in him were so close to the surface leaped to life." [48] Here a crisis arose. Why? Because man is not solely a predatory animal—he has a dual nature.

Blindly, and without knowing why, McTeague fought against it, moved by an unreasoned instinct of resistance. Within him, a certain second self, another better McTeague rose with the brute; both were strong, with the huge crude strength of the man himself. . . . There in that cheap and shabby "Dental Parlor" a dreaded struggle began. It was the old battle, old as the world, wide as the world—the sudden panther leap of the animal . . . and the simultaneous arousing of the other man, the better self.[49]

McTeague wondered why it was that this perverse urge arose to defile a love that was pure and clean. Then occurs this famous passage.

Below the fine fabric of all that was good in him ran the foul stream of hereditary evil, like a sewer. The vices and sins of his father and of his father's father, to the third and fourth and five hundredth generation, tainted him. The evil of an entire race flowed in his veins. Why should it be? He did not desire it. Was he to blame?

But McTeague could not understand this thing. It had faced him, as sooner or later it faces every child of man.[50]

Most of the critics apparently have not read beyond the first sentence of this quotation, because almost invariably they have stressed the fact that this evil was inherited by McTeague. But the rest of the quotation makes it obvious that this evil is part of the nature of man. McTeague inherited it as a man, not as the son of a particular family.

Norris' attitude toward the sexual relationship was clearly shown in McTeague's thoughts and actions. As much as he desired her, Mac realized that if he took Trina as she lay unconscious she would never be the same to him, and he stopped himself by kissing her grossly on the mouth. Here was Norris' Victorian interpretation of sex as evil. If Mac had taken Trina he would have defiled her irrevocably. "Under the shadow of her royal hair, he would surely see the smudge of a foul ordure." [51] Indeed, this was what happened when she did surrender to him—a kiss only—at the railroad station. Immediately she became less desirable; he thought less of her.[52]

Perhaps he dimly saw that this must be so, that it belonged to the changeless order of things—the man desiring the woman only for what she withholds; the woman worshipping the man for that which she yields up to him. With each concession gained the man's desire cools; with each surrender made the woman's adoration increases.[53]

After they were married, McTeague's desire for Trina changed to a simple delight in her presence. Then came the blow dealt by the loss of his practice and he became sullen. His wife no longer stirred him—she simply bothered him.[54] His inherited viciousness when under the influence of hard liquor came out, and he derived a sadistic pleasure from biting his wife's fingers. McTeague was not a free man because his brute nature lay too close to the surface and his reason was too limited. Too much an animal, it was his animal instinct—his fear of something—that finally brought about his death by forcing him to flee into the desert.

Trina also had a dual nature, but since she was a woman the problem could not be handled with such overt sexuality in 1900. She was not at all sure she loved McTeague, but when he took her in his arms, conquering her with his brute strength, she surrendered in an instant.

Why did she feel the desire, the necessity of being conquered by a superior strength? Why did it please her? Why had it suddenly thrilled her from head to foot with a quick, terrifying gust of passion, the like of which she had never known?. . . It frightened her now as she thought of it, this second self that had wakened in her, and that shouted and clamored for recognition.[55]

Norris brought this masochistic tendency to a head in the days following their reversal of fortune, when McTeague became vicious.[56]

But the crucial time for Trina was when she agreed to marry Mac. Previously she had been without sexual desires, now the woman in her clamored for recognition. McTeague had called up something in her which she could not combat. She had neither sought nor desired this, but it was there. When she thought of the rough, crude giant she did not want to marry him. It was not so much that she had no choice, but that her better self—which for Norris was the rational, sexless self— had no choice.

Norris made explicit his feelings on the whole story at the beginning of Mac and Trina's serious courtship.

Their undoing was already begun. Yet neither of them was to blame. From the first they had not sought each other. Chance had brought them face to face, and mysterious instincts as ungovernable as the winds of heaven were at work knitting their lives together. Neither of them had asked that this thing should be—that their destinies, their very souls, should be the sport of chance. If they could have known they would have shunned the fearful risk. But they were allowed no choice in the matter.[57]

Here it was evident that the destruction of the two arose from the instincts within them and the strange operation of fate or chance. As with Vandover, the basic problem was a dual nature, the evil side of which was too much for them to control. But unlike Vandover, Norris excused them from responsibility. He did not continually lecture them on their lack of will power as he had Van, but on the contrary appears to have assumed from the beginning that they would surrender to their evil, sexual instincts. Thus it would appear that the critics' emphasis on heredity and environment has been rather misplaced. In the case of McTeague, the inherited viciousness was a factor, but that seems to have been the only inherited characteristic which Norris stressed. Environment was not important at all. It is true that Norris gave some rather detailed descriptions of Polk Street, but he did not show that these conditions were causal factors in the lives of his principals. The story could have been set in another place and another social state without injury to the plot or the logic of the events. The fact was that neither in the first two novels nor in the short stories did Norris ever show that he had any real understanding of society as a complex of institutions and traditions.

Following the writing of his first two serious novels, Norris turned his hand to the adventure tales and a romance. These stories had one decided advantage over the earlier ones—they could be sold. He was never particularly proud of them, but he had to eat. The semiautobiographical romance *Blix* will be considered first because it shows how Norris came to write his first adventure novel.

The story of the novel concerned itself with the courtship of Condy Rivers and Travis Bessemer, known as Blix. In a letter to Isaac Marcosson, Norris admitted that the story was a fictionalized version of his own courtship with Jeannette Black.[58] In the novel, Condy (Norris) was pictured as a rather forgetful, weak individual who avoided any hard work, but who was transformed by the influence of Blix into a serious, hard-working, mature individual. Blix was a young, serious, mature, rational, and beautiful girl of good family. Both of them sound like characters out of an early Howells novel. Norris himself described the novel to Marcosson as follows.

It is essentially a love story. But what I have tried to do was to turn out a love story that should not slop over. No sentimentality—everything healthy and clean and natural. "Blix" does not belong to any "school" as far as I can see. It's not naturalism and it's not romanticism; it's just a story. Nothing very violent happens. There are no disagreeable people in it and it finishes—to my notion—happily.[59]

Condy and Blix at first pretend to be in love, but they were not, and consequently their relations were strained. Then, by mutual agreement, they became chums and got along fine. At the time Condy was doing hack work on a newspaper and couldn't concentrate on his serious writing. Then Blix, who had given up "society," decided to put some purpose into her life by going to New York to study medicine. In the meantime, she cured Condy of playing poker by getting him to play with her and beating him all the time. Later she gave him back his money so he could quit his job and devote his time to writing the short novel which the New York publishers had encouraged him to write. Finally this novel was accepted, and Condy was offered a job in New York. He and Blix discovered they really were in love after all and presumably lived happily ever after.

This was "bread and butter" writing and could be ignored entirely except that in it Norris developed one old theme and introduced a new one. Blix was entirely good, rational, and free, but poor Condy had the dual nature with which Norris so loved to deal. This time, however, the evil side was represented by a desire to play poker, rather than by sex. When this poker-playing urge came upon him Condy was transformed.[60] He explained to Blix, "When it comes to gambling, there seems to be another me that does precisely as he chooses, whether *I* will or not." [61] It was Blix in this case, since Condy's love was not essentially a sexual one, that appealed to the noble side of the hero. When she was with him, "he felt his nobler side rousing up and the awakening of the desire to be his better self." [62] There was nothing in this that had not been encountered previously except the suggestion that the evil side of man might not be totally devoted to sex.

What was new was an identification Norris made of the natural with the primitive, and the supplementary idea that society is a corrupting influence. The identification of the natural with the primitive occurred when Condy and Blix were sitting beside the sea, a scene which encouraged "a sensation of bigness and a return to the homely, human, natural life, to the primitive old impulses, irresistible, changeless, and unhampered." [63] If the primitive was the natural, then the good was in man and society was a corrupting influence, because society was artificial. Blix dropped out of society because she saw some men at the social functions who drank too much and behaved badly. As she decided that society was what made such people possible, she would have nothing to do with it. This, of course, was really "high society," and not society in the sense of institutions and traditions. In *Blix* and in the two adventure novels, Norris' concept of man in society concerns itself not with an inclusive society but with social life and social functions.

If the primitive is the natural and society is a corrupting influence, man must overcome temptation by an exercise of the will. When Condy made the complaint about the temptations that were laid in his path, Blix explained to him that it was the difficulty of the matter that made it worthwhile when one got there.

It's the keeping it up that makes you strong; and then when you get to be good you can make your goodness count. What's a good man if he's weak?—If his goodness is better than he is himself? It's the good man who is strong—as strong as his goodness, and who can make his goodness count—who is the right kind of man.[64]

It is obvious here, as in the rest of Norris' early writings, that traditional morality, ethical codes, codes of conduct, and theories of man still retained a strong influence on the young novelist.

But what about the so-called red-blooded adventure stories? Does this strong residue of traditional ideas remain in these works?

Although the first of these novels was named after the heroine, *Moran of the Lady Letty* is essentially the story of Ross Wilber, a young member of the San Francisco social set who was shanghaied from the pier and placed on a ship bound to hunt sharks off the lower California coast. What followed was an adventure of a civilized man in the lawless world of the open sea. For present considerations this novel is unimportant except for one factor—Ross Wilber, removed from the restrictions of civilization, still retained a moral sense that, at least in part, directed his actions.

When Ross and Captain Kitchell agreed to take the *Lady Letty* for salvage, "the predatory instinct of his Viking ancestors" rose within Ross.[65] But when he realized that Moran was the legal owner of the ship, "then the instincts of habit reasserted themselves. The taxpayer in him was stronger than the freebooter after all. He felt that it was his duty to see to it that the girl had her rights." [66] Similarly, the difference between Wilber's Lockean interpretation of their state of nature and Moran's Hobbesian one came out before the fight with the crew of the junk, when Wilber pondered over their right to take the valuable ambergris. Rights did exist for Wilber, the civilized man, even beyond the sound of the policeman's whistle.[67]

In this novel Norris also displayed his continued adherence to the sexual code of the Victorian. As Ross and Moran were lying side by side, alone on a deserted beach, he wondered what it was that kept him from making love to her on the spot. Was it moral scruples, fear, or because she did not appeal to him as a love partner? Then he leaned over and breathed the aroma of her warm body and decided that he abstained because of moral scruples.[68] Earlier Ross said he could see that to a girl like Moran, "the love of a man would appear only in the light of a humiliation—a degradation." [69]

More important for the purpose of this study is the second of the adventure stories, *A Man's Woman*. Most of the literary historians have agreed that in this novel Norris abandoned even the pretense of determinism—it is rather a glorification of the human will, the will of the superman who is outside the moral and ethical codes of society. But again this analysis collapses when one looks at the actions of the characters themselves, for Ward Bennett and Lloyd Searight are about as moral as two people could possibly be.

In this novel Norris presented his view of the primitive as a moral man. Ross Wilber was a civilized man transported into primitive conditions; Bennett *was* a primitive. This became apparent in Lloyd's thoughts when Bennett killed her runaway horse with one blow of a hammer.

There was a primitiveness, a certain hideous simplicity in the way Bennett had met the situation that filled her with wonder and with even a little terror and mistrust of him. The vast, brutal directness of the deed was out of place and incongruous at this end-of-the-century time. It ignored two thousand years of civilization.[70]

In the march southward from the North Pole, Norris pitted this giant, determined, self-controlled individual against the forces of nature. Throughout the march, nature—in the form of the frozen wasteland—was pictured as Bennett's enemy, the enemy he had to conquer if he and his men were to survive. He was a rough and brutal leader; when one man wanted to just lie down and die, Bennett forced him to his feet and made him go on. When another could not proceed under his own power, Bennett left the man behind to die and forced the others to continue their march. Most critics have pictured these acts as those of an amoral superman who is outside the dictates of conventional morality.

But still Bennett is a moral man. In the tent, after all hope had been given up, Bennett saw one of the dogs that had run off hovering on the edge of the camp. With the dog for food he

could make it to the settlements. He alone had the strength left
to do it.

He would live; he, the strongest, the fittest, would survive. Was it not
right that the mightiest should live? Was it not the great law of
nature? [71]

He had left one man to die, but that had been to save the rest.
Could he now abandon his men to death in order to save himself? He could not and did not. Even in the frozen wasteland,
with his own life in grave danger, the primitive cannot put aside
conventional morality—at least not in a novel by Frank Norris.

Both Bennett and Lloyd emerged from the story as essentially
noble savages in the tradition of Romanticism. They possessed
dual natures, and the evil side of them—again associated primarily with sex—posed problems over which both triumphed
by force of will. They were rational, free to will and act, and
essentially good. Lloyd's belief in duty and right, her conflict
between duty and self-interest, and her freedom to act apart
from the forces of heredity, environment, and social tradition
all mark her as a superwoman—but a superwoman with a strong
ethical and moral code.

Even before *A Man's Woman* was released Norris had moved
on to more thoughtful writing. It is in the Wheat Series, and
especially in *The Octopus,* that his thoughts on the ethics of
human existence reach their most complete and, at the same
time, most confused level. Again the question of whether man
directs his own affairs through ethical considerations, or is simply
a prisoner of forces which operate completely outside the realm
of morals, occupies a central position. To this question Norris
provided at least three conflicting answers.

In. *The Octopus,* Norris' main emphasis with regard to the
efficacy of human moral action was that man is insignificant in
comparison with the fecundity of the wheat and the forces of
the railroad. All of the ranchers of the San Joaquin Valley united

to defeat the railroad, but they failed. Why? Because man is an insignificant gnat in the totality of things.

What were these heated, tiny squabbles, this feverish, small bustle of mankind, this minute swarming of the human insect, to the great, majestic, silent ocean of the Wheat itself! Indifferent, gigantic, resistless, it moved in its appointed grooves. Men, Lilliputians, gnats in the sunshine, buzzed impudently in their tiny battles, were born, lived through their little day, died, and were forgotten; while the Wheat, wrapped in Nirvanic calm, grew steadily under the night, alone with the stars and with God.[72]

In this and dozens of similar passages throughout the novel, Norris presented man as an insignificant insect in an amoral universe. The railroads built themselves and the wheat grew itself; everything operated automatically through natural laws. By sheer weight of repetition this was the predominant idea which Norris presented in *The Octopus*.

But on the other hand, the most carefully presented character study in the novel was that of Magnus Derrick, whose destruction, Norris implied, lay on his own head. Magnus was a man of about sixty, tall, broad, and erect, a man of great dignity. He had always been the head man wherever he had been. People looked up to him as their natural leader and he was proud that they did so. Because he refused to lower his principles, he had abandoned politics, but it looked as though any victory over the railroad required the securing of a friendly railroad commission, and to do this he would have to acquiesce in some crooked political dealings. But what about his honor? His wife reminded him of this, and "again Magnus wavered, about to yield to his better instincts and to the entreaties of his wife. . . . His wife was right. Always she had influenced his better side." [73] In this and similar passages, Norris indicated that Magnus had a free moral choice about whether or not to enter the League against the railroad. But at other times he presented the old rancher as a prisoner of circumstances.

But now it was too late. He was pledged. He had joined the League. He was its chief, and his defection might mean its disintegration at the very time when it needed all its strength to fight the land cases. More than a mere deal in bad politics was involved. There was the land grab. His withdrawal from an unholy cause would mean the weakening, perhaps the collapse of another cause that he believed to be righteous as truth itself. He was hopelessly caught in the mesh. Wrong seemed indissolubly knitted into the fabric of Right. He was blinded, dizzied, over-whelmed, caught in the current of events, and hurried along he knew not where. He resigned himself.[74]

At still other times he speaks of Magnus as a great gambler, risking all on one cast of the dice. One wonders if Magnus was actually the free man capable of choice, the moral man caught in a dilemma where his freedom of action was limited to a choice between two evils, or "the gambler, willing to play for colossal stakes, to hazard a fortune on the chance of winning a million." [75]

Norris' solution was presented in the events of the story. Magnus, as president of the League's fight against the railroad, achieved the position he had so long sought—to be honored, well known, and respected. But it brought him no pleasure. He had suddenly aged and his old erect carriage slumped, for he could not forget that he was a briber. All his life he had been honest, but now, at this late date, he had succumbed to the harassment of the railroad; he had fallen from virtue. Consequently, he lost his old assurance, and with it his old mastery.[76] Norris' conclusion was presented when it became known that the man whom the League had elected by bribery, Magnus' own son, was really in the pay of the railroad. The author wrote, "Gambler that he was, he had at last chanced his highest stake, his personal honor, in the greatest game of his life, and had lost." [77] There seems to be no question that Norris held Magnus morally responsible for his own destruction.

Here, then, is moral and ethical confusion—a confusion in the view of man itself, man held responsible for his actions in a

only time, the problem of man and the cosmos (aside, of course, from the direct battle between the individual and some force of nature in the two adventure tales). Is there any clear view of man's ethical position presented here? Are human affairs directed by moral decisions or by amoral forces? Did Norris himself have a clear understanding of his own ideas? None of these questions can be answered completely, yet it is possible to reconcile, at least partially, the contradictions which have been pointed out. Through Magnus Derrick one sees that man can bring about his own destruction, and through another subplot one sees that man can achieve his own moral salvation. Buck Annixter did so before he was shot down by the railroad men. Man can bring about his own personal salvation or destruction, and to that degree he is free and the efficacy of the moral decision is upheld. But in his fight with the forces of evil, as here represented by the railroad, he can be defeated. Over and above this, however, is the great life force, the spirit of the universe, which, in the end, will bring about the greatest good for the greatest number. It is not a very clear view and it is clouded with confusion and contradictions, but it appears to be what Norris was trying to demonstrate in his most ambitious novel.

The essential answer which Norris presented in the second volume of the Wheat Series is quite similar to that given in *The Octopus*. Namely, that man is responsible for, and free to achieve, his own personal salvation, but he cannot control the great "forces" of the universe, in this case the wheat. Ultimately the wheat will go on its predestined way and in so doing will bring the greatest good to the greatest number. The individual may be annihilated, but the race will prosper. Norris presented some vague statements along this line in a conversation between Laura and Corthell. They agreed that the individual isn't important; it is the "type" that counts. The individual may deteriorate and, in this sense he is free, but the type never recedes and can improve. It can't regain the original good, but something

—nature or God—prevents it from going below a certain point, and it is up to the individual to lift it higher and higher.[80] All of this gives the individual a good deal of freedom and moral responsibility not only for himself, but for the future of mankind as well.

Natural forces, Norris insisted, dominate man, but these forces ultimately lead to the good. To what extent, therefore, is man morally responsible for the evil that exists? If social evil is a result solely of forces which are beyond the control of man, social reform is impossible. If Norris had totally accepted this view, he would have taken a giant step away from the traditional position. But by this time Norris was probably less ready than ever to accept such a belief, for by 1899 he seems to have acquired some interest in social reform. This is apparent in a letter to Mrs. Lilli Lewis Parks dealing with his position on the trusts.

As the title of this first book—"The Octopus"—suggests I am enlisted upon the other side. The Corporation (wh. is another name for trust) of the Southern Pacific R.R. is a very poignant issue with us in California and from what we know of it there we are not led to consider it as legitimate or tolerable, and I am afraid the S.P. is only a sample of its breed.[81]

Norris showed very little recognition of society as traditions and institutions, or of the social order, but in *The Pit* he did recognize that the consequences of the failure of the corner on wheat did not stop with Jadwin. He mentioned that smaller failures followed; banks and businesses collapsed and many small investors and depositors lost their money. The over-all impression conveyed by both volumes of the Wheat Series is that the evils in the operation of the natural laws arise from the attempts of individuals to interfere with the operation of those laws. Jadwin, and through him, man, is responsible for those evils, at least in part. And to the extent that the author holds man morally responsible for these evils, he is clinging to traditional ideas; ideas that are in direct opposition to his supposedly deterministic philosophy.

It is interesting to note also that Norris retained his rigid, Victorian outlook on sex to the very end. In *The Octopus,* where Presley finds that the daughter of one of the displaced families has been driven by hunger to her first experience as a prostitute, he abandons his attempt to help her. She had been touched by evil and was apparently beyond salvation. "Presley regained his room at the club, white and trembling. Worse than the worst he had feared had happened." [82] Similarly, in *The Pit,* Laura has a terrific battle with the sensual side of her dual nature.

Before attempting a summary of Frank Norris' adherence to traditional ideas, it is interesting to examine some of his non-fictional work. Most of these articles, the last things he wrote, deal with the writing and publication of fiction and are not of interest here as such. But in them he made assumptions which are important for the purpose of this study.

First, he made it clear that he retained his belief in, and admiration for, the man of affairs, and also that he thought all great men were a good bit alike. He stated that had Richard the Lion-Hearted been a twentieth-century American, he would have been a successful steel baron, and, conversely, had Andrew Carnegie lived in the Middle Ages, he "would have built the most ingenious siege engine and have hurled the first cast of Greek fire over the walls." [83] Along this same line of thinking he indicated an extremely strong belief in the formative power of the environment, not as society—institutions and traditions—but as training and education.

As for my part, I suspect that, given a difference in environment and training Rostand would have consolidated the American steel companies and Carnegie would have written L'Aiglon. But one dares to go a little further—a great deal further—and claims that the young Carnegie and the young Rostand were no more than intelligent, matter-of-fact boys, in no wise different from the common house variety, grammar-school product. They have been trained differently, that is all.

Given the ordinarily intelligent ten-year-old and, all things being equal, you can make anything you like out of him. . . . If a failure is a result, blame the method of training, not the quantity or quality of the ten-year-old's intellect.[84]

If an individual believes so strongly in the plasticity of human nature, perhaps it is not strange to find that same individual exhibiting a faith in "the people," which would have given pause to many a Progressive reformer.

For say what you will, the People, the Plain People who Read, do appreciate good literature in the end. One must keep one's faith in the People, the Burgesses, the Grocers—else of all men the artists are the most miserable and their teachings vain—*In the last analysis the people are always right.*[85]

Or what would a real determinist say to Norris' statement that "The people have a right to the Truth as they have a right to life, liberty, and the pursuit of happiness"? [86]

Norris frequently wrote of the more sordid side of life, as he did in *McTeague,* but he admitted that this was only one side of the picture. Writing to Howells about his review of *McTeague,* Norris said, "I believe too, you were quite right in saying that it was not the whole truth, and that the novel that is true to life cannot afford to ignore the finer things." [87] Norris contended, however, that man has a universal core and that the highest form of novel is not a study of men, but of man.[88] What, then, can this highest form of novel, whose subject is man, be used to prove? According to Norris, the novel

may be a great force, that works together with the pulpit and the universities for the good of the people, fearlessly proving that power is abused, that the strong grind the faces of the weak, that an evil tree is still growing in the midst of the garden, that undoing follows hard upon unrighteousness, that the course of Empire is not yet finished, and that the races of men have yet to work out their destiny in these great and terrible movements that crush and grind and rend asunder the pillars of the houses of the nations.[89]

And so the purpose of the novel would seem to be the instruction of man as to how great is his area of freedom and to spur him to the good by showing him that destruction follows evil doing. Further, Norris insisted, the novelist himself must be a good man if he is to produce artistic fiction.

The mind capable of theft, of immorality, of cruelty, of foulness, or falseness of any kind, is incapable, under any circumstances, or by any degree of stimulation, of producing one single important, artistic, or useful piece of fiction. The better the personal morality of the writer, the better his writing. Tolstoi, for instance; it is wholly and solely due to the man's vast goodness and philanthropy that his novels carry weight. The attitude of the novelist toward his fellow man and woman is the great thing, not his inventiveness, his ingenuity, his deftness, or glibness, or verbal dexterity.[90]

Even William Dean Howells, who has been castigated by the literary historians for his Victorian cast of mind, never indulged in more priggish assumptions than these.

Perhaps enough has been quoted to show the naïve idealism that slipped into Norris' writings and which was reflected in his view of man and morals, but one final example is here appended to show the heights this idealism reached. Making a plea for the western hero, Norris described him in terms that would bring a blush to the cheeks of a television scenario writer.

. . . a fighter for peace, a calm, grave, strong man who hated the lawbreaker as the hound hates the wolf.

He did not lounge in barrooms; he did not cheat at cards; he did not drink himself to maudlin fury; he did not "shoot at the drop of the hat." But he loved his horse, he loved his friend, he was kind to little children; he was always ready to side with the weak against the strong, with the poor against the rich. For hypocrisy and pretense, for shams and subterfuges he had no mercy, no tolerance. He was too brave to lie and too strong to steal. . . . He died in defence of an ideal, an epic hero, a legendary figure, formidable, sad.[91]

Those who have tried to present Frank Norris as a complete rebel against the Victorian code and the traditional value structure of his own day have insisted upon separating Norris' non-fiction writings, which they admit are traditionalist, from Norris the novelist. But it is evident that such a separation should not be made. The same Victorian sexual code is as prominent in the novels as in the essays. The same belief in the efficacy of human freedom in the face of naturalistic forces can be seen in both. The same insistence that personal salvation or destruction is dependent upon the moral actions of the individual forms an integral part of nearly all his writings.

This is not to say that there are no deterministic, amoral elements in Norris' writings—certainly there are. The story of the destruction of Vandover because of his surrender to the beast must be balanced by the rise of the amoral Charlie Geary and the innocent suffering of Dolliver Haight in the same novel. But it is very seldom that evil-doing is not punished in a Norris novel, and where he is deterministic, as he tries to be in the Wheat Series, that determinism is of the progressive, Spencerian variety and not strictly evolutionary and amoral.

Yet Norris has been pictured as a prime example of the development of literary naturalism in America. Here was one author who admitted a debt to Zola, who portrayed violence for the sake of violence, who pictured man as a low, vile creature imprisoned by the hereditary and environmental forces of an amoral world. All have agreed that Norris did not completely adhere to this position, but most commentators have insisted that he tried to do so. Yet an examination of his writings would seem to indicate quite strongly that these ideas were a rather thin intellectual veneer covering a solid base of traditional assumptions. Norris himself was probably unaware of the many unassimilated crosscurrents of his mind that are revealed in his writings, but they are nonetheless present.

He retained throughout his career a belief in the duality of human nature. The presentation of this duality in Magnus Derrick and Laura Dearborn lacks the strong Christian implications that Norris used in *Lauth,* but the duality itself remained. Man, for Norris, has within him the possibilities of both good and evil. The evil side of man's nature is generally, though not always, associated primarily with the sex act, and, to a greater or lesser extent in the individual instance, Norris held each of his characters responsible for controlling this evil side of his nature.

In many of the short stories and in his first two novels, *Vandover and the Brute* and *McTeague,* Norris was concerned with this inner conflict of the individual and with the operation of chance and fate. Heredity and environment were not primary causal factors in either of these novels. Norris changed his emphasis in the two adventure novels to a study of the conflict between nature and the superman, and here he identified the natural with the good and celebrated the efficacy of the human will in the triumph of man over nature. But, while he contended that society corrupted the natural man and provided but a thin veneer over the primitive impulses, the stories themselves show that man does carry his social values into the primitive world. Norris, however, does not seem to have been really aware of this latter element in the adventure stories.

In the Wheat Series, and particularly in *The Octopus,* Norris tried to incorporate all the diverse elements of his philosophy, and it is in these novels that he presents his most complete idea of the nature of man. Man in these novels is held responsible for his own personal salvation or destruction and is free to achieve either. But, more particularly in *The Pit,* he also held man responsible for much social evil through his interference with natural forces. Man, however, works out his personal destiny within a context of natural laws whose ultimate direction is to-

ward the greatest good for the greatest number, and the operation of these natural laws lies beyond human control. Again
he placed little emphasis upon the determining aspects of
heredity and environment. The forces involved are cosmic, not
social, and Norris again displayed little, if any, awareness of
society as a complex of institutions and traditions.

Like the Progressive social scientists, he saw the ultimate
outcome of evolution as the brotherhood of man, but for Norris
the forces bringing this about seem to be cosmic rather than
social and historical. More than any other writer considered, he
was inclined to accept the society in which he found himself. He
was also the only writer of the five men considered in this study
who accepted the Spencerian notion of a universal progress
apart from human control. His acceptance of the dual nature of
man and of the freedom of man to achieve his own destiny were
in the American tradition. But he stepped outside that tradition
when he placed his emphasis upon man's inability to control the
world about him. This was due largely to his tendency to place
the human struggle in a cosmic rather than a social context. The
confusion of Norris' philosophy would seem to be a result of his
failure to see any real conflict between his intellectual convictions and his inherited assumptions. This also explains the absence in his writings of the sense of tension which permeated
the mature work of the other four writers. His overriding belief
in progress and his essential optimism place Norris in the context of his own age and apart from the tension and crisis that
constituted the mental world of Crane and Dreiser.

Like most men, Norris was largely a product of the intellectual and moral climate in which he was nourished. He tried to
break out of that climate of opinion toward a new way of thinking in which he consciously believed, and it is this unassimilated
combination of strong moral and ethical assumptions with conflicting intellectual ideas that brings philosophical confusion to
Norris' novels.

4

THEODORE DREISER

The Cry of Despair

FOR the volatile Frank Norris, life was an exciting adventure; for Theodore Dreiser it was a bitter, desperate battle. Much of this difference in outlook can be explained by the difference in their personal histories. Frank Norris was the favored scion of an established upper-middle-class family. Dreiser was the twelfth child of an indigent German Catholic immigrant, a weaver by trade, and was outside the pale of traditional American society.[1] By the time Theodore was born, his father had lost all his property through illness and a series of misfortunes and was a broken man. Both Carl Van Doren and F. O. Matthiessen stress the fact that Dreiser was the first important American writer whose family was not English or Scotch-Irish.[2] This fact alone set him apart from the genteel society of the time, and he recognized the essentially rootless nature of his family. "If asked to describe our family as distinguished from others, I would say that it was of a peculiarly nebulous, emotional, unorganized and traditionless character." [3]

Because the elder Dreiser could not seem to hold a job, the family was forced to separate and move from place to place in search of a livelihood. Theodore, as one of the three youngest children, generally stayed with his mother, to whom he was deeply attached. They lived in almost unrelieved poverty, relying to a large extent on the generosity of an elder son who, under the name of Paul Dresser, was already making a name for himself as a minstrel and song writer. Theodore and his younger brother had their poverty brought home to them in vivid fashion one day, when they experienced the ignominy of being sent home from school because they did not have shoes to wear.

At fifteen, Theodore left his mother and went to Chicago, where he worked at sundry odd jobs until a former teacher provided him with money to attend the University of Indiana. His educational background was very poor; he had gone through only one year of high school. Consequently his record at the university was mediocre. He devoted a rather large section of *Dawn* to his university experience, and again the dominant note is one of isolation from the general community.[4]

Rejecting the offer of another year at the university, he returned to Chicago, where he held a number of jobs with real estate and bill collection agencies before obtaining a position on a small newspaper. Symbolically, his first really successful story dealt with Chicago's worst slums. Describing himself at that time, Dreiser wrote:

I doubt if any human being, however poetic or however material ever looked upon the scenes of this world, material or spiritual, so called, with a more covetous eye. My body was blazing with sex, as well as with a desire for material and social supremacy.[5]

He was overwhelmingly concerned with his own sexual proclivities throughout his life, and the subject occupies a great deal of space in his biographical works. In explaining this preoccupation, Matthiessen wrote:

Dreiser—on the testimony of those best able to say—would seem to have been sterile. His continually restless desire to know more and more women may have been a product of basic insecurity, of an almost desperate need to keep on proving himself.[6]

Dreiser's Chicago editor recognized his abilities and in 1892 helped him to get a job on the famous St. Louis *Globe-Democrat*. In St. Louis, and later elsewhere, Dreiser was troubled by the amorality of the newspaper world and the unfair advantages which the reporters exploited to get news and hold their jobs. He himself ruined a rather prominent politician simply to report a story.[7] Writing of his tender-mindedness of those days, Dreiser stated:

Mine was a sad case. One of the things which this point of view did for me was to give my writing, at that time, a mushy and melancholy turn which would not go in any newspaper of today, I hope. It caused me to paint the ideal as not only entirely probable but necessary before life would be what it should!—the progress bug, as you see. I could so twist and discolor the most commonplace scenes as to make one think that I was writing of paradise.[8]

Part of the blame for this he placed on a continuing belief in Christian ideals. He had long since rejected the dogmatic Catholicism of his father, but his mind "was still swashing around among the idealistic maxims of Christ and the religionists and moralists generally, contrasting them hourly, as it were, with the selfish materialism of the day as I saw it." [9]

Dreiser left St. Louis in 1894, moving generally eastward toward his final goal, New York. It was at this time, in Pittsburgh, that he made his famous discovery of Balzac and Spencer; the latter blew him "intellectually to bits." [10] Spencer and Huxley, he insisted, destroyed the last vestiges of Catholicism and Christian ideals which had lingered in his mind. He came to see that "man was a mechanism, undevised and uncreated, and a badly and carelessly driven one at that." [11] The truth of the matter, as Dreiser partially perceived, was that the English evolutionists gave form and meaning to the brutality of life which the young reporter had himself witnessed. "I was daily facing a round of duties which now more than ever verified all that I had suspected and that these books proved." [12] All disaster and tragedy seemed sadder now that he was convinced nothing could be done about it. Life was a battle, and the young reporter was not at all convinced of the strength of his own arm.

As I saw it then, the world could not understand me, nor I it, nor men each other very well. Then a little later I turned and said that since the whole thing was hopeless I might as well forget it and join the narrow, heartless, indifferent scramble, but I could not do that either, lacking the temperament and the skill.[13]

Dreiser continued to read the writings of Balzac, and he began to dream of becoming the great Frenchman's American counterpart. Years later he still maintained that Balzac, along with Hardy, constituted the chief literary influence in his life. Although critics have emphasized Dreiser's debt to Zola, he himself wrote, "I have never read a line of Zola." [14] Matthiessen, among others, has stressed rather strongly Dreiser's lack of awareness of any literary tradition.[15]

The young reporter floundered around in the newspaper world for a while longer, and then, in the fall of 1895, was lifted by his brother Paul into the editorship of the musical magazine *Ev'ry Month*. Two years later his financial position was secure enough to enable him to resign and devote himself to free-lance work for *Ainslee's* and *Cosmopolitan*. In 1898 he married Sallie White, a girl he had met in St. Louis, and at the same time he turned his hand to the writing of short stories, finding to his surprise that they were accepted for publication. Then, encouraged by his friend Arthur Henry, Dreiser began the composition of his first novel, *Sister Carrie*.

The discovery of this novel by Frank Norris, and the subsequent semisuppression of the first edition by the publishers, is a story too well known to need repetition here. More important for present purposes is that Dreiser, receiving almost nothing for his long labor and disillusioned with his marriage, was thrown into a state of depression that led to the brink of suicide and made work impossible for about three years. His wife went back to her parents in Missouri during this period, and Dreiser wandered around the country in a completely depressed state of mind. Finally Paul entered the picture once again and sent his brother to a sanitarium, where the strict regimen restored his balance. After his discharge he did physical labor in a railroad yard until he was again able to write, and he secured a position as an assistant feature editor.

From this job, paying thirty-five dollars a week, he worked himself up in the following years to director of the Butterick publications with an annual salary of ten thousand dollars. It is interesting that the magazines he edited were ones in which his own fiction could not have appeared. He summed up his editorial philosophy in the following letter to Charles G. Ross.

In fiction the Delineator buys things of an idealistic turn. We like sentiment, we like humor, we like realism, but it must be tinged with sufficient idealism to make it all of a truly uplifting character. Our field in this respect is limited by the same limitations which govern the well regulated home. We cannot admit stories which deal with false or immoral relations, or which point a false moral, or which deal with things degrading, such as drunkenness. I am personally opposed in this magazine to stories which have an element of horror in them, or which are disgusting in their realism and fidelity to life. The finer side of things—the idealistic—is the answer for us.[16]

In the light of this statement it is interesting that Dreiser lost his very remunerative position because of an affair with the daughter of one of the employees. This affair also led to another separation from his wife.

Dreiser does not appear to have been unduly dismayed at either of these events, however, and he soon completed his second novel, *Jennie Gerhardt*, which brought him considerable fame in both England and America. *The "Genius"* was already well underway; but the publishers expressed much more interest in his projected study of Charles T. Yerkes, and, partially to do research on the businessman's later career in England, Dreiser accepted the suggestion of his English publisher, Grant Richards, that he take a trip to Europe. He sailed in November, 1911, and returned to write *A Traveler at Forty* in the spring, a short delay preventing him from taking his scheduled place on the ill-fated *Titanic*.

Dreiser's chief problems in the ensuing years revolved around the conflict he stirred up with the watchdogs of American morals. The first battle came when Harper's refused to print *The Titan* after they had accepted it and set up copy for the first edition, but this novel was taken over by John Lane and no real trouble arose when it was published. The actual conflict came when John S. Sumner, the indomitable secretary of the New York Society for the Prevention of Vice, threatened suit against *The "Genius,"* the most sensual of Dreiser's novels. His publisher wanted to back down, but the author stood firm, and, with the support of the vitriolic Mencken, the battle was joined. Dozens of authors, including Winston Churchill but not Howells, signed petitions against the novel's suppression. Although no formal charge was ever instituted, the publisher did not dare risk selling the book, so it did not make its appearance until 1923 when it was issued without protest by Horace Liveright. Dreiser strained his close friendship with Mencken and nearly lost the latter's outspoken support when, at the height of the conflict over the novel, he insisted on publishing his play *The Hand of the Potter*, which related the tragedy of a sexually abnormal Jewish boy who was fatally attracted to ten-year-old girls. The play was published in 1918, however, without causing any comment at all.

It is unnecessary for the purposes of this study to chronicle the rather curious paths of Dreiser's life from 1918 to his death in December, 1945, at the age of seventy-four. The rather tragic facts of his first fifty years, however, are an important framework for an analysis of Dreiser's concept of man and society as revealed in his writings. These literary works have been divided into three groups: the first composed of *Sister Carrie* and *Jennie Gerhardt;* the second, the Cowperwood novels and *The "Genius";* and the last, the occasional writings and the two auto-biographical travel accounts written before 1918.

The story of Dreiser's first novel, based in large part on the actual history of one of his own sisters, can be stated quite briefly. In 1889, as a bright, timid young girl of eighteen, Carrie Meeber left her small home town to live with her sister and brother-in-law in Chicago. After an unsuccessful venture as a factory worker, Carrie encountered Charlie Drouet, a traveling salesman whom she had met on the train, who offered to help her. Following various complications, including the drummer's promise of marriage, Carrie and Drouet began living together. She was relatively content in this situation until George Hurstwood appeared on the scene and Carrie began to compare the two men. Hurstwood, strong, solid, well-dressed, and possessed of a sense of his own importance, was the manager of a famous saloon. He had an unsatisfactory home life with a socially ambitious wife and children, and he was immediately attracted to Carrie. Not realizing that Hurstwood was already married, Carrie offered little resistance when Hurstwood began courting her.

Drouet, with whom Carrie had continued to live, persuaded her to accept the lead in an Elks' theatrical production. Soon thereafter, both the drummer and Mrs. Hurstwood learned that their partners were technically unfaithful, and both homes were broken. At the same time Carrie also learned that Hurstwood was married and refused to see him again. She forswore the favors of all males and unsuccessfully sought a job on the stage.

Hurstwood found himself faced with a demand from his wife's lawyers for an immediate property and financial settlement or a suit for a divorce. That evening he discovered that the safe in the saloon had not been locked or the money taken to the bank. While he had the money out of the safe and was debating whether or not to take it and flee with Carrie, the door of the safe clicked shut. Since he could not open the safe to replace the money, he felt he must take it or face impossible explanations, and, by a ruse, he persuaded Carrie to accompany him on a flight to Canada, where they were married under a false name. Hurstwood, now aware of the full implications of his actions, agreed to return the money to his former employers in return for a dismissal of the charges against him. The two lovers journeyed to New York, where Hurstwood tried to start over again. This, for various reasons, proved impossible, and both Hurstwood and Carrie became steadily more dissatisfied. Carrie had more luck with her stage career, and, feeling that Hurstwood was merely a drain on her income, she forced a separation.

From this point Carrie rose rapidly in her profession, while her ex-lover was reduced to begging in the streets and ultimately to suicide. While Hurstwood was dying, Carrie sat in her rocking chair by the window of her lavish suite, contemplating the strange world in which fame and wealth had failed to bring her the expected happiness.

Dreiser's picture of man in this novel would seem to be presented on three distinguishable, though interrelated, levels— the cosmic, the ethical, and the social. As a cosmic drama it shows the purposelessness of life itself. On another level the novel can be interpreted, as it was by many contemporaries, as an attack upon personal and ethical virtue.[18] And finally, it can be seen as an exposition of the isolation of the individual in the unstable society of Dreiser's own day.[19] The essential purposelessness-of-life theme can be perceived in the preceding analysis of the story, and this theme itself stands as a repudiation of the prevalent assumption that Dreiser was a Spencerian.

The ethical problem is more complicated, since it is connected with Dreiser's view of the dual nature of man and the extent of human freedom. In the first place, he made it evident that the naturalistic Spencerian analysis of morals had not provided an answer to the problem of morality. "There is more in the subject than mere conformity to a law of evolution. It is yet deeper than conformity to things of earth alone." [20] Just what the true principles of morality are he did not say, but, in his comments on Hurstwood's state of mind as he tried to decide whether or not to steal the money, the author indicated that there is such a thing as absolute morality. For example, he wrote, "The true ethics of the situation never occurred to him," thus implying quite clearly that in the author's mind there was an ethical principle inherent in the situation.[21]

Even more important, man has a moral instinct which is operative in such instances.

To those who have never wavered in conscience, the predicament of the individual whose mind is less strongly constituted and who trembles in the balance between duty and desire is scarcely appreciable. . . . The dullest specimen of humanity, when drawn by desire toward evil, is recalled by a sense of right, which is proportionate in power and strength to his evil tendency. We must remember that it may not be a knowledge of right, for no knowledge of right is predicated of the animal's instinctive recoil at evil. Men are still led by instinct before they are regulated by knowledge.[22]

Here Dreiser not only explicitly states that man has an instinctive sense of right and wrong, but he also implies that man *can* have a *knowledge* of these things, of the "true ethics of the situation." To further clarify this point and to show the connection he made in this novel between rationality, free will, and ethics, it is essential to examine a passage in the novel which has been almost universally ignored by Dreiser scholars.

Our civilization is still in a middle stage, scarcely beast, in that it is no longer wholly guided by instinct; scarcely human, in that it is not yet wholly guided by reason. On the tiger no responsibility rests. We see him aligned by nature with the forces of life—he is born into their keeping and without thought he is protected. We see man far removed from the lairs of the jungles, his innate instincts dulled by too near an approach to free-will, his free-will not sufficiently developed to replace his instincts and afford him perfect guidance. He is becoming too wise to hearken always to instincts and desires; he is still too weak to always prevail against them. As a beast, the forces of life aligned him with them; as a man, he has not yet wholly learned to align himself with the forces. In this intermediate stage he wavers —neither drawn in harmony with nature by his instincts nor yet wisely putting himself into harmony by his own free-will. . . . We have the consolation of knowing that evolution is ever in action, that the ideal is a light that cannot fail. He will not forever balance thus between good and evil. Where this jangle of free-will and instinct shall have been adjusted, when perfect understanding has given the former the power to replace the latter entirely, man will no longer vary. The needle of understanding will yet point steadfast and unwavering to the distant pole of truth.[23]

In this passage Dreiser clearly presented his belief in the provisional dual nature of man, and he implied that man can, and will, bring himself into line with natural law through the use of his reason. This position places him in line with the thought of the eighteenth-century Enlightenment, as does his emphasis upon the essential innocence of the animal man. Drouet, the animal man, it would seem, is also capable of making his way in modern society. Dreiser explained this in connection with Carrie. "The unintellectual are not so helpless. Nature has taught the beasts of the field to fly when some unheralded danger threatens. . . . 'He keepeth His creatures whole,' was not written of the beasts alone. Carrie was unwise, and, therefore, like the sheep in its unwisdom, strong in feeling." [24]

But all of the characters in the novel were either essentially animal, as was Drouet and the early Carrie, or they were possessed of the old duality of the beast with passion and the higher being with reason and free will which warred for mastery. Is it possible for an individual to achieve the perfect understanding and complete free will which Dreiser seems to have implied in the above quotation? He gave no further explicit pronouncement on this point, but in Mr. Ames, one of Carrie's New York friends, he did present a minor character who seems to have achieved this exalted state. And in another place Dreiser implies that those individuals who do achieve this state of complete consciousness will find the personal contentment which Carrie constantly sought and never found.

It is the higher mental development which induces philosophy and that fortitude which refuses to dwell upon such things [material well-being or the lack of it]—refuses to be made to suffer by their consideration. The common type of mind is exceedingly keen on all matters which relate to its physical welfare—exceedingly keen. It is the unintellectual miser who sweats blood at the loss of a hundred dollars. It is the Epictetus who smiles when the last vestige of physical welfare is removed.[25]

Considering *Sister Carrie* on the ethical level, it would appear that in 1900 Dreiser retained a belief in a form of moral progress. This seems to be inconsistent with a view of life as purposeless, and with the strong sense of personal isolation which permeates the story, but consistency was never Dreiser's greatest virtue.

Theodore Dreiser was, however, almost the exact opposite of Stephen Crane in that he was primarily concerned with man in society rather than man alone in a meaningless cosmos. David W. Noble has analyzed *Sister Carrie* on the social level as a study of individuals "caught up in a society that had lost its capacity to believe in the values that gave it order and continuity."[26] The social scientists of the period, it will be recalled, had theorized that the machine age would destroy the evil institutional framework of middle-class society, thus emancipating the essentially good and unselfish natural man who would unite with his fellows and work for the common good. It is Noble's contention that Dreiser's acceptance of the collapse of society, with the resulting personal isolation and insecurity leading to a fierce battle for survival, was a more accurate interpretation of

the actual conditions of fin-de-siècle America than that offered
by the social scientists. And so it becomes necessary to examine
more closely the diverse fortunes of Carrie and Hurstwood.

When Carrie came to Chicago she lacked, almost entirely, any
sense of middle-class morality, traditions, and institutions, but
neither did she possess Veblen's instinct of social solidarity
which should have led her to unite with her fellow laborers.
Rather, she found them repugnant. Carrie was, or at least appeared to be, interested solely in the welfare of Carrie Meeber.
Never at any time during her rise to comparative wealth and
fame did she achieve identity with any stratum of society, and
at the end her sense of isolation and discontent was as strong as
it had been when she first entered the city.

Still it is perhaps unfair to cast Carrie in the role of the average
individual, for her quest was not solely for material welfare and
communion with her fellow human beings. According to Dreiser,
there are individuals of an intellectual temperament and those
of an emotional temperament. Among the latter are found the
poets, artists, and dreamers, and of such was Carrie. It was not
worldly goods she sought, but what they represented to her—
beauty and contentment. It was not evil covetousness, but a
quest for the finer things in life that led her to seek fame and
fortune. "Sitting alone, she was now an illustration of the devious
ways by which one who feels, rather than reasons, may be led
in the pursuit of beauty." [27] This pursuit of beauty, Dreiser suggested, would be a never-ending quest, one achievement leading
only to further search. He offered Carrie no hope.

Know, then, that for you is neither surfeit nor content. In your rocking-chair, by your window dreaming, shall you long, alone. In your
rocking-chair, by your window, shall you dream such happiness as
you may never feel.[28]

This symbolic use of Carrie as the artist engaged in the eternal
quest for the absolute in beauty somewhat hampers her useful-

ness as an agent in uncovering Dreiser's concept of man in society.[29]

No such confusion surrounds the use of George Hurstwood as a symbol of personal disintegration in modern society. At the opening of the story Hurstwood was encased in his middle-class world—safe, secure, and relatively content. In the chapter dealing with the audience at the Elks' Club play, Dreiser played up Hurstwood's position as a man of consequence among the moderately well-to-do, and he later showed that the manager was well aware of his exact position on the social scale.[30] But once Hurstwood separated himself from middle-class respectability by stealing the money and running away with Carrie, he lost his sense of individual identification and became "an inconspicuous drop in an ocean." [31] In New York he had no status, and the sordidness of his life, combined with memories of his former existence, brought ever-deepening depression and finally suicide. When the middle-class world was gone he failed to develop in himself, or to find in others, the universal core of goodness and sympathy which the social scientists promised. In some ways *Sister Carrie* was Dreiser's most optimistic novel of the period, but in it he refused to accept the human progress, rationality, and free will embraced by most of his contemporaries in all walks of life.

Dreiser's second novel was the favorite of his advocate-general, H. L. Mencken, and the title character of *Jennie Gerhardt* was the author's own favorite. This story opened in Columbus, Ohio, the home of the William Gerhardt family, in 1880. Mr. Gerhardt had been laid off, and his family was forced to go to work to pay the debts. Mrs. Gerhardt and her attractive daughter Jennie obtained work in a hotel, where Jennie came to know Senator Brander. To ease the family's financial situation, Jennie accepted gifts from the senator, entered into a sexual relationship with him, and was disowned by her father when she became pregnant. Brander, who had promised marriage, died suddenly and soon after the child was born Jennie moved to Cleveland to join her brother. There she found work as a maid, and at her place of employment she encountered Lester Kane, the handsome, forceful son of a socially prominent family, who claimed her for his own. She had almost made up her mind to stay away from him at all costs when the family received word that Gerhardt had had an accident and would not be able to work at his trade. Here Jennie faced a moral dilemma between abstract right and the good of her family, which would be poverty stricken unless she accepted Lester's offer of assistance. She made her own decision, pretended to be married to Lester, and moved the family into their home in Cleveland.

Lester was soon sent to Chicago to take over a branch of his father's carriage business, and there he and Jennie set up housekeeping in a small apartment. Later, when Lester learned the story of Jennie's relationship with Brander and discovered the existence of her daughter, Vesta, he was convinced he could never marry her—but neither could he bring himself to leave her.

Meanwhile, Lester's brother, Robert, was slowly working himself into a position to take over the business. A crisis arose when Lester's family discovered his relationship with Jennie. Slowly Lester began to feel the pressure of social ostracism in Chicago, in addition to that from his family, and he came to understand that he had to leave Jennie or he would become a social outcast. Then Mr. Kane died, and by the conditions of his will Lester was to get $10,000 a year if he married Jennie, or one fourth of the large family fortune if he left her. If he had not made a decision within three years he was to be cut off entirely. During this time, while he tried to reach a decision, Lester took Jennie on a trip to Europe. There they encountered his first love, Mrs. Gerald, who was now a widow. She and Lester still found great attraction for each other, they were obviously compatible—economically, socially, and intellectually—and she expressed her willingness to solve Lester's problems by marrying him.

As the end of the three-year period approached, Robert sent a lawyer to see Jennie, who knew nothing of the stipulations of the will, and she immediately decided she and Lester must separate. Pressured from all sides, Lester finally agreed to leave Jennie and marry Mrs. Gerald. After settling Jennie and her daughter in a small house, Lester reentered the business and social world.

The passage of years found Jennie living in quiet retirement and Lester a financial power but an unhappy man. Then he returned to Chicago on business, leaving his wife in Europe, and he became seriously ill. He sent for Jennie and told her she was the only woman he had ever loved and that the separation had been a mistake. Here was the assurance for which she had waited through the years—the testimony that made everything right; she was now happy. She stayed with Lester until his death and then faded from the picture, attending the funeral anonymously.

It is obvious from the foregoing synopsis that Jennie had many points of similarity with Carrie Meeber. Like Carrie, she was a dreamer, an idealist, one who saw the beauty of nature and was at odds with the world of the material. But, far more than with Carrie, Dreiser stressed that Jennie was an innocent. "From her earliest youth goodness and mercy had molded her every impulse." [32] In her relationship with Senator Brander she was "barren of the art of the coquette." [33] Too innocent to understand the social or even the physical implications of this relationship, she thought only of what it would mean for her family. [34]

Jennie had not sought to hold herself dear. Innate feelings in her made for self-sacrifice. She could not be readily corrupted by the world's selfish lessons on how to preserve oneself from the evil to come. [35]

This virtue of generosity, Dreiser felt, was not one which society holds dear. In society he who sells himself cheaply will find himself trampled upon. [36] Still, the innocent will be protected, for "there was always that saving sense of eternal justice in life which would not permit her to be utterly crushed." [37]

When she attracted the attentions of the rich male guests in her employer's home, Jennie wondered if there was something innately bad or evil in her that attracted them.[38] But when she finally succumbed again, it was not because of desire. Rather she was forced to decide between abstract right and the good of her family. "She realized, as she sat there, that fate had shifted the burden of the situation to her. She must sacrifice herself; there was no other way." [39] Later, of course, she came to love Lester, but her decision was based neither on love, nor desire, nor self-interest.[40] Lester's death-bed confession of love made life worthwhile for Jennie, for it was a confession of their spiritual union, a union never sanctioned by their own world.[41] It is clear that society was operative upon her through its pressure on Lester and her own family, but in each case Jennie had to make a choice. The basic one was whether or not to accept Lester, and here her course was made inevitable only by her own feeling of responsibility to her family. In making a choice, she exercised free will. Jennie as a dreamer, an innocent, was limited in her freedom of will by her lack of rationality and awareness as much as by the forces of society surrounding her.

This was not true of Lester Kane. Lester's father had amassed a fortune by just methods and, with his wife, was an example of an older business world of responsibility and respect. The other son, Robert, a hard, incisive character, was the financier of the family. Cold and conventional, he combined hard business tactics with strict adherence to society's moral code and he probably represented to Dreiser the middle-class businessman of his own day.

Thus Lester Kane was born a member of the financially powerful social elite, but by the time he met Jennie he had ceased to believe that his birth meant innate superiority. He had subjected the whole of his social, spiritual, and material heritage to close scrutiny and found it wanting, but he had devised nothing to replace it.[42] Lester accepted life as he found it, but tempered this with a personal standard of right and wrong. "The man had a keen sense of justice and fair play. Above all things he wanted to be decent in his treatment of people." [43] Here was a man cut loose from the moorings of his social tradition, floundering about in a world that he did not quite understand.

Dreiser described Lester as "an essentially animal-man, pleasantly veneered by education and environment," and this combination constituted the essence of his problem.[44] In explaining Lester's attraction to Jennie, Dreiser brought into play his idea of "chemic" affinities.

There is a fate in love and a fate in fight. This strong, intellectual bear of a man, son of a wealthy manufacturer, stationed, so far as material conditions were concerned, in a world immensely superior to that in which Jennie moved, was, nevertheless, instinctively, magnetically, and chemically drawn to this poor serving-maid. She was his natural affinity, though he did not know it—the one woman who answered somehow the biggest need of his nature.[45]

Here was a force which drew Lester to Jennie and held him there. But there was also a countervailing force that tended to pull them apart, for "he was hedged about by the ideas of the conventional world in which he had been reared." [46]

This countervailing force of social convention is victorious in this novel, and it has a direct bearing on the important question of Lester's free will. It must be remembered that for Dreiser the sexual relationship was a natural one, and therefore it was good, even outside social sanction.[47] But the reaction of society to an infraction of its social code he considered to be almost automatic. When Jennie was about to have a child out of wedlock, he wrote:

The ignorance and immobility of the human beings about her made it impossible for them to see anything in her present condition but a vile and premeditated infraction of the social code, the punishment of which was ostracism.[48]

Finally, even Lester was forced to see that "the people of his time believed that some particular form of social arrangement was necessary, and unless he complied with that he could, as he saw, readily become a social outcast." [49]

But this was not the only thing that tended to separate Jennie and Lester, for they were from different extremes of the social scale. After a preliminary discussion showing how fish, animals, and birds are limited to their own domains, Dreiser made this parallel on man in his social stratum with particular reference to Lester.

In the case of man, however, the operation of this theory of limitations has not as yet been so clearly observed. The laws governing our social life are not so clearly understood as to permit a clear generalization. Still, the opinions, pleas, and judgments of society serve as boundaries which are none the less real for being intangible. When men or women err—that is, pass out from the sphere in which they are accustomed to move—it is not as if the bird had intruded itself into the water, or the wild animal into the haunts of man. Annihilation is not the immediate result. . . . And yet so well defined is the sphere of social activity that he who departs from it is doomed. Born and bred in this environment, the individual is practically unfitted for any other state.[50]

This is the determinism which has been emphasized by most Dreiser scholars in their discussions of this novel, and it is the force which Dreiser used at the conclusion. There Jennie was separated by a fence from the body of her lover which was being loaded on a train, and "wealth and position in this hour were typified to her mind as a great fence, a wall, which divided her eternally from her beloved." [51]

Was Lester then simply a pawn of his environment, social position, and conventions? Lester indicated his own opinion when he said to Jennie, "All of us are more or less pawns. We're moved about like chessmen by circumstances over which we have no control." [52] But at the time of the separation he suffered from "that painful sense of unfairness which comes to one who knows that he is making a sacrifice of the virtues—kindness, loyalty, affection—to policy." [53] He became soured on life because he felt that in forsaking Jennie he had done the first ugly, brutal thing in his life. Then occurs this statement which seems to fly in the face of social determinism.

Worst of all, his deed could not be excused on the grounds of necessity. He could have lived on ten thousand a year; he could have done without the million and more which was now his. He could have done without the society, the pleasures of which had always been a lure. He could have, but he had not.[54]

Dreiser also made Senator Brander responsible, at least for his seduction of Jennie. When Brander realized Jennie was his for the taking, Dreiser wrote:

There are crises in all men's lives when they waver between the strict fulfilment of justice and duty and the great possibilities for personal happiness which another line of conduct seems to assure.[55]

This is not the language of one who excuses man from moral responsibility by denying him free will.

As in *Sister Carrie*, Dreiser again injected the optimistic note of the spiritual nature of man into his second novel. This spiritual nature, he asserted, had in his own day been overwhelmed by the whole social complex of a materialistic civilization which produced "what may be termed a kaleidoscopic glitter, a dazzling and confusing phantasmagoria of life that wearies and stultifies the mental and moral nature." [56] Thus it appears that some people, at least the innocents like Jennie, do have something of a spiritual, moral nature. But these innocents must expect to be buffeted about by the materialistic society in which they live. Yet, cast out by society, they can still find compensation in something more important.

Nature is not ungenerous. Its winds and stars are fellows with you. Let the soul be but gentle and receptive, and this vast truth will come home—not in set phrases, perhaps, but as a feeling, a comfort, which, after all, is the last essence of knowledge. In the universe peace is wisdom.[57]

This peace is to be found in a larger view of things. While on a trip to Europe, after the full realization of her social perfidy was revealed to her, Jennie saw this.

Admitting that she had been bad—locally it was important, perhaps, but in the sum of civilization, in the sum of big forces, what did it all amount to? They would be dead after a little while, she and Lester and all these people. Did anything matter except goodness—goodness of heart? What else was there that was real? [58]

To the innocent, harassed by his own civilization, Dreiser held out one further hope. As Jennie was in a state of hypermelancholia over the death of her daughter, he wrote, "If only some counselor of eternal wisdom could have whispered to her that obvious and convincing truth—there are no dead." [59]

Dreiser's next novels dealt with the career of the financier Charles T. Yerkes. Two volumes of the complete trilogy were published during the period before 1918. These two volumes, together with *The "Genius,"* constitute what C. C. Walcutt has called the second stage of Theodore Dreiser's naturalism. Having found "that life was meaningless and morals absurdly inadequate, the next step was to conclude that the only good lay in exercising one's will to power." [60] In the first two novels Dreiser dealt with essentially weak individuals who were rather easily maneuvered by the forces of society. Now, in *The Financier, The Titan,* and *The "Genius,"* he turned his attention to individuals endowed with the Nietzschean will to power. It is interesting in this connection that Dreiser had by this time read

Nietzsche, although his acceptance of the German philosopher's teachings is open to question. Writing to Mencken in regard to the Baltimore apostle's edition of Nietzsche's works, Dreiser commented, "If the outline of Mr. Nietzsche's philosophy in the introduction is correct, he and myself are hale fellows well met." [61] But later, when he read the works themselves, the novelist said of Nietzsche, "I can't say I greatly admire him." [62]

It is obvious that the lives of the weak individuals in the first novels were to a large extent under the control of social forces. But what about the superman? Can he, in Dreiser's opinion, withstand the force of society and by exertion of his will walk his own path freely? An examination of the statements Dreiser made in the novels, compared with the history of Cowperwood as he presented it, provides the answer.

The plot of *The Financier* and *The Titan* is a complex one, but the major events can be stated quite briefly. Frank Algernon Cowperwood was born and raised in pre-Civil War Philadelphia, where his father was a modestly successful man. Frank was born with a penchant for things financial, and he completed his first business coup at the age of thirteen. At seventeen he quit school to enter the business world, where his rise was rapid and dramatic until the Chicago fire of 1871. This event caused a momentary financial flurry, precipitating a series of events that ended in Cowperwood's financial failure. This was complicated by a political situation in which Frank, who, along with others, had made use of city funds, was made the scapegoat by the party machine. He had been married for several years, and a further complication arose from an affair with the daughter of a powerful politician. As a result of these events, Cowperwood received a jail sentence and served thirteen months, getting his release in time to regain his fortunes during the panic of 1873.

Aware that he would not be able to achieve the desired social position in Philadelphia, Frank moved to the freer air of Chicago with the politician's daughter, Aileen Butler. His wife finally consented to a divorce, allowing Frank and Aileen to legitimize their union and attempt to enter Chicago society. They could not break through the social barriers, but Frank did manage to carry off some very successful financial deals with the aid of John J. McKenty, the suave boss of the Chicago underworld. These deals, in addition to one particularly unwise choice of a partner in an extramarital affair, consolidated the social and financial powers of the city in opposition to him. All this was complicated by Frank's numerous affairs and the gradual disintegration of his second marriage. He did manage to consolidate the traction companies, his chief aim, but he failed to obtain the long-term franchise which was essential to his complete success. At the conclusion of the second novel Frank was being consoled in his failure by the young and charming Berenice Fleming, his latest and deepest love, who was to be his partner in the London venture, the subject of the final volume of the trilogy, which Dreiser did not complete until the 1940s.

Most literary and intellectual historians have interpreted the Cowperwood novels in one of two rather extreme ways. Some, like Stow Persons, have contended that through Cowperwood, Dreiser was pillorying the financier as "a parasitic growth on the body social." [63] Most critics, however, have found in these novels a prime example of Dreiser's rejection of conventional moral standards, his celebration of the efficacy of human will, and his presentation of life as a battle where the victory goes to the strong rather than to the virtuous.

The specific statements made in the novels, both by direct interpolation and through the words of Cowperwood, indicate that the latter interpretation is the correct one. The view of man and morals presented in these comments is not an optimistic one. Dreiser presented the conventional mind as "a petty piece of machinery," [64] whose thought processes rarely come in contact with reality, and the subtlety of life goes by unperceived except for an occasional accidental discovery. [65] In the entire battle between Frank and his opponents in Chicago, Dreiser seems to show that the public—democracy—cannot really act in its own interest.

As a matter of fact, Dreiser asserted that the average man is greatly attracted to the Machiavellianism of a man like Cowperwood. "Your cautious citizen of average means, looking out through the eye of his dull world of seeming fact, is often the first to forgive or condone the grim butcheries of theory by which the strong rise." [66] Perhaps partially for this reason Dreiser expressed little faith in the possibility of deliverance by the political reformer, the political leader "who preaches a new doctrine of deliverance, and who, out of tenderness of heart, offers a panacea for human ills. His truly shall be a crown of thorns." [67] In *The Titan* he treated Bryan very kindly, as he did also the reform governor, Swanson (probably Altgeld), but he had no faith that they would be able to show the deluded public the path of its own self-interest.

Some individuals can, however, conduct their lives largely in accord with reason. Of Cowperwood he wrote, "He was not without sensibilities of the highest order, only they were governed and controlled in him by that cold iron thing, his reason, which never forsook him." [68] But this was not wholly true, for even the highly rational Cowperwood was not immune to the lapses in rationality which occurred in the heights of passion.[69]

In the psychology of the "human animal," the first and the oldest controlling principle is self-preservation.[70] And in such a life, as he presented it during the battle in the state legislature, even self-preservation is quite a problem. Here, he said, was "life at the full, life knife in hand, life blazing with courage and dripping at the jaws with hunger." [71] But the picture of life as a battle is not usually presented in such physical terms; it is seen in its more subtle aspects in the thoughts of the Philadelphia financier and politician, Mollenhauer, when one of the political hacks came to him on his knees for protection.

How often had he seen weaklings no more dishonest than himself, but without his courage and subtlety, pleading to him in this fashion, not on their knees exactly, but intellectually so! Life to him, as to every other man of large practical knowledge and insight, was an inexplicable tangle. What were you going to do about the so-called morals and precepts of the world? This man Stener fancied that he was dishonest, and that he, Mollenhauer, was honest. He was here, self-convicted of sin, pleading to him, Mollenhauer, as he would to a righteous, unstained saint. As a matter of fact, Mollenhauer knew that he was simply shrewder, more far-seeing, more calculating, not less dishonest. Stener was lacking in force and brains—not morals. This lack was his principle crime. There were people who believed in some esoteric standard of right—some ideal of conduct absolutely and very far removed from practical life; but he had never seen them practice it save to their own financial (not moral—he would not say that) destruction. They were never significant, practical men who clung to these fatuous ideals. They were always poor, non-descript, negligible dreamers.[72]

But what about the force of social control that had exerted such a strong influence in the earlier novels? These forces of social tradition and convention are still operative, even though the individual himself does not subscribe to them.[73] The social control was still operative, but for an intelligent man, like Cowperwood, all that was necessary was the semblance of conformity.

One found oneself in a given social order, theory, or scheme of things. For purposes of social success, in order not to offend, to smooth one's path, make things easy, avoid useless criticism, and the like, it was necessary to create an outward seeming—ostensibly conform. Beyond that it was necessary to do nothing. Never fail, never get caught.[74]

It appears that to be successful a man need only be intelligent enough to consider his own self-interest rationally, shrewd enough to conform outwardly to the dictates of the social code, and clever enough to manipulate the deluded creatures about him. This would seem to be the meaning of the allegory of the Mycteroperca Bonaci with which Dreiser concluded *The Financier*. This fish lived a comfortable existence because of its extreme ability to adapt itself to its environment. Dreiser concludes:

What would you say was the intention of the overruling, intelligent, constructive force which gives to Mycteroperca this ability? To fit it to be truthful? To permit it to present an unvarying appearance which all honest life-seeking fish may know? Or would you say that subtlety, chicanery, trickery, were here at work? An implement of illusion one might readily suspect it to be, a living lie, a creature whose business it is to appear what it is not, to simulate that with which it has nothing in common, to get its living by great subtlety, the power of its enemies to forefend against which is little. The indictment is fair.[75]

This is an obvious parable on the life of Cowperwood and would seem to justify the interpretation that these two novels are a study of life as a battle in which the clever individual triumphs over all, a celebration of the freedom of the human will. But did Frank Cowperwood, the example in which Dreiser worked out his philosophy, rise and achieve his goals by an exercise of human will and rationality, or were other factors involved?

As a boy of ten, Frank witnessed the uneven battle between a lobster and a squid, and he learned from this how life was organized. "Things lived on each other—that was it." [76] As he grew up, "I satisfy myself" became his motto. Even after he was charged with his crimes in Philadelphia Frank was calm and collected, never losing his courage or his head. He was not troubled by a conscience, for he saw life not in terms of right and wrong, good and evil, morality and immorality, but of strength and weakness. He saw himself as merely unfortunate, not evil.[77]

This was one side of Frank Cowperwood, but there was another side as well. Though he had little consideration for the strength or rights of the people, he was in sympathy with the fate of individuals.[78] He was a ruthless competitor, but when the victory was won he was gentle and sympathetic and did not take advantage of the fallen enemy. In one instance he tried to bribe an idealistic and honest governor by offering to bail him out of his financial difficulties; when the governor refused to be bribed and vetoed the bill which Frank had forced through the legislature the financier still gave him the loan he needed so badly.[79]

Along with this strain of human sympathy Frank also possessed a peculiar kind of idealism. Dreiser asserted that if he had not become a great financier, Cowperwood would have become a philosopher,[80] for he was in the main an introspective man and "the pathos of broken ideals were not beyond him." [81] This side of Cowperwood's nature was expressed in his quest for the ideal, a quest that took place along two seemingly incongruous lines. In the first place, he was an art collector of some distinction, and he found release from the pressures of his financial affairs in his gallery.[82]

The other line of this quest was connected with Frank's extramarital affairs. For Dreiser, the sexual relationship seems to be connected with art and beauty only so long as the woman retains the sacrificial, solicitous attitude of the mistress, for this connection disappears when the relationship descends to the "grasping legality of established matrimony. . . ." [83] The logical conclusion of this attitude is seen when Cowperwood finally came to perceive "that the ultimate end of fame, power, vigor was beauty, and that beauty was a compound of the taste, the emotion, the innate culture, passion, and dreams of a woman like Berenice Fleming." [84]

This was the rather complex individual who was Frank Cowperwood. Was he, then, responsible for his own destiny or was he not? The point should be made (a point which most commentators have chosen to ignore), that Frank was not in the end successful. The fact of his ultimate failure does violence to the interpretations of these novels as amoral and makes it necessary to determine both the reason for Cowperwood's rise and the cause of his fall. The logic of the story seems to indicate that Frank rose because of his own abilities and his willingness to participate wholeheartedly in the battle of life. Similarly, it seems that he caused his own downfall by an unfortunate ability to choose the wrong mistresses. These are the facts emphasized by those who see Cowperwood as a free individual in charge of his own destiny.

But Dreiser made it difficult to adhere to this position by his own interpolations. Cowperwood, himself, was at a loss to explain the reason for his success. Why, he asked, had he been given a fine mind; why had he achieved financial success? Not because he had earned or deserved it, certainly. He rejected the notion that it could have been simply the result of an accident in favor of a belief in his lucky star—his destiny.[85] Speculating on success in general, Dreiser indicated that Providence of some description does shape men's lives.

It is one of the splendid yet sinister fascinations of life that there is no tracing to their ultimate sources all the winds of influence that play upon a given barque—all the breaths of chance that fill or desert our bellied or our sagging sails. We plan and plan, but who by taking thought can add a cubit to his stature? Who can overcome or even assist the Providence that shapes our ends, rough hew them as we may.[86]

Man, it would seem, can "rough hew" the plan of his life, and perhaps, as David Brion Davis suggests, he can find fleeting or momentary happiness in contemplation of the art spirit—as Cowperwood, for example, sought momentary release in visits to his art gallery—but in the end he cannot control his own destiny.[87]

The destiny of man is not, however, left solely to chance. The life of the individual may be controlled largely by chance, but in the end it is part of the eternal equation which controls the destiny of society as a whole. In the final pages of the second volume of the Cowperwood series, Dreiser gave an over-all interpretation of the movement of society. The world, he says, has too much religion. We should spurn the teachings of moralists and seek knowledge of life, instead, in life itself, where we would find that the life force, in essence or in society, is an equation. The individual may rise up and appear to be master of all he surveys—for a while. Then the mass will rise up to subdue him and restore the eternal equation. The value words of our language—right, justice, truth, morality, and the rest— are, he felt, simply expressions of the need for balance, a recognition of the equation. In Cowperwood's case he states it as follows:

Rushing like a great comet to the zenith, his path a blazing trail, Cowperwood did for the hour illuminate the terrors and wonders of individuality. But for him also the eternal equation—the pathos of the discovery that even giants are but pygmies, and that an ultimate balance must be struck.[88]

This does not mean that man must meekly submit or that he must work for the realization of that equation which will be the inevitable result. Cowperwood, for one, continued his attempt to impose his will upon society and to search for the ideal, but Dreiser insisted that he would achieve neither.

And this giant himself, rushing on to new struggles and new difficulties in an older land, forever suffering the goad of a restless heart— for him was no ultimate peace, no real understanding, but only hunger and thirst and wonder. Wealth, wealth, wealth! A new grasp of a new great problem and its eventual solution. Anew the old urgent thirst for life, and only its partial quenchment.[89]

Even for the great and mighty Cowperwood there would be no loss of isolation. Rejected by a society whose mandates he would not, or could not, obey, he continued a quest that would end only in death.

Dreiser's final novel of the pre-World War I period is the highly controversial story of Eugene Witla, *The "Genius."* Any reader who comes to this novel with a knowledge of the author's life is struck immediately by the close similarity between the story of Witla and the biography of Theodore Dreiser, for *The "Genius"* is essentially a fictionalized version of the author's life up to the time he separated from the Butterick organization and returned to his more serious literary pursuits. Partially for this reason, the events of the novel must be related in some detail.

Eugene Witla was a rather weak child with a moody disposition and an intense sense of beauty, who was born into a small-town, middle-class family. Like most of Dreiser's characters, Eugene chafed at his modest circumstances and left home to seek his fortune in the city—Chicago. He had some vague ideas about art school or newspaper work, but had to take various jobs for which he was totally unsuited, and as he viewed the extreme gap between rich and poor, the brutality of the city soon manifested itself to him.

On one job Witla managed to save a little money, with which he was able to enter the art school. Then, on a trip home, he made the acquaintance of a farm-bred schoolteacher, Angela Blue. She was five years older than Eugene and as conventional in her outlook on life as he was unconventional—but "sexual affinity" made itself manifest.

Back in Chicago, Eugene was thrilled by the Bohemian atmosphere of the art school, and he entered into a sexual relationship with a young model at the same time he was carrying on a nonphysical courtship of Angela. By this time Eugene had obtained a position as a newspaper illustrator where he first learned that he could write as well as paint.

The thought of marrying Angela and keeping the model as his

mistress entered his mind, but he could do neither without a good deal more money than he was making. So, again irked by his lack of means, he left to seek greener pastures in New York. At this point Dreiser first presented Eugene's sexual adventures as a perpetual quest for beauty, as he wrote:

He was an idealist by temperament, in love with the aesthetic, in love with love, and . . . there was no permanent faith in him for anybody —except the impossible she.[90]

In New York Eugene was again struck by the fixed state of wealth and luxury and the distance which separated the ordinary man from their attainment; again he had to do battle with a new and frightening world. But by the spring of his second year in the city moderate success had been attained and he made his first trip to Angela's home in Wisconsin. Witla found the whole Blue family to be possessed of stability and quiet force; they were well grounded, not in church dogma but in religious precepts, and they made him wonder at his own moral laxity. When he left, Eugene had had an idyllic interlude in the bucolic atmosphere of the Blue family farm, and he found their respectable relationship to society an admirable one.

Back in New York, he took a studio with two fellow artists and that winter placed his first work in a leading magazine. During the same period he met Miriam Finch, a sophisticated woman with whom, Dreiser said, he came to the sanest understanding he had yet reached with any woman—an intellectual companionship, not an affair. But at the same time he was flattered by the admiration of the beautiful, sensuous Christine Channing. The following summer, in a mood of philosophic doubt as to the meaning of life, Eugene accompanied Christine to the mountains instead of going to Angela. This again was an idyllic interlude for, in Christine, Eugene found for the first time a combination of physical and intellectual compatibility. He was shocked, however, by her amorality for

her parents. There he found that most of his friends avoided him, and after a few abortive attempts to sell his paintings he took a job as a railroad hand. He was relatively content with this position until his landlady's married daughter came to town. They began an affair which was hampered but not terminated by Angela's return, and her subsequent discovery of his latest infidelity brought on new conflicts and mutual recriminations.

Ultimately Eugene became convinced that success meant hard work. This brought home to him his own dual outlook on life. From his study of other men Eugene concluded that some men were honest, moral, and virtuous, at least to some degree, and some men, such as Angela's father, had all these qualities. He saw that these men rose in life by persistent hard work and rigid adherence to duty. When he examined his own being he saw none of these qualities. It occurred to him that other men did not think much of a man who was as obsessed by women as he was; that a man who had this vice would never get anywhere. "Conscience was his barrier, a conscience unmodified by cold self-interest." [94] On the other hand, his intelligence told him that it was the strong and the amoral who got ahead in the world, that most people were not controlled by moral standards, and that there was no real justice in life. If there was an order, a system in society it did not seem to work very well. He found himself torn between his conscience and his philosophy, and this left him feeling altogether mean and contemptible.[95]

Nonetheless, he acted upon the notion that success meant hard work with no philandering and found a job as a newspaper illustrator. He then moved to an advertising agency where he became a real success, and from there he moved straight up the ladder until he became co-manager of a large publishing house.

At this time Eugene became acquainted with the wealthy Mrs. Dale and her daughter, Suzanne, whose fresh, young beauty immediately attracted him. "For a fourth or a fifth time Eugene was imagining himself to be terribly, eagerly, fearsomely in love." [96] By this time he had made a success of the publishing company, but he and Suzanne confessed their love and he gradually lost all sense of responsibility and interest in the business of publishing. Then one night Angela caught her husband and Suzanne in each other's arms and the usual scene ensued. Hoping to hold her husband, Angela then told Eugene, truthfully, that she was pregnant, but instead of rendering him repentant, this revelation only convinced him that she was trying to trap him into staying with her.

Mrs. Dale found out about the affair and complained to Eugene's employer. This, plus all the other elements working against him at the publishing company, led the owner of the firm to give Eugene what amounted to a dismissal. At almost the same time he lost all his savings in a real estate deal and gradually came to see the extent of damage Mrs. Dale could do to his career. Meanwhile Suzanne was thinking seriously about the matter for the first time, and under a barrage of fire from all sides she agreed to go away with her mother for a year.

These events precipitated another period of despair for Eugene and he was saved from suicide only by the gradual return of his desire to paint.[97] He was also, at this time, suffering from a sharp pain in his groin and his sister urged him to go to a Christian Scientist practitioner. But Christianity as a whole was repulsive to him. He knew that his naturalistic philosophy made room for a first cause, and he admitted that there was a spirit called God, but he doubted that this spirit concerned itself with human affairs.[98] "He was a doubter ever. All life . . . went to pieces under his scalpel, and he could not put it together again logically, once he had it cut up." [99] Finally he did go but could not reconcile the Christian Science concept of a universe of goodness with the world as he knew it, for Mary Baker Eddy's teachings were diametrically opposed to his own conviction that the universe was cruel and malicious.[100]

His desire for Suzanne was still strong, but as the time for the birth of Angela's baby approached he began to see the danger of childbirth for a woman of Angela's age, and he repented of his earlier desire for her death. Thinking of someone other than himself for the first time in months, he vowed to reform if Angela pulled through, but she lived only long enough to hear Eugene confess his sins, swear reformation, and pledge his care to the child.

During the three years following the death of his wife, Eugene passed through all the byways of philosophy and religion to arrive finally at the conclusion that life was only ceaseless change. Dreiser said that Eugene was not really changed by all this; he was "only hardened intellectually and emotionally— tempered for life and work." [101] He worked feverishly and brilliantly at his art, and his next exhibition was a success. Still lured by beautiful women, Eugene was now in control of his faculties and managed to live a comparatively normal life with his sister's family and his own child.

The story of this novel and of Eugene Witla has been developed at some length for two reasons. First, because it provides insight into the life of Dreiser himself, particularly in so far as it may be read as a rationalization of his own sexual adventures. Secondly, it is in this novel that Dreiser gives the most complete fictional treatment of some of the aspects of his concept of man that were mentioned earlier. The search for beauty—for the ideal—through painting and women, which was mentioned as one side of Frank Cowperwood's nature, was even more important to Eugene Witla.[102] Here again Dreiser presented an individual's varied sexual relationships as essentially a quest for beauty arising out of the artistic side of the man's nature. But again he failed to clear his mind entirely of the traditional notion that such activities are evil, and, as with Cowperwood, they were certainly one of the reasons why Eugene encountered so many difficulties. This continuing sense of sin is further emphasized by the artist's pangs of conscience during each affair, and by the fact that his most serious affair, that with Suzanne Dale, never reached a physical culmination.

This equivocation about the nature of the extramarital sexual relationship is a segment of the first two major conflicts in the novel. Throughout the novel Dreiser portrayed Eugene's mind as being pulled in two directions; his conscience telling him that he was the most vile of men, while his intelligence told him that he lived in an amoral world where such actions are justified.[103] Here Dreiser recognized the most perplexing ethical problem of his age—the conflict between social tradition and the apparent implications of the new industrial society and the new science. Even the "genius," the artist, and in all probability the author as well, could not escape this inner conflict. The degree to which Dreiser retained elements of traditional morality, a morality that based responsibility on free will, can again best be investigated by examining the three levels, or points of view, from which Dreiser mentioned the conflict—the individual, the social, and the cosmic.

"Human nature is a subtle, irritable, irrational thing," Dreiser wrote. "It is not so much governed by rules of ethics and conditions of understanding as a thing of moods and temperament." [104] This was certainly true of Eugene's passion for women, and Dreiser indicated that this inability of the mind to control the passions is a human characteristic. "It is a question whether the human will, of itself alone, ever has cured or ever can cure any human weakness." [105] Man is urged forward by "blood moods" which both social convention and reason condemn. Perhaps Dreiser saw that if he pushed this ability of the passions to dominate man to its ultimate conclusion, Eugene would be reduced completely to the animal level, and this does not seem to have been his intention. He continually compared the artist's thirst for women to the alcoholic's thirst for liquor, but he did not really make him a confirmed alcoholic. Eugene could, and sometimes did, triumph over his passions by the use of his reason.

Dreiser did not, in this novel, consider sexual passion a sufficient basis for a lasting marriage. With both Christine Channing and Suzanne Dale, Eugene had some intellectual compatibility, but with Angela "his only urge was his desire, in the gratification of which he might find compensation." [106] And Dreiser suggested, "It was a thin reed to lean on; there could be no honest satisfaction in it." [107] Spiritual love, he considered, was the only enduring kind.

It is written that love is deathless, but this was not written of the body nor does it concern the fevers of desire. The marriage of true minds to which Shakespeare would admit no impediment is of a different texture and has little sex in it.[108]

This intellectual love between man and woman is "deathless in so far as it reflects the spiritual ideals of the universe—not more so. All else is illusion of short duration and vanishes in thin air." [109] Nor is man exempt from the consequences of his surrender to passions simply because the world does not find him out. Dreiser wrote, "We think that our actions when unseen of mortal eyes resolve themselves into nothingness, but this is not true. They are woven indefinably into our being, and shine forth ultimately as the real self, in spite of all our pretences." [110] So, on the personal level, it would seem that Dreiser retained many elements of traditional morality which held man responsible for his actions. But this must be offset by his view from the social and cosmic level.

The social stratification and social tradition that were mentioned in connection with *Jennie Gerhardt* are strongly operative in *The "Genius."* Here Dreiser wrote of the various classes of human society "and the barriers which these offer to a free migration of individuals from one class to another." [111] The forces of environment, including the particular social stratum which one occupies, exert such a strong influence that priests and lawyers, as well as laborers, *appear* to be born with their particular attributes.[112] This social stratification and environment endows one with an instinct toward the social norm which constitutes a force for the continuation of social tradition. When Eugene's friends deserted him, Dreiser commented that it is natural for people to avoid the man whose conduct violates the social code.

Our social life is so organized, so closely knit upon a warp of instinct, that we almost always instinctively flee that which does not accord with custom, usage, preconceived notions and tendencies.[113]

Adherence to the social norm would seem to be instinctive when viewed from the social point of view, but what happens when the problem is approached from the cosmic level? In the period before he went to Christine in the mountains, Dreiser put Eugene through his own period of philosophic doubt. He was thrown into a turmoil by his reading of Spencer, Spinoza, Schopenhauer, Epictetus, and Marcus Aurelius, and concluded that life had no meaning, that it is nothing but ceaseless change. His reading of Darwin and Huxley showed him some form in nature's methods but did not dissipate his gloom, and it made him all the more eager to live and be loved.[114] In the mountains with Christine, Eugene wondered why the momentary peace and beauty which he discovered there could not remain forever, and he concluded that even this would become deadly after a while. "The call of the soul is for motion, not peace. Peace after activity for a little while, then activity again. So must it be." [115] Dreiser said that Eugene went through many philosophic byways during his life but he never really changed his mind to any great extent, and this final statement of his cosmic view of life is not vitally different from that which he had held all along.

He then reached a state not of abnegation, but of philosophic open-mindedness or agnosticism. He came to know that he did not know what to believe. All apparently was permitted, nothing fixed. Perhaps life loved only change, equation, drama, laughter. . . . He realized that at worst and at best it was beautiful, artistic, gay . . . this large thing which he at once loved and detested was sparkling on. . . . He was negligible—but, oh, the sting and delight of its inner shrines and favorable illusions.[116]

In the light of these views on society and life, one can understand Dreiser's most complete statement on the validity of morality in the social and cosmic contexts. This statement occurred when Eugene found himself impressed by the solid morality of the Blue family on his first visit to their home, but it was a view that the remainder of the novel did not really alter.

He was glad to see them, believed they had a place in society, but was uncertain whether they bore any fixed or important relationship to him. He was always thinking in his private conscience that life was somehow bigger and subtler and darker than any given theory or order of living. It might well be worthwhile for a man or a woman to be honest and moral within a given condition or quality of society but it did not matter at all in the ultimate substance and composition of the universe. Any form or order of society which hoped to endure must have individuals like Mrs. Blue, who would conform to the highest standards and theories of that society, and when found they were admirable, but they meant nothing in the shifting, subtle forces of nature. They were just accidental harmonies blossoming out of something which meant everything here to this order, nothing to the universe at large.[117]

So it would seem that for Dreiser whatever disorientation and increase in the sense of isolation immorality might bring to the individual, whatever its social consequences, it means nothing at all in the cosmic vastness where life is nothing but change ruled over by the great god, Whirl.

Before leaving this complex novel brief mention must be made of the conflict which Dreiser saw in contemporary society between the pursuit of beauty—the ideal—and material success. In the life of Frank Cowperwood these two pursuits were more complementary than conflicting, except when the quest for beauty found expression in extramarital affairs. But they formed an important conflict in the life of Eugene Witla, just as they did in the life of Theodore Dreiser. Especially after his rise in the advertising and publication world, Eugene found himself torn between his desire for material success and his desire to paint. And, as was true in Dreiser's own career, Eugene was not able willingly to forego material success for art until he was forced to do so by the scandal of an affair. Actually, Dreiser did not really show the desire for material success to be a socially inculcated value until the writing of *An American Tragedy,* after the close of the period under consideration here, so the importance of this conflict for present considerations is simply to show another struggle which Dreiser, at that time, saw taking place within the individual.

So far, little mention has been made of the mass of Dreiser's writings other than novels. In grouping these other writings together, the assumption is made that Dreiser's concept of man remained fairly constant from the time he started publishing (at about thirty years of age) to the end of the period under consideration. His emphasis on particular aspects of this concept changed or, perhaps more accurately, shifted from time to time, but this does not mean, as some commentators have maintained, that there was a basic change in the concepts themselves. The preceding analysis of the novels indicates that no such fundamental change took place.

For purposes of analysis, the shorter and nonfictional writings have been divided into four general categories: Dreiser's direct statements on human nature as such; his view of man in society, which involves also the problem of Dreiser as a reformer; his ideas on man in the cosmic drama of life itself; and, finally, the question of free will and the allied issue of ethical values. All of these questions are, of course, interrelated, and to separate them is to impose an artificial order on Dreiser's writings, but this seems necessary for purposes of clarity.

Dreiser generally considered man in connection with society

or with the cosmos, and he seems to have been little concerned with human nature apart from the context in which he found it, thus making it somewhat difficult to ascertain what he believed man would be under considerations different from those of his own age. Nevertheless, he did make a few general comments on the subject in various writings. In the first place, it is fairly clear that he considered human nature to be relatively constant, not varying unduly from age to age, society to society, or class to class. In *A Traveler at Forty*, he suggested that national characteristics are not simply the product of environment but are strongly dependent on the continuity of racial stock. "Races like animals," he wrote, "have an origin above soil and do hold their own in spite of changed or changing climatic conditions." [118]

I think we make a mistake when we assume that the manners, customs, details, conversations, interests and excitements of people anywhere were ever much different from what they are now. . . . Life works about the same in all times. Only exterior aspects change.[119]

Although human nature is fixed and all men are essentially alike, some individuals are certainly better off than others, and this inequality is also embedded in the nature of man. In reply to an English aristocrat who was denouncing the leveling tendencies of democracy, Dreiser contended:

Not so, I thought and said, for democracy can never alter the unalterable difference between high and low, rich and poor, little brain and big brain, strength and weakness. It cannot abolish differences and make a level plain.[120]

This belief in the fixity of human nature and in the inability of democracy to abolish the inequalities between men should be borne in mind when one considers Dreiser as an environmentalist.

Also, it should be pointed out that, despite his comments on the human animal, no character in Dreiser's fiction was presented as essentially animal. Mencken took violent exception to the contemporary references to Dreiser's characters as animals. The conduct of these characters, he said, was "no more merely animal than the behavior of such acknowledged and undoubted human beings as Woodrow Wilson and Jane Addams." [121]

The truth is, of course, that Dreiser viewed man as a compound of good and evil, but since, as he believed, Americans and nearly all contemporary authors were deluded about the nature of man, he took it upon himself to enlighten them by stressing the evil side.[122] For Dreiser, truth was to be discovered "in life itself," and life taught "that man in all his relations is neither good nor evil, but both." [123] H. L. Mencken was one of the few contemporaries of Dreiser to see that one of the basic conflicts in his writings was that which takes place within man himself, between the two sides of his dual nature. He pointed this out in his defense of *The "Genius."*

The whole point of the story of Witla . . . is this: That his life is a bitter conflict between the animal in him and the aspiring soul; between the flesh and the spirit, between what is weak in him and what is strong, between what is base and what is noble.[124]

Mencken, in this statement, has obviously oversimplified the problem in *The "Genius,"* but he did point out one of the most important conflicts, not only in the life of Eugene Witla, but of Frank Cowperwood as well.

But if the major conflict is within the mind of the individual, what is the connection between the individual and the society of which he is a part? Authorities again have differed in their opinions on the extent to which Dreiser subjected his characters to the control of society. Part of this confusion arises from a similar confusion in Dreiser's own comments. At one time he insists, "The so-called standards of right, truth, justice, law, are no more than the wire netting of a sieve through which the water of life pushes almost uninterrupted." [125] At other times he wrote of social custom as operating with crushing force, as in this statement of the thoughts of a young reporter as he watched a crowd preparing to lynch a Negro who had raped a white girl.

Custom seemed to require death in this way for this. It was like some axiomatic, mathematic law—hard, but custom. The silent company, an articulated, mechanical and therefore terrible thing, moved on. It also was axiomatic, mathematic. [126]

From these and other remarks it would seem that Dreiser considered society to be a force which could encourage but could not control the evil that was in man.

Just as the critics have disagreed on the extent to which Dreiser subjected man to the control of society, so, too, have they disagreed about his views on man's capacity to change his environment—to bring about reform. [127] Here the difference of opinion arises from a confusion of Dreiser's sympathy for suffering, with a belief in the possibility of reform. "I could weep just at the sight of a large, drab, hungry manufacturing town," wrote Dreiser. "I feel sorry for ignorant humanity." [128] In his early days he expressed some belief in the possibility of reforming human conditions and even in later years he retained a soft spot in his heart for the idealistic reformer. It may sound foolish, he said, to talk about the dreamings of an idealist at a time when America was saddled with a ruling oligarchy, but

we always want to help the mass, we idealists, *at first*. We look about and see human beings like ourselves, struggling, complaining, dying, pinching along with little or nothing, and our first thought is that some one human being or some group of beings is responsible, that nature has designed all to have plenty, and that all we have to do is clear away the greed of a few individuals. . . . I used to feel that way and do yet, at times. I should hate to think it was all over with America and its lovely morning dreams. [129]

Here, too, Dreiser mentioned the equilibrium theory which has been explained in connection with *The Titan*. Contrasts between the fortunes of men are constant, but when these contrasts become too great, "up rises some tender spirit," among whom Dreiser mentioned several biblical and religious figures as well as Henry George, Whitman, Altgeld, and Bryan. "These men," he wrote, "are not always thinking of themselves, you may depend on it." [130] He went on to say that limited reform is possible—"a rough equation can be struck always." [131] But really meaningful reform is probably not possible—utopia is unachievable, and, he suggested, also undesirable.[132] The heart of Dreiser's attitude is summed up in the following statement.

Messieurs, I know the strong must rule the weak, the big brain the little one, but why not some small approximation toward equilibrium, just a slightly less heavily loaded table for Dives and a few more crumbs for Lazarus? I beg you—a few more crumbs! [133]

Here is evidence of the mind of a man whose capacity for sympathy was overwhelming, but who could find no means of bringing lasting help to those for whom he grieved.

The source of Dreiser's pessimism, with regard to improving man's lot in society, can be found, at least in the philosophic sense, in his belief that the whole human struggle is insignificant when seen in the light of cosmic vastness. He described man as a slave, a grain of sand, and an infinitesimal shell. Such references are scattered throughout his fictional and nonfictional works.[134]

Yet here on earth these atoms called men must participate in the battle of life. In one of his early short stories, Dreiser told of a man who fell asleep in the park and, dreaming he was an ant, found life in miniature in a battle of the ants.[135] In *Life, Art and America*, he assailed the unthinking American for his faith in the inalienable rights of man when life itself teaches that there are no such rights.[136] Occasionally the battle that is life became too much even for Dreiser. "Now and then, very frequently, in fact, life becomes too much for my hardy stomach," he says. "I withdraw, chilled and stupefied by the way strength survives and weakness goes under." [137] Yet the hardness and cruelty of man to man is as nothing compared to the cruelty of nature itself. "I indict nature here and now, as I always do and always shall do, as being aimless, pointless, unfair, unjust." [138]

These insignificant beings, participating in the battle of life, have tried to cast the mysteries of the universe into a mold. But Dreiser contended, "Life will not be boxed in boxes. It will not be wrapped and tied up with strings and set aside on a shelf to await a particular religious or moral use." [139] For Dreiser, life was a mystery, a puzzle, a constant wonder. One of the best expressions of his sense of the mystery of life is the poem, "Ye Ages, Ye Tribes," written in 1916.

> Ye ages, ye tribes, long parade of nations!
> I dream, and ye come back, the strong, the proud,
>   the beautiful,
> Rockcave and temple, burrow and throne, hunter
>   and army.
> The mighty show and concealment, unrest and
>   prayer, shrines and tombs!
> How have ye strewn the earth, how burned with
>   your insatiate passions, how fallen, fallen.
> Oh, the loves alone, the tears alone, the strifes alone
>   —how innumerable.
> How has man reveled with woman, master driven
>   slave, Caesars slain with armies!
> How agonies have sweated brows, pains racked
>   bodies, the unattainable lured all.
> What of chains, gibbets, hearts of stone?
> Has it brought order out of disorder, faith out of
>   fear, aim out of turmoil?
> Has it answered "Why?"
> Lo, the earth resounds with the bells of creed, and
>   all men pray.

They bow down in wonder, and know not.
They gaze upon one another, and find no answer.[140]

But, like Eugene Witla and Lester Kane, once Dreiser had destroyed the traditional framework of the value system—social tradition and religion—by the use of the new science, he then found that science could neither replace that value system with a new one nor provide satisfactory answers to the mystery of life. As Robert Shafer has pointed out, Dreiser took from Spencer and the naturalistic philosophers only what he wanted, and what he wanted contained little that was characteristic of that philosophy. In life he found accident, chaos, and disorder which was "abruptly contradictory of the Synthetic gentleman's grandiose fancy of one eternal universal law infallibly working to bring about perfection in all things earthly." [141] Dreiser himself stated that Darwin had not provided him with answers to the questions that troubled him.

The great question with me always was, how did people come to be, in the first place? What were the underlying laws of our being? How did it come that human beings could separate themselves from cosmic solidarity and navigate alone? . . . The fact that Darwin had already set forward his facts as to evolution did not clear things up for me at all.[142]

Since science could not provide ultimate answers, Dreiser had no real objection to religion as such. "I have no deadly opposition to religion," he wrote. "The weak and troubled mind must have something on which to rest." [143]

In a universe where man is insignificant and yet is forced to participate in a battle of life, the significance of which is beyond his comprehension, is there any chance for progress, and, if so, what part will man play in bringing it about? Burton Rascoe has called Dreiser "a tragic optimist, trembling with profound pity over the dismal contortions of life, but ever hopeful that somehow, some time, man's burdens will be lightened and his afflictions healed." [144] There is considerable evidence that, at least in his early days, Dreiser did believe in some form of progress. As he grew older, however, Dreiser apparently lost his early belief in universal progress, although he retained a faith in limited progress in some areas. He was much impressed by the work of some of the labor leaders and felt that their efforts might bring about a lessening in the severity of the human experience—a form of limited progress in which individuals would play a significant and creative role. [145]

In most of his statements concerning an order in the universe, however, Dreiser contended that nature's plan took no notice of man. In both *A Traveler at Forty* and *A Hoosier Holiday*, Dreiser repudiated his former position that nature is simply blind force. He wrote, "I have always felt, in spite of all my carpings, that somehow in a large way there is a rude justice done under the sun. . . ." [146] This does not mean that nature or God takes any notice of the individual; it is simply an extension of Dreiser's theory of the eternal equation. He asked man to believe that there is a "larger intelligence at work" which has an over-all plan for the universe, but which takes no notice of man, who is at best a tool. [147] Since the universal planner takes no particular notice of man as an individual, the individual's actions are not necessarily determined, and Dreiser left room in his cosmic plan for the operation of human will and social forces. [148]

Dreiser's individuals existed in a universe which did not regard them as important, participated in a battle called life which they could not understand, and dwelled in a society that oppressed them with its unnatural restrictions but provided them with no lasting human relationships. And science, the only road to truth, provided no promise that man's lot would ever be any better; progress, while possible, was certainly unlikely. Man's life was tragedy, a tragedy arising out of the discrepancy between the human dream and human capabilities. In one of his sketches Dreiser told of an artist of extremely varied talents who died suddenly on the threshold of success. This man's story was the story of mankind.

We toil so much, we dream so richly, we hasten so fast, and, lo! the green door is opened. We are through it, and its grassy surface has sealed us forever from all which apparently we so much crave—even as, breathlessly, we are still running.[149]

Considering the many contradictions in Dreiser's writings, it is not strange that commentators have disagreed rather violently as to whether or not he considered man to have free will. There can be little doubt that as a philosopher Dreiser tended to deny free will. The following is a typical statement from Dreiser, the philosopher.

All good things are gifts—beauty, strength, grace, magnetism, swiftness and sublety of mind, the urge or compulsion to do. Taking thought will not bring them to anyone. Effort never avails save by grace or luck or something else. The illusion of the self made is one of the greatest of all.[150]

Yet in the very act of denial he frequently showed how torn he was between his philosophical convictions and his longing for human freedom. Time and again he celebrated the optimistic innocence of the American who believes himself to be free to act. [151]

Deciding on the free will of his fictional characters is a far more difficult job. Gerald Willen, in one of the most careful studies of Dreiser to date, has contended that Dreiser does endow his characters with wills. The characters may find themselves in situations arising from accident, but once there they take willful action.[152]

As a conscious thinker there is no doubt that Dreiser believed the individual incapable of making a free choice; as a novelist, however, he invariably projected his characters into situations calling for the exercise of the will.

This may be an overstatement of the case in both directions, but the dichotomy between Dreiser the philosopher and Dreiser the novelist does exist. This dichotomy can be clearly seen in the play *Laughing Gas,* which was one of the author's favorites. In this work he expatiated at length on the meaninglessness of life and the insignificance of the human will. Yet the patient, in whose mind these thoughts on life and man took place, saved himself in the end by his own efforts and by his own will to live.[154]

As C. C. Walcutt has pointed out, some of the confusion about free will in Dreiser's writings can be clarified by separating volition and action.[155] This separation can be demonstrated by a brief discussion of the four-act play *The Hand of the Potter,* to which Mencken objected so violently.[156] This play tells the story of Isadore Berchansky, son of a poor Jewish family, whom Dreiser described as

a tall, lithe, broad-shouldered young man of twenty or twenty-one, so strangely composed mentally and physically that he is bizarre. He is so badly compounded chemically that he seems never to be of one mood, and has a restless, jerky, fidgety gait and manner. . . . Also, he has an affliction of the left arm and shoulder, which causes it to twitch or jerk involuntarily.[157]

He was sexually abnormal in that he was so attracted to girls that he couldn't control himself. Unfortunately, this attraction was particularly strong toward girls of eight or ten, and before the opening of the play he had served a prison term for assaulting a very young girl. During the course of the play he assaulted and then killed the child of a neighbor. Isadore was the natural suspect, and, although the police failed to find him, he followed the urgings of his father and committed suicide.

Isadore realized that his sexual attraction to young girls was abnormal, and in his rational moments, away from temptation, he abhorred his urges. He did not wish to commit such acts, but, faced with temptation, he could not help himself. In Isadore's case, the hand of the potter had slipped. Dreiser did not contend that Isadore's actions were acceptable, but he did insist that the boy was not to blame for them. His own ideas were placed in the mouth of one of the Irish reporters who said:

Aal men are naht balanced or normal, be their own free will an' say-so, any more than they're free an' equal in life, an' that's naht at aal. They're naht aal endowed with the power or the will to do an' select, aal the rules ave the copybooks to the contrary nahtwithstandin'. . . . Sometimes I think we're naht unlike those formulae they give ye in a chemical laboratory—if ye're made up right, ye work right; if ye're naht, ye don't, an' that's aal there is to it—laa or no laa.[158]

Here, certainly, is a case of an individual who is free to make up his mind what he wants to do or, in this instance, what he does not want to do, but who is not free to translate that decision into action. A fair conclusion would seem to be that Dreiser retained for his fictional characters a small vestige of the traditional free will, but almost wholly denied the equally traditional idea of human creativity—the ability of the individual to change or alter his environment. Not one of Dreiser's characters showed any real capacity in this regard. Even the dynamic Cowperwood ultimately failed in his attempt.

Of the three major literary figures of the period, Theodore Dreiser is, in many ways, the most difficult with which to deal. In his writings one is faced with the exact opposite of the epigrammatic style of Crane, who made few direct references to his concept of man. With Dreiser the problem is one of too much direct comment—comment which is not only contradictory, but is also in conflict with the picture of man he presents in his fiction. In trying to understand and present his underlying concept of man, one is forced to rely on general tendencies and over-all impressions to a much greater extent than with the other writers considered.

Dreiser recognized the fact that he was outside the mainstream of American letters from both a cultural and an economic standpoint, and this was one of the most important influences operating upon him. He viewed the contemporary economic struggle from the inside to a far greater extent than any other writer considered in this paper. Stephen Crane also was immersed in the economic struggle, but that was largely his own choice, for he could have fallen back on his family at any time. Howells, Norris, and Churchill were never in any real danger of destitution. Perhaps this is the main reason why Dreiser, more than any other writer except Crane, found it impossible to accept the traditional picture of life, of society, and of man. Social forces were so ever-present in the life of the novelist that he found it difficult, perhaps even impossible, to visualize what man might be apart from that society. He was less concerned with the natural man—man apart from institutions and traditions—than any of the four other writers considered here.

Man, for Dreiser, was an insignificant atom in a vast cosmos where neither he nor his society was considered to be important. There was a plan in nature, perhaps even a master planner, but this plan or planner took no notice of the hopes and aspirations of the individual, who was but a slave, a tool, to be utilized by nature, then cast aside. Even though man could not interfere with the plan of the universe, a plan which Dreiser conceived of as a tendency toward equilibrium, he could "rough hew" the edges of his own life.

Thus man was endowed with a very limited freedom to act, and his acts took place in a social context where he was hedged about with unnatural restrictions, yet forced to take part in an almost unmitigated battle for life. In this society man could seldom, if ever, achieve lasting human contacts. The one exception

to this might be the spiritual love of two individuals, unhindered
by legal restrictions, but Dreiser never portrayed anyone who
actually achieved this relationship. Man hindered himself in
the social context by adhering instinctively to the illusions about
life and human nature which were perpetuated in social and
religious tradition, and by ostracizing those who broke this code.
His only hope for progress was to free himself of these illusions,
and this Dreiser did not feel was likely to happen because of
man's weakness.

Hedged about by social restrictions and drawn by chemical
compulsions, most men found it impossible to order their lives
in the light of reason. Dreiser does not wholly deprive man of
either reason or moral faculties but he does insist that, in most
cases, these are not strong enough to overcome his animal appetites. The traditional dual nature of man thus remains an
integral part of Dreiser's concept, and his novels depict many
battles between the two sides of man's nature. His divergence
from tradition lies in his greater emphasis on the weakness of
man, but he still wanted man to try to curb the evil within himself and to overcome the social and natural forces allied against
him.

So while Dreiser joined his fellow novelists and the social
scientists of his day in condemning contemporary society, he
rejected the notion of the latter that man was essentially a free
and creative being who could and would utilize the new industrialism to bring about progress toward utopia. His own life
experience would not allow him to accept their view of the
social nature of the unselfish natural man who, cleansed of the
corruption instilled in him by historic society, would revert to
his natural goodness.

Dreiser's boundless capacity for sympathy has misled many
interpreters into picturing him as a reformer who believed in
the doctrine of progress.[159] It was certainly true that he clung
to the traditional ethical verities and longed to improve the

conditions of suffering humanity, but he was sincerely convinced that man could accomplish little in this direction. Since he admitted that he could not comprehend the plan of the universe, he did not deny that some progress or reform was possible, but if it came about as the reformers planned, it would be by accident. This combination of sympathy for his fellow man and longing for the ethical verities, joined with his belief in the essential impotence of human effort, produced in Dreiser a sense of the tragedy of life which in his day was equaled only by that of Stephen Crane.

It was only when his sympathy carried him away that he gave voice to the rebellion that was still strong in him. Man is an animal who can dream of something better than animality; he can dream of things he can never achieve. Life itself is tragedy. But, still, as Mencken said, Dreiser was only halfway between "Warsaw, Indiana, and the Socratic grove." [160] He had seen too much of life to subscribe to the doctrines of Progessivism; he retained too much sympathy to give up once and for all the ethical values which he shared with his contemporaries. In the end he had to acknowledge the Furies, for he had "heard the disastrous beating of their wings." [161]

5

WINSTON CHURCHILL

The Conservative Revolution

THE three authors just considered, Stephen Crane, Frank Norris, and Theodore Dreiser, are generally considered to be among the most important American literary figures of their day. No course of study in American literature of the Progressive period could afford to ignore any one of them. Yet, if it were possible to go back to, say, 1915 and ask the average educated American to name the three most prominent authors of the period since 1890, it is highly doubtful that any of these three men would appear on the list. A man whose name would almost certainly be on the list is Winston Churchill. In today's literature courses he is mentioned with condescension if he is mentioned at all, yet during the Progressive years Churchill's novels probably outsold the works of Crane, Norris, and Dreiser combined.

All of Winston Churchill's novels except *The Celebrity* and *The Dwelling Place of Light*—the first and last that he published—ranked among the ten best-selling fiction works for the year of their publication, and even *The Dwelling Place of Light* is listed among the one hundred most popular fictional works published between 1895 and 1920. Five of his novels ranked first in sales in the year they were published: *The Crisis,* 1901; *The Crossing,* 1904; *Coniston,* 1906; *Mr. Crewe's Career,* 1908; and

The Inside of the Cup, 1913. *A Modern Chronicle* in 1910 and
A Far Country in 1915 placed second; *Richard Carvel* came in
third in 1899. His most popular novel, *The Crisis,* sold over a
million copies and was outsold by only twenty-five other novels
from 1895–1945.[1]

Nor was this popularity simply among the female readers of
what William Dean Howells would have called "romances."
Theodore Roosevelt, for example, was an enthusiastic advocate
of Churchill's work.[2] The high regard in which the novelist was
held is shown in the following two quotations. Morris E. Speare
wrote of Churchill:

His works . . . have become great light-houses warning against the
shoals and reefs, and showing the way to the safer paths beyond. Of
Mr. Winston Churchill, the sociologist, there can be no conflict of
opinion as to the value of his works to American moral development
and its national growth. It would be difficult to find another writer of
our time with such balanced emotions, such ingrained common sense,
possessing his freshness and eloquence in discussing moral issues, and
having the contagion of his patriotism.[3]

And John G. Underwood, in *Literature and Insurgency,* 1914,
said:

In an era of mob rule in literature and in life, Winston Churchill
stands distinguished by qualities that old St. Louis and Annapolis
. . . still inculcate; qualities that still make for justice, courage,
truth, dignity and the distinction of conscious rectitude.[4]

In contrast to the view of Churchill's contemporaries, the general
attitude taken by more modern scholars is exemplified by Henry
S. Commager, who found Churchill to be the literary equivalent
of Theodore Roosevelt in politics.

Not without convictions, Churchill was without passion; . . .
Churchill subscribed to admirable ideas but to nothing that can be
called a philosophy, and the ideals were sicklied over with senti-
mentalism. His insights were shrewd rather than profound, his moral

judgments facile rather than conclusive. His villains had hearts of gold, he could not forego the happy ending, and—notwithstanding his own experience in New Hampshire politics—he retained to the end faith in the healing power of the democratic dogma. It is precisely because he was so sensitive a seismograph that his record of the impact of Darwinian ethics upon the older morality has more than an antiquarian interest. He is the perfect historian of the Rooseveltian phase of Progressivism.[5]

Who was this man who was so loved by his contemporaries and so scorned by succeeding generations? Born November 10, 1871, in St. Louis, Winston Churchill could lay claim to a very distinguished American ancestry. His mother, Emma Bell Blaine, was a descendant of Jonathan Edwards and the famous Dwight family; another line of her family moved from colonial Virginia to Kentucky and thence to Missouri, where they became prominent in St. Louis. On his father's side, the American Churchills went back to John Churchill, who settled at Plymouth in 1643, where many of the family became prominent in the West Indies trade.[6]

Like many of his fictional characters, Winston was orphaned at an early age and reared by a maternal uncle and aunt. After graduation from Smith Academy he worked in a warehouse until he received an appointment to the Naval Academy. He graduated from Annapolis in June, 1894, with a fairly good record, but he resigned his commission in order to become a writer. The prospective author then spent a few months editing the *Army and Navy Journal* and a few months with *The Cosmopolitan,* where he soon became managing editor. Then, on October 22, 1895, he married Mabel Harlakenden Hall of St. Louis, a union which provided him with independent means and enabled him to devote full time to writing. He had begun both *Richard Carvel* and *The Celebrity* by April of 1896 when he and Mrs. Churchill sailed for Europe, where he did research for *Richard Carvel. The Celebrity,* published in January, 1898, won him considerable notoriety, for it was thought to be a parody of the ever-popular Richard Harding Davis, but it was *Richard Carvel,* issued in June, 1899, that brought him real fame. With fame came a confusion of names and a personal association (never a friendship) with Winston Leonard Spencer Churchill, later Sir Winston, who in this period was overshadowed by his American namesake.

In the fall of 1898 Churchill bought a hundred acres of land near Cornish, New Hampshire, overlooking the Connecticut River. There he built the later famous Harlakenden House, which gained additional publicity when it was used as a summer White House by President Woodrow Wilson. In the meantime Churchill became the local Sir Walter Scott, known for his grace and dignity, his fashionable dress, and his carriage, complete with footmen and coachmen. The courtly hospitality of Harlakenden House became famous.

Aware that experience in politics would provide him with good literary material, Churchill first became interested in local political affairs in 1902. Like Humphrey Crewe, in *Mr. Crewe's Career,* he proclaimed his candidacy for the legislature by inviting the people of Cornish to Harlakenden House, where he announced his intention of standing for office as a conservative Republican. He was elected to the lower house of the state legislature in 1903 and reelected in 1905. Political leaders saw him as a rich young man with aristocratic tendencies and treated him kindly, telling him stories about Ruel Durkee, one-time political boss of the state and the model for the lead character in *Coniston,* Jethro Bass. He was freely admitted to the headquarters in the Eagle Hotel in Concord from which the Boston and Maine Railroad ran the state, but his legislative career was as frustrating as that of Humphrey Crewe. His bills for minor reforms of various sorts—conservation, highways, and the like— were lost in committee, and his venture into practical politics left him disgusted and revolted.

Then in 1906, following the publication of *Coniston,* the smoldering revolt against the domination of the Boston and Maine burst forth. During this time Churchill became convinced that the Progressives of the Roosevelt variety were the true conservatives, and backed by the reform Lincoln Republican Club he ran for governor of the state. The organization was assured of the support of President Roosevelt, it put forward the usual Progressive platform, and Churchill made it quite clear that his was a fight against "The Trust." But none of the Republican leaders in the state supported him, and he had only a month and a half to campaign before the primary. Nonetheless, by the time of the convention, known as the "fire-escape convention" because of the many nonqualified delegates present in the hall, the machine was unnerved and denounced the novelist-politician vehemently. The result was a riotous affair. Churchill started out fourth on the first ballot and gained the lead by the eighth, only to have his opponents band together and defeat him.

After this defeat Churchill issued a statement that he and the Lincoln Club would continue to battle for their platform, and he remained active in politics for some years. In 1908 he worked actively for Taft but refused to run again himself. He entered the race in 1912 as a Bull Moose candidate for governor, but, as in the national election, the split in the Republican vote gave the election to the Democrats. Although he was skeptical of many of its current ideas, Churchill remained in the national councils of the Progressive party until it collapsed in 1916, but did not again run for office.

When the war broke out Churchill, like most Progressives, did what he could to support the cause. He helped with naval recruiting, wrote articles explaining naval organization, and also visited war fronts at the request of the allied governments. Upon his return he wrote *A Traveller in War-Time,* which contained his essay on America's contribution to the democratic idea. Then, sometime between 1918 and 1922, he decided definitely to withdraw from politics and literature, a resolution he maintained until the publication of *The Uncharted Way* in 1940.

During the years after World War I Churchill lived in semi-retirement. In 1930 he was quoted as saying:

Do you know I've almost forgotten that I ever did write? I never thought much of books anyway. I realize now that I have no deep interest in sociology, for instance. . . . Life goes according to fashions and fads. I am not deploring it. I think everything in life has its place, and one can hardly say that life progresses. . . . It is all temporary. My interests are more timeless than that. That is why I live as I do. After all, it's a question of fun, and I get more fun this way, living apart, painting and carpentering.[7]

This rather pessimistic statement was certainly a far cry from the optimistic Progressive of 1915, but it was an attitude Churchill seems to have maintained for the remainder of his life. When his long life was ended by a heart attack on March 12, 1947, a few of the literary journals noted his passing but, on the whole, he died a forgotten man.

Why should an author's star shine so brightly for two decades, then, almost without flickering, slip from view? At first glance this may seem to be a question for the literary historian or, in more practical terms, for the research department of a publishing company. But at another level it has important implications for a study of American attitudes toward man and society during the period of Churchill's popularity.

One could argue, of course, that Churchill's novels were best-sellers simply because he was a good storyteller writing on popular themes. The difficulty with this interpretation is that it leaves too many problems unsolved. First of all there is the rather obvious problem of the large number of equally effective storytellers who wrote on similar themes, yet did not achieve mass popularity. Secondly, there is the difficulty that Churchill was not considered by his contemporaries primarily as a man of letters or as a storyteller. He was regarded, rather, as a serious student of contemporary problems, and he thought of himself in the same light. He believed completely in the solutions he suggested—at the time they were presented—and he wrote the novels for the specific purpose of dramatizing these solutions. His closest friends were not men of letters and he did not really regard himself as part of the literary world.[8]

Richard Hofstadter is the only one who has attempted to come to grips with the problem of Churchill's tremendous popularity with the Progressive generation at a somewhat greater depth.[9] Hofstadter suggests that "a popular writer's appeal is a commentary on the needs and desires of his public," [10] and thus provides an insight into the mind of his own generation. Putting it another way, the popular novelist or author is popular because he dramatizes ideas nascent in the public mind. Hofstadter's idea of what was in the mind of the Progressive generation is a variation of his well-known hypothesis of the "status revolution." For a variety of reasons, according to his analysis, the rising generation of the 1890s, the Progressive generation, found it impossible to duplicate the epic achievements of its predecessors and "in psychic self-defense many sons and daughters of the middle class, and even of the rich, were driven to condemn what they could not emulate." [11] In other words, they rejected the business ethic of their fathers and everything that outlook implied. They read Churchill because he provided them with heroes and heroines who clung to the ethics of the family rather than to the ethics of trade.

This is a fruitful hypothesis and to an extent it is quite accurate. A number of difficulties arise, however, when one contends that several million people bought Churchill's novels for this reason. There is very little in Hofstadter's thesis that would separate Churchill from William Dean Howells or a dozen other novelists of the period who did not find their books on the best-seller lists. More important, it distorts, in the opinion of the present writer, the picture of the generation he is trying to explain. It makes the Progressive generation, and Churchill, almost totally conservative, even reactionary, in their desire to return to the ethics of the family—an ethic supposedly based upon benevolence and cooperation. Conservative in some important ways the Progressives were, but they, and Churchill, were far more complex than Hofstadter's thesis would lead one to believe. His answer to the problem of Churchill's appeal to his contemporaries, important as it is, must be greatly supplemented by other factors.

In the first place, what was Progressivism? In essence, as Hofstadter implies, it was a reaction against the anarchy and destructiveness of the late nineteenth-century business community with its theory of cut-throat competition based on the Spencerian evolutionary concept of the survival of the fittest. From the Civil War on, there had been a reaction against this world without ethics or manners or values on the part of the older, established families—the Liberal Republicans and the mugwumps or, in the terminology of Eric Goldman, the Patrician Reformers.[12] These older, established families rejected the prevailing society of the late nineteenth century as a corrupting influence that brought out the evil, selfish side of man's dual nature. With William Dean Howells, they looked to society, in the sense of inherited tradition, as a civilizing influence which could save man from the evils of contemporary society.

Hofstadter, in his *Age of Reform,* suggests that this Anglo-Saxon, Protestant, upper middle-class segment of the population was led into the reform movements of that period by the "status revolution" then under way.[13] This status revolution had displaced the cultured leaders of the community and replaced them with a crass group of newly rich whose opportunistic methods had allowed them to overshadow the old gentry. Thus the mugwumps, trained in the genteel tradition of social responsibility, lined up against the *nouveaux riches,* who rejected social responsibility for tooth-and-claw competition. But the mugwumps were a small group and, like Howells, they lacked a program of positive reform. They could not compete with the formidable opposition of the business community and its popular philosophy of the Gospel of Wealth.

Then by the 1890s there developed in America a new social philosophy which justified social order without sacrificing the tradition of American individualism. During the nineteenth century it was generally believed that if man is unhindered by institutions and is free of the burden of inherited traditions, he will give expression to the better side of his nature. In other words, the natural man, while possessing a dual nature, is primarily good, rational, and benevolent. But in society, where he finds himself plagued by institutions and traditions, man gives expression to the evil, irrational, selfish side of his nature. The late nineteenth-century version of this philosophy was contained in the laissez-faire pronouncements of the Gospel of Wealth. This theory was inverted by a revolution in American social philosophy during the 1880s and 1890s, led by the sociologists and social psychologists mentioned earlier, and this revolution must be examined in greater detail because it is the key to an understanding of Churchill's writing and his popularity.

The ideas of these Progressive social scientists are exemplified in the writings of the psychologist Charles Horten Cooley, who insisted that the social man is the good man and the atomistic man of the Lockean tradition and the Gospel of Wealth is the evil man.[14] Like the mugwumps or Patrician Reformers, Cooley and the Progressive social philosophers rejected the business society of the late nineteenth century. But Cooley went far beyond the mugwumps in his attempt to square individualism with the need for social planning. To do this he had to solve the dilemma created by the commitment of his generation to the idea that man is a free and creative individual who is good as long as he is apart from institutions and traditions. This traditional notion, Cooley argued, was a fundamental misunderstanding of the nature of man. According to Cooley, man is by nature social and his meaningful environment is not nature, but society. The infant is born and reared as part of the family group, as part of society. In the primary groups, such as the family, man learns all the ideals which form his basic nature and these are the ideals of cooperation, not competition. Here he finds love, truth, loyalty, benevolence, and moral unity. The natural man, who Cooley asserts is social, is therefore good, rational, and benevolent.

It was when man stepped out of his primary groups that he encountered evil. Men have not followed the altruism of their basic instincts because there was no unity among the primary groups. Misunderstanding among these groups had bred conflict and competition. Thus, while man in the society of prehistory had been good, rational, and benevolent, the history of man in historical society had shown him to be evil, irrational, and selfish. This was because there is a plastic side to the nature of man which had been corrupted by historical society.

The unique promise of the historical society of the late nineteenth century was that industrialism was destroying the evil institutions and traditions of the past and, at the same time, it was providing a revolution in communications that, for the first time, would bring all men and all primary groups into everyday contact with each other. This everyday social intercourse would destroy the misunderstandings of the past and allow the natural man to blossom forth in fruitful cooperation.

It is important to note that while Cooley and the Progressive social scientists asserted that the process of evolutionary progress was the wave of the future, they did not think it was automatic. Man was a necessary and active agent. He was free to fight a battle which was already won; free to create a new social order that was preordained. Victory was assured both because of the unfolding of sociological law and because of man's ability to rationally comprehend that law. Cooley and his fellow academicians thus laid a rational basis for replacing competition with cooperation and, at the same time, retained the American commitment to the creative individual.

Nor was this new social philosophy a completely secular argument, for these men were committed as well to a religion of progress.[15] Because of the force of the attitudes implanted in man by a corrupt contemporary society, Cooley asserted, only a new religion could break the shackles. This new religion would teach man to blend himself into society, to cherish that part of himself that contributed to the whole. The idea of God would merge with that of the social state. The individual, awakened to his spiritual unity with God and with society, would be the agent of God in an evolutionary process which would remake the world in His image.

It is important to note that Cooley, and many of his contemporaries, believed that America could achieve this utopia of social solidarity without major institutional changes—a revolution could be brought about through a change in attitude alone. Here one can see the side of Progressivism that Hofstadter and many other historians have tended to ignore. The Progressives were conservative in their social attitudes, in their desire to preserve most existing institutions, and in their wish to save the free and creative individual of the American tradition. But at the same time they could be radically millennialistic, they could look forward with certainty to a massive spiritual change that would be truly revolutionary.

It is the unique importance of Winston Churchill that he unites, exemplifies, and displays all of these various aspects of Progressivism. In his writings one can see the strength of the conservative mugwump tradition, witness the crucial debate on the nature of man and society, and feel the emotional pulsations of the radically millennialistic fervor that produced the almost incredible optimism which permeated Progressivism. He was a man intimately associated with the climate of opinion during the Progressive period. The following analysis will attempt to show the extent of this association and will also offer a possible explanation for his sudden retirement at the height of his popularity.

The works which Churchill published before 1904 (*The Celebrity, Richard Carvel, The Crisis, The Crossing,* and several short stories) contained very little serious thought about the human situation. All of the heroes were free, rational, moral individuals who fell in love with sweet, self-sacrificing women. The villains were a bad lot, but were easily recognizable by their oily ways, their lack of honor, and their dissipated lives. Virtue, as one might expect, triumphed, and all perfidy was revealed in the end.

There were, however, certain assumptions which Churchill made in these writings that are of value in understanding his views. Perhaps the most enduring of these is his assumption that nobility of character is directly connected with an aristocratic background. In the mugwump tradition, nearly all of his heroes and heroines were descended from high-ranking families, though frequently they themselves did not know this until late in the story. The villains were nearly all moneygrubbers of lowly origin.[16]

Churchill's habit of drawing an elaborate picture of the historical situation in which the action took place has, however, led some critics to classify him as an environmentalist. Underwood, for example, said of *Richard Carvel:*

It is characteristically American in the best sense: in its hatred of snobbery, pretense, treachery and injustice. . . . It is true to life. It transcends the ordinary historical romance of considerable literary pretensions in that it makes its major and minor villains, Chartersea, and his fellow-duelist, Grafton Carvel, Richard's old rector and tutor, and Dorothy Manner's father, more the products of untoward environment than of the evil in their own natures.[17]

This is absurd. Grafton, Chartersea, and Richard's tutor, Allen, were rogues at the time they were introduced into the story and we know little of their environment; what we do know makes it identical with that which spawned such noble characters as Comyn and Richard. Cooper's statement is much more accurate.

Mr. Churchill's heroes and heroines belong with hardly an exception to this dominant, self-sufficient class. Even as small children, they have a precocious assurance; they foreshadow, with surprising accuracy, the men and women they are destined to become. . . . The impression he leaves, in one and all of his books, is that his characters have become what they are, not because of environment, but in defiance of it.[18]

Connected with this faith in the aristocratic tradition was Churchill's espousal of the leadership principle. That is, the good man draws others to him through a power, not defined but demonstrated, which emanates from his personality. This principle was introduced in Churchill's first novel, *The Celebrity* (1898), and in his two early short stories, *Mr. Keegan's Elopement* and *By Order of the Admiral*.[19] Mention is here made of this seemingly secondary aspect of Churchill's view of man because of the overwhelming importance which he later attached to the creative power of the "reborn" individual.

Then, as Churchill turned his attention from the historical romance to the sociopolitical life of his own day, his novels took on a more serious tone. His two so-called political novels, *Coniston* (1906) and *Mr. Crewe's Career* (1908), mark the turning point between the first two phases of his career. The action of the first novel takes place in the small New Hampshire village of Coniston, where the love story of Jethro Bass and

Cynthia Ware is unfolded. Jethro, the village tanner, was beyond the pale religiously, socially, and politically, while Cynthia
was the daughter of an orthodox minister. The political aspect of
the story emerged when it was learned that someone was
making a secret drive for power in Coniston. The respectable
people were shocked at this upsurge of the unlettered and un-
orthodox, but Jethro won the election for head selectman—a
position he then held for thirty-six years.

Before the meeting, Cynthia, believing that Jethro could not
be wicked enough to carry through this unrighteous plan if he
were instructed as to the ethics of the affair, went to him with
an appeal not to use his power in this manner. But when she
saw that he would not or could not stop the move, she fled and
a short time later moved to Boston, where she met and married
Will Wetherell. Before they were married she admitted to Will
that she did not love him, and he accepted the fact that Jethro
was the only man she had ever loved. She died very young,
leaving a daughter who was also named Cynthia and who left
Boston with Will when he was told by his physician that he had
to go to Coniston for his health.

In the twenty-seven years since the first Cynthia had left,
Jethro had risen to become political boss of the state, running
things from his "Throne Room" in the state capital's Pelican
Hotel. Young Cynthia and Jethro almost immediately became
intimate friends, and after Will had conquered some of his fear
of the political boss he, too, became Jethro's friend. Cynthia, by
then a young lady, also frequently encountered Bob Worthington, whose father had been in love with her mother and was now
a big industrialist. The senior Worthington was interested in a
railroad franchise bill, and he was forced to ask Jethro's aid to
get it through the legislature. Will died soon after and Cynthia
went to live with Jethro.

Meanwhile, a political battle was shaping up as the railroads,
led by Worthington, tried to take political control from Jethro.

During this time Jethro had induced Cynthia to remain in Boston with friends and go to school, and there Bob Worthington became a serious suitor. Then a newspaper article appeared which revealed the facts of Jethro's career and methods. Churchill's position on the relative evil of Jethro and Worthington in this matter seems to be expressed by Mr. Morrill, president of a railroad line, who said that while he couldn't defend Jethro's career, the political boss had been a true friend to many, and if Worthington took control then all the personal kindness with which Jethro had mitigated the evils of the system would disappear and the people would be debased a hundred times worse than before. But Cynthia did not see matters in such relative terms and she returned home, brokenhearted, to Coniston, where she confronted Jethro with the articles, begging him to tell her they were not true. When the old man confessed, admiration broke through Cynthia's sorrow as she told the old man that she loved him more than ever before. But she could not eat bread bought with tainted money, and she took a job in a neighboring village.

In the meantime Jethro had, just at the crucial time, dropped out of the political battle, but Worthington, who had just learned of his son's love for Cynthia, made the fatal mistake of forcing her dismissal as a schoolteacher. This brought Jethro roaring back into the fight, and after much excitement he won the greatest political battle of his career. But he himself was unhappy, for he believed that he had forfeited Cynthia's love, the one thing he held dear. Nonetheless, he sent for Worthington, rejected the latter's offer of a bribe, and forced the railroad president to agree to the marriage of Bob and Cynthia. This done, he returned to Coniston, a broken and supposedly defeated man, because he had accomplished this only by conceding his own political power. But Cynthia, realizing what he had done, welcomed him with open arms. Bob rushed back to Cynthia and they were married, and both they and Jethro lived happily ever after. Churchill did not emphasize the fact that this personal happiness was purchased at the expense of turning the state over to Worthington and the railroads.

Jethro Bass was the main character in *Coniston* and the best character study in all of Churchill's writings. He was low-born and therefore naturally lacking in native nobility of character, but at the crucial point in the story Churchill left his motives unclear. During the early chapters of the novel, Jethro was represented as a sober, hard-working individual, slow, stuttering, and unlettered, and it was never clear just why he wanted to become a powerful politician. Writing of the meeting of Cynthia and Jethro, when she came to plead with him not to seize power in Coniston, Churchill stated, "But what she asked was impossible. That wind which he himself had loosed, which was to topple over institutions, was rising, and he could no more have stopped it than he could have hushed the storm." [20]

Here Churchill appears to have taken refuge in ambiguity as he made Jethro responsible for starting the Democratic upsurge but denied him the power to curb it. Then, at the town meeting, he pictured the orthodox as all-righteous and the rising Jacksonian Democrats as all-pernicious. "There is no moral to the story," he says. "Alas—it was one of those things which inscrutable Heaven permitted to be done." [21] The reader is left wondering to just what extent Churchill held Jethro, as an individual, responsible for all this.

The problem was that, by 1904, as Churchill's interest turned from the past to the political-economic life of his own age, he became increasingly aware of the formative powers of man's social environment. In *Coniston*, he came face to face with the basic problem—if man is free and creative, that is, if he is able to make and reform society and is also essentially good, benevolent, and unselfish—how does one explain the hard fact of social and political corruption? If man is both good and creative, whence social evil? If man is not both good and creative, how can he hope to reform his society? These were questions that the conscious Progressive, as a believer in the goodness and creativity of man, and as a believer in the possibility of social progress, had to answer. Churchill's problem here was the problem of the Progressive movement.

It would have been easy to fall back upon that sport-of-chance, the villain. Churchill had used this devil theory in his early romances and, as a political boss who had used corrupt means to gain and retain power, Jethro Bass was a natural for the villain's role. But Jethro was no villain. This is made abundantly clear when he manfully admitted to the one person whose love he cherished that the charges of political corruption against him were true—and this despite his certainty that such an admission would result in the loss of that love.

Jethro was basically a good man who forfeited his political power to his fatherly love of a young girl. What then? Does Churchill still, in some way, hold Jethro responsible for the evil social conditions, or were the conditions responsible for Jethro? At one point he wrote, "Jethro Bass himself was almost wholly responsible in that state for the condition of politics and politicians." [22] But at the time of Jethro's triumph over his enemies, Churchill commented, "Who will judge him? He had been what he had been; and as the Era was, so was he." [23] What this appears to mean is that Jethro was responsible for the evil in his state, but that he himself was a product of a corrupt age in American politics, a state of affairs that Churchill, like the mugwump-liberals, tended to identify with the Jacksonian movement.

What then is the source of the primary evil—the corruption of the era? The answer to this question is more clearly and fully formulated in the second political novel, *Mr. Crewe's Career,* published in 1908. This novel had its setting in Ripton, New Hampshire, the home of Hilary Vane, who was chief counsel of the Imperial Railroad. Hilary's chief burden in life was his son,

Austen, who had inherited an unconventional temperament from his deceased mother. Austen had returned home from the West after shooting a man in self-defense, and when he agreed to practice law with his father matters ran smoothly for a period of two years and it appeared that the prodigal had returned.

Then a bad accident occurred at a railroad crossing, and Austen's quick action saved the victim's life. He suggested to the man that he take the case to court rather than accept the usual settlement. When Augustus P. Flint, president of the railroad and Hilary's boss, learned of Austen's suggestion, the young lawyer immediately received a pass which stated that the recipient should accept it as a retainer. Indignantly returning the pass directly to Flint, Austen took the case to court and won, a result that secured for him the wholehearted approval of the common people and the secret approval of his father.

At this point the millionaire Humphrey Crewe entered the story. A pompous individual with great faith in his own abilities and in the idea of aristocratic stewardship, Crewe had done a great many things for the community, although the natives did not seem to appreciate them adequately. He had decided to become the state representative from the town of Leith, and he ran his campaign in a very businesslike manner. But he soon found that there was a political boss in the area, one Job Braden, who was of the old Jethro Bass school, and the millionaire-politician was forced to compromise his moral position by asking Braden's approval. Crewe was what might be termed a sophisticated innocent in his dealings with the politicians, and part of Churchill's picture of the millionaire was an obvious parody of his own naïve efforts as a neophyte politician. As a millionaire, Crewe received enormous publicity and was greeted with excitement when he arrived at the capital, where Jethro's system had been replaced by the empire of the railroad. Hilary now occupied the famous Number Seven at the Pelican House, which connected by folding doors to the governor's suite.

In the meantime, Austen had met Victoria Flint on various occasions and they were attracted to each other, but he restrained himself because she was Flint's daughter. His antirailroad position had made him quite popular, and like all good men in Churchill's writings he attracted people to himself by the force of his personality. Consequently, he was asked by a delegation of country members to enter the race for governor in the next election—a request which he treated with modest levity.

Humphrey Crewe was not similarly inclined. He had turned against the railroads and led an antirailroad bill through the House, an action that placed him in a position to run for governor as an antirailroad man. The ensuing campaign was not going well for Crewe. His opponent, Adam Hunt, did not campaign at all; he had purchased the position from the railroad and didn't need to make speeches. But Hilary saw that a railroad candidate couldn't win the nomination and he dropped Hunt for another man who was not so closely connected with the railroad.

During the campaign, Hilary and Austen had a violent disagreement which caused Austen to move from his father's house, and Hilary, heartsick over the break, began to doubt the righteousness of his own position. Then the old attorney and his boss had a fight, and when the railroad president insinuated that Austen would step in at a moment's notice and accept the nomination, Hilary resigned on the spot, effective after the convention. Flint was not born to the purple and consequently could not understand that it would be impossible for Austen to enter the fight against his own father.

At the convention, which Churchill patterned directly on the "fire-escape" convention in which he himself had participated, the three candidates were running very close, and it looked like defeat for the railroad until Hunt finally gave in and combined votes with Hilary's candidate to defeat Crewe. Hilary was quite ill by this time, and Austen came to take him home—the victor in his last battle. Austen interpreted the meaning of the convention when he returned his father's papers to Flint. He told the railroad man that he, Austen, could have been nominated but had remained aloof because of his father. But the real point of the whole matter was that railroad rule was doomed anyway, so this particular contest was of no lasting importance. [24]

The key character in this novel was, of course, not Humphrey Crewe, but Austen Vane. Austen played the part of the hero and the Greek chorus at one and the same time, for he both participated in and explained the events that took place. The problem in this novel resulted again from Churchill's assumption that man is essentially good and that he is free to adjust or change his environment in the light of his reason. He then had to account for the corruptness of the existing institutions. Churchill's answer, which Austen reiterated again and again was that the corruption was the result of an evolutionary process. [25] Since man is both good and creative, he can not be positively responsible for this evil, but he is negatively responsible. In the past men had grown careless; they had been engrossed in moneymaking and had allowed the corruption to creep in. Therefore, when men became conscious of the conditions, as the new generation was becoming conscious, they would exert their creative powers to correct the situation. A "generation of ideals" was springing from a "generation of commerce." [26] Men remained, in this interpretation of Churchill's, essentially good, free, and creative.

Thus Churchill, in a rather confused way, arrived at the same answer as the contemporary social thinkers such as Cooley. In a more sophisticated and philosophical manner, they, too, had maintained that the natural goodness of man had been suppressed by historical forces which had developed the plastic side of man, making him appear evil and selfish. Man, as he became aware of the corruption, would rebel against the existing conditions and reform the world. He could do this because his basic nature remained rational, altruistic, and uncorrupted. Secure in this faith, Churchill could put into the mouth of Austen Vane an expression of belief in the good sense, rationality, and freedom of the average voter as extreme as has ever been written.[27]

So by 1908 Churchill had risen above the devil theory of popular tradition to the more sophisticated level of the social scientists. In his novels the people received a simplified version of the reform ideas being formulated by some of the best minds in America. These new ideas, however, were combined in his novels with Churchill's old belief in the importance of inherited tradition. The noble Austen Vane, for example, inherited his good qualities from his mother's distinguished lineage. Churchill felt that leadership from the old, aristocratic families was necessary if society was to survive. This rejection of contemporary historical society at the same time he accepted the importance of the aristocratic tradition of social responsibility places Churchill squarely in line with one of the main cultural traditions of his day—that of William Dean Howells and the mugwump-liberals.

Churchill did not, however, content himself with vague promises of a new "generation of ideals" which would reform the world; he went beyond this to provide a map of the road to utopia. This map he unrolled in what have been termed his sociological novels where he ostensibly dealt with the problems of divorce, the social gospel, and the political-economic struggle. The central issues of these novels were not, however, the ones listed above, nor were these works, in the usual sense, sociological novels at all.

Churchill was really interested in exploring two important problems. First and foremost, he was concerned with how the individual could rise above the evils of contemporary society and achieve self-realization. Then, once the path of the individual was made plain, he was concerned with the reform of society as a whole, the achievement of the Kingdom of God on earth. Here was a real problem for the novelist. As a good American traditionalist, his first concern had always been with the individual; yet, like the other Progressives, he fully realized the necessity of reforming society, a reformation that was seemingly dependent on the subordination of the individual to social unity. Somehow he had to combine these two objectives by devising a plan that would reform the corrupt contemporary society while it retained the individual as the primary good. And here again his position is strikingly close to that of the Progressive social theorists.

In *A Modern Chronicle* (1910), Churchill made explicit his rejection of the philosophy of the Gospel of Wealth. [28] Here he showed the disorientation in both the individual and the family that takes place in the world of business; he has rejected the atomistic concept of society that viewed a competitive life as a fruitful one. The real problem in this novel was not the superficial one of divorce, but the quest of the individual for moral roots in a society that placed its emphasis on material prosperity. In the heroine, Honora Leffingwell, Churchill presented for the first time his belief that personal integration is to be found in a sacrifice of self. But, though personal integration through sacrifice of self provided a means of individual self-realization, it did not, of itself, accomplish the second purpose of providing a means for the reform of the primary evil—social corruption.

It was apparently during the three years that separated the publication of *A Modern Chronicle* and the publication of *The Inside of the Cup* (1913), that Churchill clarified his hitherto rather vague ideas, for in the latter novel he managed to unite the two problems of self-integration and social reform. Because this novel contained the first and, in many ways, the most complete expression of Churchill's over-all view of man, and because it demonstrates some of the factors involved in his own conversion to social Christianity, it must be considered at some length.

This story took place in one of the largest cities of the Middle

West, probably St. Louis, where the old established order had been shaken by the new prosperity. St. John's Episcopal was the church of the old and the wealthy families of the city, and had been presided over for many years by the kindly and beloved Dr. Gilman. During the opening chapter the author presented a discussion of religion and its place in modern life. It took place in the home of Asa Waring, head of one of the old families, and it is made clear that the encroaching industry of the city had left both the Waring residence and St. John's in a less than desirable neighborhood.

The story then turned to the career of Eldon Parr. Parr had started at the bottom, married into one of the old families (this is significant because a Churchill heroine—Parr's daughter, Alison—must have at least a partially aristocratic background), and worked his way to the top. As the story began, the widowed Parr was in command of the vestry of St. John's. The current problem which concerned Parr and the other members of the vestry was the selection of a replacement for Dr. Gilman, who had just died. The heart of the matter, as stated by Nelson Langmaid, a legal genius closely connected with Parr, was their desire for a "level-headed clergyman about thirty-five years old who will mind his own business." [29] John Hodder seemed to be a man who would fill the bill. He was a firm believer in the absolute truth of the doctrines of the Church, and he preached orthodox theology from the Virgin Birth to the Apostolic Succession.

But Hodder had not always been a sober-minded clergyman. His youth had been rather wild, and he realized that women were still his weakness.

This he did know—for he had long ago torn from his demon the draperies of disguise—that women were his great temptation. Ordination had not destroyed it. . . . Yet with his hatred of compromises, he had scorned marriage.[30]

He had been very popular in college and at Harvard Law School, but just at the time he was to start law practice he was drawn to the Church by a form of conversion. After winning, at least partially, his fight with his friends and his "demon," he entered the ministry and became the most orthodox of clergymen. Once in the city Hodder became intimately acquainted with Parr, whose importance it was impossible not to recognize, and Parr, like Langmaid and most others, was soon conscious of the force of the rector's personality.

As the church of the rich, St. John's attracted few of the working people and the "down-and-outers" who lived so close to its doors, but the rector became increasingly interested in work among the poor. While his assistant seemed content to keep these people off the streets, Hodder worried because they were not making orthodox Christians of them. The slums, poverty, and vice of Dalton Street began to oppress him. Why couldn't he reach them? He was getting on well with the congregation, yet even among these, the ones whom he most wanted to touch, such as the Waring family, he was unable to reach.

Then one day Mrs. Goodrich, Waring's daughter, came to Hodder and told him of her lack of certainty about the doctrines of the Church. Hodder tried to show her that the doctrines were sound and necessary, and especially to show her that independent thinking on such matters resulted in anarchy. But when she left he knew that he had failed to convince her—a woman whose sincerity and courage he respected. Other, similar incidents also left him troubled.

His intimacy with Parr, however, continued, and one evening the financier told his rector the story of his son, Preston, a lad of great promise who had become "wild." Preston had wanted to marry a girl of the streets, and when Parr got her out of the way the boy left him. He then told Hodder of his daughter, Alison, a moody and intense girl whom he had never been able to understand. She had broken with him when he wanted her

to marry Gordon Atterbury, who was a pillar of the Church but
otherwise a cipher. Again Hodder saw in the actions of the
daughter and son the evils of individualism, but though he
could blame them for their actions, he was not wholly un-
sympathetic toward them.

The following winter the rector entered into his duties with
great energy and zeal but seemed to make no progress, for little
by little he found himself following the line of the other churches
toward institutional work rather than religious conversions, and
he accepted the vestry's offer to build a new, modern settlement
house. Then one night at a party he overheard a conversation
among the business leaders of the city which led him to believe
they did not want the world changed, that the aspirations he
held for the Church were foreign to them. The next Sunday he
attempted to shatter their complacency with a sermon in which
he denounced their materialistic attitude. But they missed the
point entirely and simply told him it was a wonderful sermon.

At this juncture Alison finally entered the picture personally.
Parr had supported the settlement house wholeheartedly, and
at dinner Hodder listened while father and daughter debated
the question—Alison maintaining that the charity work was
nothing but a sop to their consciences and of no real value. She
denounced the doctrines of orthodox Christianity and by her
arguments forced Hodder to face facts that he had been avoid-
ing. Her analysis of her father as one who would have crucified
Christ as an agitator, as one who feared the vital spark that lay
at the bottom of Christianity, forced him to recognize the truth.
She laid bare what he immediately perceived was the core of
the problem when she contended that the drift from the Church
was caused by the alliance between the clergy, who preached
the brotherhood of man, and the capitalists, who were unalter-
ably opposed to such ideas. She pointed out to him the division
within his own mind. As a rector of the Church, he believed in
orthodox dogmas, but as a moral man he perceived that the

authority of the Church was not a satisfactory support for a meaningful religious faith.

During the ensuing months, Hodder passed through a crisis. Did he dare submit his beliefs to the test of truth? Gradually he came to the conclusion that in his present state of confusion he could not continue to conduct the services, and consequently he decided to go away until his mind cleared.

In preparation he purchased the books of modern religious criticism, philosophy, and history, but on the day he was to leave he encountered a woman crying in the church and, escorting her to a slum hotel on Dalton Street, he discovered her sick child. Hodder wanted to send for the doctor but the woman became terrified and tried to send him away because her husband was very bitter toward the Church. She told the rector her husband had invested all their savings in the Traction Company, which Hodder knew Parr and Langmaid had organized in such a fashion that the important financiers could pull out before the company collapsed, although it destroyed the small investors. This loss had resulted in the physical breakdown of the woman's husband and his ensuing bitterness toward Parr and his Church.

While they were talking, Horace Bentley came to the door. Once a wealthy man, Bentley had lost everything to Eldon Parr. At the time he had declared that he was glad to be rid of his fortune, had deeded his pew back to St. John's, and dropped out of sight. Hodder learned something of Bentley's work among the people on Dalton Street, and he came to the conclusion that the whole conventional concept of charity was a crime against civilization. Bentley sensed Hodder's power and urged him to stay and lead the fight for enlightenment, but the rector felt that in his state of unbelief he could not be an advocate of Christianity. He could, however, remain in the city without preaching and study the conditions of Dalton Street, working with Bentley and the young people of the area.

Meanwhile, he tested each of his old beliefs in the crucible of truth as revealed by history and modern criticism and found them wanting. Filled with the desperate longing for adventure that had been so intrinsic to his youth, and drawn by the temptations of Dalton Street, Hodder wandered into a restaurant frequented by many prostitutes. There he fell into conversation with a prostitute named Kate Marcy, and in the course of their talk he discovered she was the girl Parr had bought off to get his son away from her. She also told him of the pay-off that occurred between her profession and the local political boss, the same politician backed by the parishioners of St. John's. Hodder won her confidence and with the assistance of Bentley and Sally Grover tried to cure her of alcoholism. It was Miss Grover's statement that they must trust Kate as God trusted individuals which led Hodder to his own grand conclusion—individual responsibility. This was the principle upon which the world ran, and upon this principle he saw visions of a new order in government and religion. Going to the church for the first time in months, Hodder found the answer to his prime problem—he would not leave the Church.

He began to sense a guiding hand on his shoulder. From Josiah Royce, and elsewhere in the work of the nonnaturalistic modern philosophers and scientists, he discovered that faith meant personal belief, and that the will of the spiritual world must be revealed through the individual. He had found it revealed in Bentley; he himself must stay in the Church and reveal it to others. The basic principle of this new Christianity was "the development of the individual into an autonomous being." [31] Hodder's rebirth was now complete. [32]

When Hodder reentered the pulpit his congregation sensed almost immediately that their rector had changed, and the church powers began to fret. With the backing of Alison, who had viewed his evolution, Hodder informed Parr of his change in outlook. The two former intimates engaged in a battle royal, during which Parr denounced Hodder as a socialist and was in turn informed that he was no Christian. But this was only a preview of the reaction to Hodder's first sermon, and he was soon presented with a request for his resignation.

Meanwhile, Hodder's actions had attracted the people of the neighborhood to the church, and the unity between social Christianity and reform politics which Churchill had been trying to show was symbolized by the union of Hodder and Bedloe Hubbell, the reform leader who was led back to Christianity by the rector. During these events Alison and Hodder finally proclaimed their love. When she informed her father of their impending marriage, he again threatened disinheritance. The lovers then went to Bentley's and, as he greeted them, "the light from his face, that shone down upon them, was their benediction." [33]

Churchill stated in a postscript to this novel that his own ideas coincided with those of the rector after his change in outlook,[34] and an analysis of those ideas reveal the author's conclusions about man and society. The basic premise of this view was the traditional American belief in individual responsibility and it was upon this assumption that Hodder constructed his new theology.

God trusted individuals—even such as Kate Marcy. What did that mean? *Individual responsibility!* He repeated it. Was the world on that principle, then? It was as though a searchlight were flung ahead of him and he saw, dimly, a new order—a new order in government and religion.[35]

Churchill also adhered to the traditional view in making this responsible individual "a mixture of good and evil, selfishness and unselfishness." [36] Man, in other words, has a dual nature. Hodder set forth this concept in explaining his new interpretation of original sin. "It means," he said, "that we are all apt to follow the selfish, animal instincts of our natures, to get all we can for ourselves without thinking of others, to seek animal pleasures. And we always suffer for it." [37] Original sin is thus reduced to a surrender to the lower, evil side of man's nature. Hodder was well aware that he himself possessed such a dual nature and that the lower side of that nature was his continuing sex drive.[38] During the crisis of his loss of faith, what he most feared was the unchaining of that "other man," the man of sensual appetites.[39] But he really presented Churchill's most careful formulation of the dual nature of man in his attempt to explain the existence of a sense of sin. He stated the following as the theory of modern psychologists, with which he was in agreement.

It is that we have a conscious, or lower, *human* self, and a subconscious, or better self. This subconscious self stretches down, as it were, into the depths of the universe and taps the source of spiritual power. And it is through the subconscious self that every man is potentially divine. Potentially, because the conscious self has to reach out by an effort of the will to effect this union with the spiritual in the subconscious. Apparently from *without,* as a gift, and therefore, in theological language, it is called *grace.* This is what is meant by being "born again," the incarnation of the Spirit in the conscious, or human. The two selves are no longer divided, and the higher self assumes control.[40]

This statement not only affirms the dual nature of man, but it also proclaims once again that each individual is responsible for, and therefore free to achieve, his own personal salvation. Further than this, by asserting that each man is "potentially divine," Churchill was saying that the Kingdom of God can be achieved on earth. Even the manner in which the kingdom will be brought about is made fairly explicit.

If all men and women were reborn we should have the paradox, which only the reborn can understand, of what is best for the individual being best for society, because under the will of the Spirit none can transgress upon the rights and happiness of others. The Spirit would make the laws and rules superfluous.[41]

Here, as for the social scientists, each man achieves his personal salvation by the act of wilfully uniting his better self with God and with society. Churchill, like the good Progressive he was, saved his individualistic orientation by making the individual responsible for his own salvation, and still offered a solution to the corrupt society—a religion that will teach all men to be brothers, or, in the language of the social scientists, to rediscover the virtues of the primary group. He had now fully embraced the radically millennialistic doctrines of the social philosophers such as Cooley.

Churchill was also following the path of the Progressive social thinkers in proclaiming the social nature of man. This was made perfectly clear in an article written in 1916 entitled, "A Plea for the American Tradition." [42] And he seems to have agreed with these other writers that this end of history, this achievement of the Kingdom of God on earth, would come about in the foreseeable future. This is the implication of the extremely optimistic temper of his writing during this 1912–15 period. Also, the idea that truth will be victorious was a constant comment in Churchill's writing, and with Hodder he had discovered truth. "I shall leave them crippled," Hodder said of his enemies, "because I have the truth on my side, and the truth is irresistible." [43] Indeed, Churchill felt that triumph was already underway. Hodder's opponents were disturbed, the author contended, because they themselves had gradually developed a critical attitude toward the ways of modern tooth-and-claw business practices, and they had uncomfortable sensations that the rector was right. They simply couldn't face the disagreeable consequences that such a change would make in their lives. They could not conquer the evil, selfish side of their own natures. "What these did not grasp," Churchill wrote, "was the fact that that which they felt stirring within them was the new and spiritual product of the dawning twentieth century—the Social Conscience." [44]

These same ideas were placed in a different context in *A Far Country*, published in 1915. Like Honora Leffingwell, John Hodder, and Alison Parr, the main character of this novel was on a search for personal integration, and again this salvation was achieved. But beyond this Churchill managed here to unite his new social ideas with the old genteel mugwump tradition, providing a new synthesis for the salvation of society.

The story of *A Far Country* is told by the hero, Hugh Paret. Describing his youth, he said, "What I seem to see most distinctly now is a young mind engaged in a ceaseless struggle for self-expression, for self-development, against the inertia of a tradition of which my father was the embodiment." [45] He inherited from his father—a successful, well-educated, and respected lawyer—not only a belief in the moral government of the universe, but also a belief in the tariff and the Republican party. As a student at Harvard, Hugh learned that scholarly eminence was not necessary, and probably was detrimental to one's social success, and he fell into the collegiate whirl. Nonetheless, it was at Harvard that he first made the acquaintance of the most important single influence in his life, Hermann Krebs. Krebs was the son of a German forty-eighter, and he was working his way through college for the incredible reason that he wanted to get an education. He was not only an idealist but was also a social misfit who wanted to become a lawyer to protect the innocent. Hugh was impressed by Krebs, but saw him as a revolutionary—a menace to the stability of the order with which he had cast his lot.

At the home of a rich friend, Hugh became definitely committed to the commercial struggle. The impression of wealth, especially as personified by Mr. Watling, a successful lawyer from his home town, now took possession of Hugh and he entered Watling's law firm. He was cautioned by his uncle, who was of the old aristocratic tradition, about Watling's methods, but Hugh considered his uncle's moral outlook to be old-fashioned and out of date. In Watling's office he quickly learned the new order of things, and as he strove for success the old human ties, ties with the responsible aristocracy, became strained.

When Hugh was sent to the state capital to guide the passage of a bill favoring one of Watling's clients, he witnessed the inner workings of corrupt politics and the passage of legislation by wholesale bribery.

And I reflected that the world was for the strong, for him who dared reach out his hand and take what it offered. It was not money we coveted, we Americans, but power, the self-expression conferred by power. A single experience such as I had had the night before would suffice to convince any sane man that democracy was a failure, that the world-old principle of aristocracy would assert itself.[46]

While at the capital, he discovered that Krebs was a member of the legislature. He had gone through law school and been elected in opposition to the state machine. When he learned about Hugh's bill, the young legislator denounced it as criminal and led a fight in the legislature to defeat it. During this battle, Hugh realized his own divided feelings in regard to the socialist. He found himself wishing, on the one hand, that Krebs would be defeated and humiliated, and, on the other hand, hoping that the man would be true to himself.[47]

During a campaign to send Watling to the United States Senate, Watling imparted to Hugh his creed that democracy was a failure, that leadership had to come from the few, that industrial and financial trusts were a necessity, and that capital had to have free rein. Hugh accepted the creed, and when he met and married Maude Hutchins the creed was more in his mind than the marriage.

When Hugh and Maude returned from their European honeymoon, Nancy Willett, his childhood sweetheart, had married and was enjoying her position as the social leader of the city.

Maude, however, had little use for the social whirl and turned to Hugh's friends among the old aristocracy rather than to Nancy. This distressed Hugh, and he found little time for his family. Instead, his whole being cried out for a renewal of the old intimacy with Nancy. In a world where men took what they wanted, why not?

About this time there was a political storm brewing in the country as the people grew restless under the leadership of a dynamic President (obviously Theodore Roosevelt). A small storm was also building up in Hugh's home town where Krebs was supplying the reformers with proof of political corruption. By this time, Hugh was regarded as an important figure and was called in by the "Banker-Personality in New York," who was being sued by the government under the Sherman Act. This was a real boost to Hugh's career, and it was Nancy rather than Maude who understood the honor he had been accorded. Then one evening Maude announced she was taking the children to Europe—indefinitely. Since Nancy had complete freedom in her marriage, Maude's departure accorded Nancy and Hugh their real chance, and after considerable moral wavering she surrendered to him.

Meanwhile it became known that Watling was going to retire from the Senate and Hugh was chosen by the party leaders as his successor. This was a great honor, but Hugh saw immediately that he could not have the Senate seat and Nancy too. With this problem on his mind, Hugh was forced to enter into the political campaign which the reformers were conducting against the party bosses. Hugh saw Krebs, who was running for district attorney, as the heart of this movement, and he took to the stump to fight him. To do this he had to read Krebs' speeches, and when he did so he found himself greatly impressed. Then Hugh discovered a plot to smear Krebs by luring him to a girl's room and exposing him there. Horrified at this, Hugh went to the hall where the socialist was speaking and was there when Krebs suffered a heart attack. The following day Hugh went to see him, and after listening to the socialist's ideas he himself suffered a breakdown.

He soon recovered, but Krebs' dramatic death swung the election to the reformers—the first time in Churchill's writing that they actually won. Hugh, in the meantime, was fighting a battle between his old self, seeking power and success, and the self that had responded to Krebs; again Churchill showed that it is the fight within the individual that is important. Hugh began to dip into the new evolutionary scientific theories and found a unity between these and the new social Christianity.

His wife had not been informed of his illness, and he had to make up his mind whether or not to go back to her. Finally he decided that his duty was to join his wife and help prevent his children from making the mistakes he had made; his career would have value by creating in them what he might have been. Reunited with Maude, he told her that, though he still loved Nancy, he wanted to devote the rest of his life to her and to the children—to teach them the true path which she had known all along, but which he had only recently discovered.

It may seem that Churchill was rather preoccupied with the relatively minor problem of divorce. His thinking on this subject seems to have undergone a rather subtle change. The overall impression conveyed by *A Modern Chronicle* is that he disapproved of divorce even for such mismatched souls as Honora and her husband, Howard Spence. But in 1912 he stated in a symposium on divorce that it should be left to the individual conscience.[48] He made this much more clear in another article in which he said that our American government and society are based on the principles, started by Adam Smith, of noninterference with the individual's pursuit of his own self-interest. This materialistic attitude, he maintained, was the cause of modern divorce. The reborn individual did not need divorce laws, which were made for the natural man, not the spiritual. Divorce laws, and all other laws for that matter, were made to protect society from the natural man. Since the natural man and woman were not really married, at least not in Churchill's interpretation of the Christian sense, it was perfectly all right for them to be divorced.[49] The social aspect of divorce was brought out in *A Far Country*, in which Hugh Paret made the following observation on this question:

> The "wrongness" or "rightness," utility and happiness of all such unions depend upon whether or not they become a part of the woof and warp of the social fabric; in other words, whether the gratification of any particular love by divorce and remarriage does or does not tend to destroy a portion of that fabric.[50]

Hugh's divorce would apparently destroy a portion of the social fabric, so, in line with the theme of personal integration through self-sacrifice, he sacrificed his personal passions to the good of the whole. Here again is an expression of the mugwump belief that the civilized man has a definite obligation to uphold the morals of society.

The important aspect of this novel, however, is the political philosophy of the "Socialist," Hermann Krebs. At the end of the novel Hugh achieved personal salvation largely by accepting Krebs' philosophy and it is relatively safe to assume that the author expressed his own views through Krebs. This is especially true since Krebs integrated his political theory with the social and religious ideas Churchill had set forth earlier.

Through Krebs, Churchill again stressed the idea that man is not individually responsible for the evils of society. "I don't make the mistake of blaming a few individuals for the evils of modern industrial society." [51] "The wickedness they complained of did not reside merely in individuals: it was a social disorder." [52] But if man were not responsible individually for the social disorder, Churchill made it clearer than ever that mankind as a whole bears the responsibility. The evils of society, he said, "were merely the symptoms of that disease which had come upon the social body through their collective neglect and indifference." [53] Krebs denounced the people and told them they had received the government they deserved.

The old reformers had made the mistake of conducting their campaigns on the lines of Sunday school morality. Krebs' new morality was common sense—a combination of the new science and the new religion. The scientific point of view and the religious point of view, Krebs contended, were really one, for God intended man to weigh his beliefs in the light of the only means of achieving truth—human reason. [54] "The new education, the new viewpoint was in truth nothing but *religion made practical*," [55] and "socialism, in the proper sense, is merely the application of modern science to government." [56]

The development and spread of the new religion, the new culture, depended upon leadership, and Krebs repudiated the traditional Jacksonian notion that any man could handle a public office. "Leadership, and the wisdom it implied, did not reside in the people, but in the leaders who sprang from the people and interpreted their needs and longings." [57] Hugh correctly saw a close connection between this leadership principle and the assumptions of the conservative business leaders, like Mr. Watling. But there was also an important difference. Watling's leaders, in line with the business ethic and the Gospel of Wealth, were to be the fittest, those who survived the struggle; Krebs' were to be the reborn.

It has been argued that in accepting the leadership principle Churchill abandoned his earlier Jeffersonian political slogan of giving the government back to the people in exchange for the aristocratic Hamiltonian principles advocated by his neighbor Herbert Croly. [58] But this apparent shift is really only a slight change in emphasis. If the leadership was to be made responsible, as Churchill indicated it was, the people would still have the final word. They would still have to be trusted. Also, the idea of leadership, in the sense that people are attracted to the good man who draws strength from his goodness, had been a part of Churchill's view of man from the first, and was exemplified by the mugwump-liberals of his own day. Indeed it was perfectly embodied in Churchill's political idol, Theodore Roosevelt. It was simply that the complete emphasis on the necessity for leadership from the reborn was first brought out in *The Inside of the Cup* and made explicit in *A Far Country*.

Churchill was still convinced in 1915 that the new generation was becoming more aware of the evils that existed, and that, aided by the "new science" and the "new religion," they could and would reconstruct society in the light of human reason. After his conversion, Hugh Paret issued this declaration of faith in the freedom and creativity of man.

The birthright of the spirit of man was freedom, freedom to experiment, to determine, to create—to create himself, to create society in the image of God! [59]

Here certainly is another parallel to the radical millennialism of Cooley.

If it was not clear from Krebs' highly individualistic approach that Churchill was not really espousing any known variety of socialism, he made it perfectly clear in an article written in 1916 called "A Plea for the American Tradition." [60] In this article he opposed any form of collectivism as un-American. The American tradition, he said, was a system of the voluntary cooperation of individuals. Salvation and social reform would be achieved by transforming the old material individualism of classical economics into spiritual individualism. Then the pursuit of happiness would become self-realization, and this self-realization of the individual Churchill equated with the good of the whole. By a kind of spiritual "invisible hand" the self-interest of the individual would be in accord with that of society.

For Churchill, man retained his traditional dual nature, but the natural man was essentially good and could achieve a re-birth, or a conversion of his material self-interest to a spiritual self-interest. In all previous societies the evil side of man had to be restrained by institutional controls, but the reborn individual would not need to be so restrained because he would perceive that his real self-interest coincided with that of the whole society.[61] Thus when all men, by the exercise of their reason and free will, and guided by the new science and the new religion, fully realized themselves, or were reborn, the Kingdom of God on earth would be inaugurated, utopia would be achieved, and the end of history would have arrived.

It can easily be seen that Churchill's role was not that of a creator of new ideas, but, rather, that of a sensitive popularizer. His familiarity with the writings of contemporary social philoso-phers is obvious. But it is through Churchill's novels that one can see most clearly the Progressive combination of genteel mugwump conservatism with a radical millennialism which held that salvation for man and society is here and now. He was an index to the spiritual hopes of the American middle class and in 1915 those hopes were still riding the crest of a wave, a wave that was soon to smash itself against the hard rocks of reality. Here, too, Churchill's thought provides a guide, for by 1917 he had lost much of his previous optimism—a loss that appears to have grown out of his increasing sense of the power of society to corrupt the natural man and hold him prisoner. This change appears in his last novel, *The Dwelling Place of Light,* published in 1917.

Janet Bumpus, the heroine of this tale, was the elder daughter of an old and respected New England family which had failed to keep pace with modernity and consequently had slowly sunk to the bottom of the economic ladder—victims of Hofstadter's status revolution. Janet worked as a stenographer in the Chipper-ing Mills until Claude Ditmar, manager of the mills, was at-tracted to her and made her his private secretary. In a rather

that Ditmar had been shot by an insane Italian. When Janet recovered, Insall asked her to marry him. Not having foreseen that he could possibly grow to love her, she was in despair because she had to hurt him one way or the other. Choosing the moral path, she told him about Ditmar and the impending birth of her child, which so shocked the poor fellow that he left Silliston immediately. The two women then went to Canada, where Janet's daughter was born; there she received a letter from Insall explaining his momentary shock and his continuing desire to marry her. But Janet insisted she could not accept his sacrifice. She realized she was going to die and decided it was better that way, since she had not come to love Insall and would only ruin his life. The story closed as Mrs. Maturin told Janet that she wanted the infant and said, "I will take her, I will try to bring her up in the light, and Brooks Insall will help me." [62]

It seems to this writer that in this novel Churchill was trying to point up the difference between contemporary society, which is evil, and the older social tradition, which is good. The tension of the novel occurred as a result of the fact that a representative of this older tradition, Janet Bumpus, found herself trapped by the web of modern society. Consequently, the best means of analyzing this novel is to present the conditions of modern society and those of the older tradition in order to see how these two interacted to make a tragedy of the life of Janet Bumpus.

As is evident from the analyses of the earlier works, Churchill viewed modern society as essentially an amoral, industrial world in which the individual seeks his own self-interest. For Churchill, it was a decrepit social order and was subject to disease.[63] One of the individuals formed by this society was Claude Ditmar, whom Churchill described as "a creature rather wonderfully adapted to his environment." [64] He had taken over the management of the Chippering Mills, removed the old-fashioned methods, and made the business a paying proposition. When faced with the wretched living conditions of his workers, he replied:

Isn't it because these people want to live that way? . . . They actually like it, they wouldn't be happy in anything but a pig-sty—they had 'em in Europe. And what do you expect us to do? Buy land and build flats for them? [65]

Ditmar was the modern man who knew what he wanted, went after it, and got it.

Janet's sister, Lise, was also a product of modern society, but unlike Ditmar she was not one of the fittest who survived. She was a rather "cheap" type—a worshiper at the shrine of wealth and worldly success.

Success to Lise meant money. Although what some sentimental sociologists might call a victim of our civilization, Lise would not have changed it, since it produced not only Lise herself, but also those fabulous financiers . . . she read about in the supplements of the Sunday newspapers. . . . In short, her philosophy was that of the modern, orthodox American, tinged by a somewhat commercialized Sunday School tradition of an earlier day, and highly approved by the censors of the movies. The peculiar kind of abstinence once euphemistically known as "virtue," particularly if it were combined with beauty, never failed of its reward.[66]

But Lise never tasted these rewards. Although she discovered that she was not pregnant and an abortion was unnecessary, she still could not return home, and the implication was that she ended in that walking cemetery of fallen girls, the streets of New York.

A third example of the products of modern society was the tall, slim, eloquent Italian, Leonard Rolfe. Though Rolfe was not born an American, he typified the syndicalist leaders and exemplified those whom modern society had formed yet had passed by, and who sought revenge in a doctrine of violence. His ideals and moral standards, or rather the lack of each, were those of the new industrialist—to take what one can get. "He lived on the plane of the impulses and intellect, discarded as inhibiting factors what are called moral standards, decried individual discipline and restraint." [67]

These were the conditions of modern society and three types of individuals who allowed themselves to be formed by that society. The other force that Churchill saw at work was the older social tradition, symbolized by Silliston Academy and personified in Brooks Insall and Mrs. Maturin. Silliston was a sheltered spot in "a chaotic world of smoke and struggle," [68] where Churchill saw enshrined the stable order of an earlier age.

Silliston, indifferent to cults and cataclysms, undisturbed by the dark tides flung westward to gather in deposits in other parts of the land, had held fast to the old tradition, stood ready to do her share to transform it into something even nobler when the time should come. Simplicity and worth and beauty—these elements at least of the older Republic should not perish, but in the end prevail.[69]

Almost the same terms used to describe Silliston could be used to characterize Mrs. Maturin and Insall. They were strong, vital, and dependable, almost wholly apart from the turmoil of the modern world. Their social attitude was exemplified by Insall's answer to Janet when she asked if he were on the side of the capitalists in the strike. "I? I'm a spectator—an innocent bystander." [70] The heart of these two individuals would appear to be their belief that "to understand is to pardon." [71] In this light, the strike was not the fault of the employers,

not in a large sense. . . . When people grow up to look at life in a certain way, from a certain viewpoint, it is difficult, almost impossible to change them. It's—it's their religion.[72]

These were the two forces at work upon the character of Janet Bumpus, inheritor of the old tradition, inhabitant of the modern, chaotic society. "She was one of the unfortunate who love beauty, who are condemned to dwell in exile, unacquainted with what they love." [73] Unlike Lise, she could not find joy and forgetfulness in dance halls and movie houses, and if she desired wealth it was only because it would provide a means of escape from her sordid surroundings. When she walked to Silliston, the architectural beauty of the academy electrified her and she felt that at last she had come to the home for which she longed.

For the first time in her adult life she stood in the presence of tradition, of a tradition inherently if unconsciously the innermost reality of her being: a tradition that miraculously was not dead, since after all these years it had begun to put forth these vigorous shoots.[74]

Janet knew she had been given the position as Ditmar's secretary because of her sex appeal, and in his presence she experienced alternate waves of antagonism and attraction, "revealing to her depths and possibilities of her nature that frightened while they fascinated." [75] She was thrilled that he wanted her, but her pride revolted because he wanted her clandestinely. Marriage, however, never occurred to her, for "she was not so commonplace." [76] She did not shrink from Ditmar's embrace because she believed, in the orthodox sense, that it was wrong, but because it involved a surrender of her own personality. "The core of her resistance was the very essence of an individuality having its roots in a self-respecting and self-controlling inheritance." [77]

As she worked with Ditmar, she began to accept his point of view, the modern point of view, on life. She saw men striving for prominence and power and was intoxicated by her own power over her boss. If one could get power and refused to take it, he was a fool; virtue had little if anything to do with success. This feeling of unity with Ditmar was destroyed when she learned of Lise's planned abortion, and "the scorching revelation of life's injustice lighted within her the fires of anarchy and revenge." [78] It did not take long, however, for her to discover that the philosophy of syndicalism was really no different from that of capitalism, and that Rolfe's attitude toward her was the same as Ditmar's.

It was then she began to frequent the soup kitchen. There

she admired the lack of intellectual narrowness in Insall and Mrs. Maturin, and sensed a wider culture of which they were a part—a culture not harnessed to a "cause." [79] Janet wondered at the friendship which these two cultured people offered her, but to them she typified the strike—"the protest, the revolt, the struggle for self-realization, that is beginning to be felt all over the nation . . . that is not yet focused and self-conscious, but groping its way, clothing itself in any philosophy that seems to fit it." [80] Churchill himself characterized Janet as typical of the individual in the modern world when he said, "Janet's problem was in truth . . . the supreme problem of our time: what is the path of self-realization?" [81] Mrs. Maturin put it another way in her reply to Janet's question on whether or not she believed in God.

I like to think of Him as light, Janet, and we are plants seeking to grow toward Him—no matter from what dark crevice we may spring. Even in our mistakes and sins we are seeking Him, for these are ignorances, and as the world learns more we shall know Him better and better. It is natural to long for happiness, and happiness is self-realization, and self-realization is knowledge and light.[82]

Before her death Janet achieved this self-realization, and she had the assurance of Mrs. Maturin that her daughter would be brought up "in the light." In so far as Janet was meant to exemplify modern man, as Churchill indicated she was, it would seem that he was still holding to the notion that there would be an end to history, that man would achieve utopia. But it surely must have been apparent to him that Janet was in no way typical of man in modern society. Where was the average individual to get the social tradition into which Janet had been fortunate enough to be born, and which Churchill indicated was all-important to her salvation? One might argue that the average man could not obtain it, but he could be led by those who did have that tradition. This would have been in line with Churchill's leadership principle and a few years before would probably have been his answer to the question. But Brooks Insall was no leader. He was an "innocent bystander" who deplored all forms of organization. The whole tone of this novel is different from anything Churchill had written previously; it was more somber, less optimistic, and, for the first time, the heroine had to die within its pages. Was it possible that Churchill had lost the effervescent optimism of his earlier days? The feasibility of general salvation was still present, but by 1917 Churchill had lost much of his confidence that it would be achieved in the foreseeable future. The reason for this loss of confidence in a general rebirth of society may be that Churchill had finally made up his mind that only the actual possessors of the old tradition could withstand the pressures of modern society.

This interpretation is further strengthened by Churchill's last major work, the three-act play *Dr. Jonathan,* which was published in 1919.[83] The title character is a slightly older Brooks Insall, a thinker, a unified individual in his own right, but in no sense an active reformer. The play concludes with the hope that labor and management might work together, that everyone would learn from the war that political democracy was meaningless without economic democracy, and that social unity might be achieved. But the optimism is far more suppressed here than in the earlier works, and the pleas for social cooperation contain an almost desperate note. Dr. Jonathan's quiet acceptance of life is a far cry from the reforming zeal of John Hodder and Hermann Krebs. The doctor's course of action was not far, however, from the actions of his creator, who in the years following the war withdrew from society, living apart from the modern, industrial world which he apparently no longer felt he could conquer by either practical politics or the novel.

C. C. Walcutt, in his excellent study of Churchill's compromise between romanticism and naturalism, had this to say on the evolution in the novelist's thought.

This novel [*The Dwelling Place of Light*] represents a third stage in Churchill's growth. First he wrote pure romance. Then came problem novels with a sociological bias that did not deny individual freedom and that represented economic and political evils as caused by *man*. In them he could *blame* people and institutions, like the clergy, and he did so. The third stage embodies his attempt to get behind personalities to the determining forces that control them. Here he is even more urgently required to abandon the ethical presuppositions that brought confusion to the novels of the second stage. He came nearer to doing so, because he sees that the problem is no longer a moral one; but he cannot face it through to the end. Hence his evasion in this last novel is his most conspicuous failure.[84]

But this analysis of Churchill's writings is inaccurate on several points. Churchill did not, in the so-called second stage, blame men as individuals or even groups for the evils that exist. The evils are a result of conditions which arise because of the neglect of society as a whole, and, except in *Coniston*, where his position on the responsibility of Jethro Bass was equivocal, he did not blame individuals for these evils. And secondly, in the last three novels of the second stage—*A Modern Chronicle, The Inside of the Cup*, and *A Far Country*—Churchill was not primarily concerned with how the evils came about, but how man can rise above them to achieve self-realization. To place the emphasis upon society is to distort the meaning. Churchill was from first to last, even in the romances and the political novels, interested primarily in the salvation of the individual. In this sense his philosophy did not evolve at all, except that toward the end he became considerably less confident that mankind in general could achieve this salvation.

Churchill had accepted the social scientists' notion that the natural man was essentially good, rational, and unselfish; he had also accepted their theory that historical society, and especially classical economics, had corrupted the natural man by teaching him that he was an atom of self-interest. He had turned to the new religion, sociology, and psychology for an aid to man in the campaign to reform society and achieve utopia through the use of his reason and creativity.

Something between 1915 and 1917, perhaps the outbreak of a widespread war after a century of peace, perhaps his own growing awareness of the power of contemporary society to corrupt man, caused Churchill to lose his faith in the inevitability of social unity and reform. His own answers and those of the Progressive social scientists no longer seemed applicable. Utopia no longer seemed to be around the next bend in the road. In addition to this, the continuing status revolution made it increasingly clear that the civilizing tradition of the nineteenth-century social aristocracy would have no place in the revolutionary, industrial world of the twentieth century. Thus by 1920 Churchill had lost both supports for his dream of social salvation—the leadership of the socially responsible aristocrats and the radical millennialism of Cooley and the social scientists.

The shock of World War I and the debacle of the peace settlement led an increasing number of Americans to share this loss of faith in man and in man's ability to create his own society in the light of human reason. America did not move to a mood of stoic resignation, but the old sense of inevitability, the radical millennialism of the Progressive years, receded from their thinking. While the work of the social scientists contained other ideas that made their writings acceptable to the more skeptical postwar generations, the novels of Winston Churchill apparently did not. And this loss of popularity was seemingly preceded by the author's own loss of faith in his own ideas, a fact which may help to explain the sudden retirement of one of the most popular novelists in American history. Neither he nor his work managed to survive the changing climate of opinion.[85]

CONCLUSION

THE Introduction to this study suggested that an analysis of the concepts of man held by representative novelists during the Progressive period would shed light on a number of problems in American intellectual history. First, it should help to evaluate the nature and extent of the Progressive revolt against tradition; this in turn should be of assistance in delineating the dominant patterns of thought during the years from 1890 to 1917. Finally, such an analysis may be of value in establishing the usefulness of the literary community as an underdeveloped source for the intellectual historian.

Throughout the study I have contended that the central feature of traditional American ideas about human nature was a continued debate on freedom and creativity. But the question, in the final analysis, was not really whether or not man has this freedom to will and act; it was to what extent he is free. In one sense, this whole debate may seem absurd—either man is free or he is not—but most Americans before 1917 refused to accept this proposition. While some did lean toward total freedom, no significant group accepted a philosophy of absolute determinism. This fact has been obscured by intellectual historians through an overconcentration on the problem of heredity versus environment. While this question is, of course, an important one, a more salient consideration for the American has been to what extent social, hereditary, or cosmic forces, alone or in combination, limit man's freedom to will and act. And this is a question which is crucial to any conscious reformer concerned with improving the society in which he lives.

It has been further suggested here that Americans shared the political theory of the seventeenth-century English middle class, with its emphasis on the duality of man. As in Locke's state of nature, there is, on the one hand, a belief in a rational, benevolent, free man capable of forming and reforming his society; and, on the other hand, the concept of a selfish, irrational individual who must be curbed by society—by government. Man, in other words, has within him a capacity for both good and evil. Until the late nineteenth century, Americans generally contended that man, if he were unhindered by institutions and traditions, would give expression to the good side of his nature. Within this context opinions about human potential varied considerably, differences running from the quiet skepticism of the Founding Fathers to the exaggerated enthusiasm of the mid-nineteenth-century democrat.

Following the Civil War a series of social and intellectual changes took place which constituted a threat to the old way of life and to the traditional assumptions about man and society. For the majority of Americans, however, this threat did not produce any drastic changes in their ideas about the basic nature of man. Rather they found new assurances for their old ideas in the laissez-faire pronouncements of the Gospel of Wealth, itself a restatement, often in scientific terms, of the traditional faith in the free and creative individual.

It was against this background of traditional ideas and assumptions that the writings of a representative of the older generation were examined. This analysis of William Dean Howells shows that during the early years of his writing career, he shared much of the optimism of his contemporaries. But after 1885 he began to alter his ideas, to present a less optimistic picture of man and society. He started to question human potentiality within the context of contemporary society. Torn between a desire to preserve the feeling of aristocratic responsibility for social stability and his dreams of Altruria, he lost much of his earlier optimism. And gradually his popularity began to fade as a new generation of Americans reached intellectual maturity. Most critics and historians have suggested that the major reason why Howells lost his popularity was because he was too Victorian, too unrealistic for the more sophisticated Progressive generation.

The weakness of this assertion clearly emerges from a survey of the articulate opinion of the Progressive generation, the generation which reached maturity around 1890 and thus felt the full force of the intellectual and social challenges to tradition. The first of this generation to be examined were the philosophical founders of Progressivism, the social scientists. Applying the methodology of science to human society, these men altered the older interpretation of human nature by depicting the atomistic individual of the Gospel of Wealth and the Lockean tradition as the evil side of man, and insisting that man is by nature a social animal. The revolution had arrived; tradition had at last been destroyed by science. But had it? For these men went on to assert that their new natural man was a product of the altruistic family group, and since contemporary society, which assumed with the Gospel of Wealth that man in society is selfish, was being destroyed by the forces of the industrial revolution, man could establish a new general society expressing the cooperativeness of the original family group. The final result of the new interpretation of human nature by the Progressive social theorists was a renewed faith in man's basic freedom, goodness, and creativity. This, obviously, is not revolution.

Indeed there is no intellectual revolution in America before 1917. Important changes in basic attitudes and assumptions, however, did take place during this period, changes that would reach their full fruition only after 1917. And these fundamental changes in the general concept of man came not in the widely acclaimed writings of the social scientists, but in those of the literary men. Stephen Crane, Frank Norris, and Theodore Dreiser, to differing degrees and in different ways, challenged the customary assumptions of freedom and creativity. My major concern in the analysis of these men has been to show that each of them felt the pull of tradition as well as the pull of scientific realism; the conventional cluster of ideas had at least as much force in directing their thinking as did the new concepts. While they consciously tried to accept the conclusions of scientific, matter-of-fact knowledge and the realities of the world around them, even these more sensitive members of the literary community could not totally rid themselves of their intellectual heritage. To ignore this conflict within the minds of individual men of this period is to miss the absorbing intellectual drama of their generation. And many intellectual and literary historians have missed this drama and have consequently distorted the Progressive pattern of thought in their honest attempts to solve the difficult problem of periodization and dramatize the changes in the intellectual atmosphere during the dynamic years between 1890 and 1917. The conclusion seems inescapable that this was a period of uneasy transition, not of intellectual revolution.

This conclusion, however, should not be allowed to obscure the equally vital fact that there were men, notably Crane and Dreiser, who did repudiate the easy optimism of their contemporaries. If William Dean Howells' books did not sell because he was too unrealistic, too optimistic for the skeptical Progressive generation, then the writings of Crane and Dreiser should have been high on the best-seller lists. But they were not. This is, at least in part, because the intellectual audience of the

Dreiser's pictures of the world in which they had lived seemed to be an accurate account of the Progressive years. Their contention that utopia would not be achieved by simple changes in the social structure appeared to be more realistic than the ideas put forward by their contemporaries. Gradually more and more American intellectuals came to agree that simple social engineering would not resolve the human dilemma.

And this alteration in popularity of the novelists suggests an answer to the other question posed by this study. The literary community does constitute an important source for the historian, but the intellectual historian who seeks to use the products of the literary world as a reflection of the dominant thought patterns of a given age must use extreme caution. Churchill and the early Howells may be fairly good mirrors of popular thought. One would certainly get a distorted image, however, if he assumed that Crane and Dreiser reflected the common attitudes and assumptions in Progressive America. But these two artists do serve a different and equally important function, for their pictures of the actual world in which they lived, their ideas about man and society, were at least as accurate as those of the social theorists. This bears out the assertion that the literary man, as a sensitive observer of his own society, can serve the intellectual historian and the historical profession in general, as more than a simple reflection of contemporary opinion. He can also serve as an interpreter of the real world. Rising as far as humanly possible above the dominant thought patterns, he can provide deeper insights into the actual human condition than those provided by most of the more traditional sources.

In quite another vein, this analysis also suggests that Progressivism lost its dynamism after 1917, not so much because the conservative aspects of its ideology would not allow the Progressives to make drastic changes in the social and economic structure, but because of the radical millennial strain in their thinking. This led them to expect a utopia of social solidarity

3. This latter interpretation is presented in Stow Persons, *American Minds*, pp. 217–451.

4. John C. Greene, "Objectives and Methods in Intellectual History," *Mississippi Valley Historical Review*, XLIV (June, 1957), 58–74.

5. Ralph L. Ketchem, "James Madison and the Nature of Man," *Journal of the History of Ideas*, XIX (January, 1958), 62.

6. (Minneapolis, The University of Minnesota Press, 1958).

7. The best example of this interpretation is Commager's *American Mind*.

8. There have been very few attempts to deal with traditional American concepts of man in any general way. For a more complete development of the statements made here the reader may wish to consult Chapter I of my "Man and the Progressive Novelists," (Unpublished Ph.D. dissertation, University of Minnesota, 1959). The only other real attempt to outline American concepts of man in an over-all pattern can be found in two articles by Merle Curti, "Human Nature in American Thought: The Age of Reason and Morality, 1750–1860," *Political Science Quarterly*, LVIII (September, 1953), 354–75, and "Human Nature in American Thought: Retreat from Reason in the Age of Science," *Political Science Quarterly*, LVIII (December, 1953), 492–511. Some of the best work in this area of American intellectual history can be found in articles analyzing a particular segment of the topic. The following are among the most interesting and useful: C. Arnold Anderson, "Human Nature: The Common Concern of the Humane Disciplines," *Ethics*, LXIV (April, 1954), 169–85; Robert G. Binkley, "The Twentieth Century Looks at Human Nature," *Virginia Quarterly Review*, X (July, 1934), 336–50; Merle Curti, "Woodrow Wilson's Concept of Human Nature," *Midwest Journal of Politics*, I (May, 1957), 1–19, and "Jane Addams on Human Nature," *Journal of the History of Ideas*, XXII (April–June, 1961), 240–53; R. C. Davis, "American Psychology, 1800–1885," *Psychological Review*, XLIII (November, 1936), 471–93; R. L. Humphrey, "Human Nature in American Thought," *Political Science Quarterly*, LXIX (June, 1954), 266–70; Ralph L. Ketchem, "James Madison and the Nature of Man," *Journal of the History of Ideas*, XIX (January, 1958), 62–76; R. D. O'Leary, "Swift and Whit-

man as Exponents of Human Nature," *Ethics,* XXIV (January, 1914), 183–201; Philip Rieff, "The American Transference: From Calvin to Freud," *Atlantic,* CCVIII (July, 1961), 105–7; James F. Scanlan, *"The Federalist* and Human Nature," *Review of Politics,* XXI (October, 1959), 657–77; Joseph Schiffman, "Edward Bellamy's Altruistic Man," *American Quarterly,* VI (Fall, 1954), 195–209; Richard A. Thompson, "Francis Parkman on the Nature of Man," *Mid-American* (January, 1960). The following books deal with American concepts of man in a nonspecific way, but shed interesting light on the subject from a variety of points of view: John M. Anderson, *The Individual and the New World* (State College, Pa., Bald Eagle Press, 1955); Commager, *The American Mind;* Robert H. Bremner, *From the Depths: The Discovery of Poverty in the United States* (New York, New York University Press, 1956); Merle Curti, *The Growth of American Thought* (New York, Harper and Bros., 1951); Ralph H. Gabriel, *The Course of American Democratic Thought* (New York, Ronald Press, 1956); Richard Hofstadter, *The Age of Reform* (New York, Alfred A. Knopf, 1956), *The American Political Tradition* (New York, Vintage Books, 1956), and *Social Darwinism in American Thought;* Louis Hartz, *The Liberal Tradition in America* (New York, Harcourt, Brace and Co., 1955); R. W. B. Lewis, *The American Adam: Innocence, Tragedy and Tradition in the Nineteenth Century* (Chicago, University of Chicago Press, 1955); Perry Miller and T. H. Johnson, *The Puritans* (New York, The American Book Company, 1938); Samuel Eliot Morison, *The Intellectual Life of Colonial New England* (Ithaca, University of Cornell Press, 1960); Noble, *The Paradox of Progressive Thought;* Russel B. Nye, *The Cultural Life of the New Nation* (New York, Harper and Bros., 1960); Saul K. Padover, *The Genius of America* (New York, McGraw-Hill, 1960); Vernon L. Parrington, *Main Currents in American Thought* (New York, Harcourt, Brace and Co., 1930); Persons, *American Minds,* and *Evolutionary Thought in America;* A. A. Robach, *History of American Psychology* (New York, Library Publishers, 1952); Herbert W. Schneider, *A History of American Philosophy* (New York, Columbia University Press, 1946), and *The Puritan Mind* (Ann Arbor, University of Michigan Press, 1958); Henry Nash Smith, *Virgin Land: The American West as*

16. I am concerned here only with American thought. The inclusion of Locke in this category is Hartz' idea, and it is not essential for present purposes whether his analysis of Locke's philosophy is a valid one or not.

17. On this point see David W. Noble, "The Religion of Progress in America, 1890–1914," *Social Research* (Winter, 1955), pp. 417–40.

CHAPTER 1

WILLIAM DEAN HOWELLS: The Mugwump Rebellion

1. The primary source for the biographical information on Howells is the two-volume biography by Edwin H. Cady: *The Road to Realism: The Early Years, 1837–1885, of William Dean Howells* (Syracuse, New York, Syracuse University Press, 1956), and *The Realist at War: The Mature Years, 1885–1920, of William Dean Howells* (Syracuse, New York, Syracuse University Press, 1958). Unless otherwise stated biographical information is taken from this work.

2. Howells understood very well the in's and out's of practical politics and was quite willing to use personal influence to get what he wanted. See letters in *Life and Letters of William Dean Howells*, ed. Mildred Howells (2 vols., Garden City, New York, Doubleday, Doran and Co., 1928), I, 16–27, 37–38, 39–40, 53–55.

3. (Boston, Houghton Mifflin Co., 1957).

4. *A Modern Instance*, pp. 332–33.

5. *Ibid.*   6. *Ibid.*, p. 75.

7. *Ibid.*, p. 277; see also pp. 132, 333.

8. (New York, Rinehart and Co., 1957).

9. Three types of society can be found in the writings of Howells. The first of these is society in the sense of an aristocratic, humanizing moral tradition. This was the society Howells found in the Cambridge literary circle, and for purposes of clarity it will be termed civilization. The second use of the term society, which will be termed contemporary society, is the existing society of Howells' day which encouraged tooth and claw competition. A third type of society, utopian society, is essentially what one would have if the type of society termed civilization was extended to include the whole. It is unfortunately necessary in making the analysis to use the term society in its more accepted

form as the totality of institutions and traditions. Whenever the word is used in this chapter an attempt will be made to distinguish which type of society is meant.

10. (New York, Rinehart and Co., 1958).

11. *A Hazard of New Fortunes* (New York, E. P. Dutton and Co., Inc., 1952), pp. 286–87. This passage is a direct interpolation by the author.

12. *Ibid.*, p. 288.   13. *Ibid.*, p. 245.   14. *Ibid.*, p. 244.

15. *Ibid.*, pp. 247–49.   16. *Ibid.*, pp. 254–55.

17. *Ibid.*, p. 304.   18. *Ibid.*, p. 372.   19. *Ibid.*, p. 540.

20. *Ibid.*, pp. 486–87.   21. *Ibid.*, p. xxii.   22. *Ibid.*, p. 503.

23. *Ibid.*, p. 304.   24. *Ibid.*, p. 503.

25. (New York, Harper and Bros., 1903).

26. *Ibid.*, pp. 29–30.   27. *Ibid.*, p. 31.   28. *Ibid.*, p. 35.

29. *Ibid.*, pp. 157–58.   30. *Ibid.*, p. 161.   31. *Ibid.*, p. 166.

32. *Ibid.*, p. 474.   33. *Ibid.*, p. 116.

34. (New York, International Book and Publishing Co., 1900).

35. *Ibid.*, pp. 345–46.   36. *Ibid.*, p. 452.   37. *Ibid.*

38. *Ibid.*, p. 453.

39. *The Son of Royal Langbrith* (New York, Harper and Bros., 1904), see especially pp. 119, 192.

40. *Ibid.*, p. 207.   41. *Ibid.*, p. 208.   42. *Ibid.*, p. 118.

43. *Ibid.*, p. 207.   44. *Ibid.*, p. 213.   45. *Ibid.*, p. 216.

46. *Ibid.*, pp. 301–2.   47. *Ibid.*, p. 275.

48. *Ibid.*, pp. 225–27.   49. *Ibid.*, p. 228.   50. *Ibid.*, p. 350.

51. *Ibid.*, p. 282.   52. *Ibid.*, p. 360.   53. *Ibid.*, p. 368.

54. *A Traveler from Altruria* (New York, Sagamore Press, 1957), pp. 9, 37, 65.

55. *Ibid.*, p. 41.

56. *The Writings of William Dean Howells* (New York, Harper and Bros., 1910), VI, 281.

57. January 7, 1884, *Life in Letters*, I, 357–58.

58. *Imaginary Interviews* (New York, Harper and Bros., 1910), p. 319.

59. *Traveler*, p. 12.   60. *Ibid.*, pp. 94, 169.

61. *Ibid.*, pp. 78, 99, 105.

62. *Through the Eye of the Needle* (New York, Harper and Bros., 1907), p. 219.

63. *Traveler*, pp. 196–97.   64. *Ibid.*, p. 203.

65. *Ibid.*, p. 200.   66. *Ibid.*, pp. 209–10.

67. *Eye of the Needle*, pp. 187–233.

68. "The Social Criticism of William Dean Howells" (Unpublished Ph.D. dissertation, New York University, 1939), p. 258.

69. See *Traveler*, pp. 187–90.   70. *Ibid.*, p. 187.

71. *Ibid.*, p. 190.   72. *Eye of the Needle*, pp. 131, 154.

73. Another aspect of Howells' environmentalism was his preference for American to European society. On this point see Howells' letters to his sister, Victoria, in *Life in Letters*, I, 46–48, *passim;* and letter to James Russell Lowell, *Ibid.*, I, 85. See also Everett Carter, *Howells and the Age of Realism* (Philadelphia, J. B. Lippincott Co., 1950), p. 59.

74. *Literature and Life* (New York, Harper and Bros., 1902), p. 13.

75. Letter to Samuel Clemens, May 1, 1903, *Life in Letters*, II, 175.

76. "The Social Consciousness of William Dean Howells," *The New Republic*, XXVI (April 13, 1921), 192–93.

77. Quoted in Cady, II, 130.   78. *Eye of the Needle*, p. 12.

79. *Ibid.*, p. 24.   80. *Ibid.*, p. 3.   81. *Ibid.*, p. 96.

82. "Equality as the Basis of Good Society," *Century*, LI (November, 1895), 67.

83. *Men of Good Hope* (New York, Oxford University Press, 1951), p. 203.

84. *Stops of Various Quills* (New York, Harper and Bros., 1895), No. IV, no pagination.

85. *Ibid.*, No. XXVI.   86. *Ibid.*, No. VII.

87. *Ibid.*, No. VI.

88. May 7, 1888. *Life in Letters*, I, 415.

89. "Editor's Easy Chair," *Harper's*, CXII (January, 1906), 309–12.

90. (New York, Harper and Bros., 1896), *passim*, particularly pp. 122–50, 245–81.

91. Howells to Hamlin Garland, January 15, 1888, *Life in Letters*, I, 407–8.
92. *Writings*, VI, 184.   93. *Ibid.*
94. October 8, 1888, *Life in Letters*, I, 418–19.
95. *Century*, LI (April, 1896), 935–36.
96. Letter to William C. Howells, July 10, 1892, *Life in Letters*, II, 25–26.
97. *Traveler*, pp. 148–53.   98. *Life in Letters*, II, 26.
99. "Howells' Opinions on the Religious Conflicts of His Age as Exhibited in Magazine Articles," *American Literature*, XV (November, 1943), 264.
100. *Ibid.*   101. *Eye of the Needle*, p. 3.
102. Letter to William C. Howells, April 27, 1890, *Life in Letters*, II, 3.
103. Same to same, November 9, 1890, *Ibid.*, II, 8–9.
104. *Hazard of New Fortunes*, p. xxiv.
105. *Life in Letters*, II, 58–59.

CHAPTER 2

STEPHEN CRANE: The Promethean Protest

1. Ernest Marchand, *Frank Norris, A Study* (Stanford University, California, Stanford University Press, 1942), p. 96.
2. Crane's life is detailed in two biographies. One is Thomas Beer, *Stephen Crane* (Garden City, New York, Garden City Publishing Co., 1927), and the second is John Berryman, *Stephen Crane* (New York, William Sloan Associates, 1950). Beer, however, is very inaccurate and out-of-date, and Berryman is vague. For a clear presentation of the simple facts of Crane's life consult the *Dictionary of American Biography*, ed. Allen Johnson and Dumas Malone (New York, Charles Scribner's Sons, 1928–44), IV, 506–8.
3. Letter from Crane to an unknown recipient, 1900; *Stephen Crane An Omnibus*, ed. Robert W. Stallman (New York, Alfred A. Knopf, 1958), p. 693.
4. On Crane's educational experience see Berryman, pp. 15–23. Also interesting are Harvey Wickham, "Stephen Crane at College,"

American Mercury, VII (March, 1926), 291–97; C. Jones, "Stephen Crane at Syracuse," *American Literature*, VII (March, 1935), 82–84; and L. U. Pratt, "Formal Education of Stephen Crane," *American Literature*, X (January, 1939), 460–71.

5. Letter from Crane to John Hilliard, included in an article by Hilliard, *New York Times Supplement*, July 14, 1900, pp. 466–67.

6. Berryman, p. 24.

7. Corwin K. Linson, *My Stephen Crane* (Syracuse, New York, Syracuse University Press, 1958), p. 2.

8. *Ibid.*, pp. 31–34.   9. *Omnibus*, p. 648.

10. Crane to a friend, 1894, *Omnibus*, pp. 605–6.

11. Berryman, *Stephen Crane*, p. 125.

12. Letter from Crane to an editor of *Leslie's Weekly*, about November, 1895, *Omnibus*, p. 629.

13. Robert H. Davis, Introduction to Vol. II of *The Works of Stephen Crane*, ed. Wilson Follett, (12 vols., New York, Alfred A. Knopf, 1925–27), xviii-xix.

14. Quoted in Berryman, *Stephen Crane*, p. 188.

15. See Daniel G. Hoffman, *The Poetry of Stephen Crane* (New York, Columbia University Press, 1957), p. 111.

16. Berryman, *Stephen Crane*, p. 218.

17. See for example "Horses—One Dash," *Works*, XII, 203–20; and "Five White Mice," *Ibid.*, 157–75. In both of these stories the hero is involved in trouble that is circumstantial but extrication is brought about by human action.

18. *The Collected Poems of Stephen Crane*, ed. Wilson Follett (New York, Alfred A. Knopf, 1930), p. 8.

19. *Ibid.*, p. 101.   20. *Works*, XII, 241–68.

21. *Ibid.*, p. 242.   22. *Ibid.*, p. 248.

23. *Ibid.*, pp. 64–84.   24. *Poems*, p. 31.

25. Crane to an editor of *Leslie's Weekly*, November, 1895, *Omnibus*, p. 628.

26. Crane to Copeland and Day, *Omnibus*, p. 602.

27. *Poems*, p. 14.   28. *Ibid.*, p. 21.

29. *Ibid.*, p. 83.   30. *Ibid.*, pp. 129–30.   31. *Ibid.*, p. 130.

32. Van Wyck Brooks, *The Confident Years, 1885–1915* (New York, E. P. Dutton and Co., Inc., 1952), p. 14.

33. Hoffman, *The Poetry of Stephen Crane,* pp. 13–14.
34. *Poems,* p. 41.   35. *Ibid.,* p. 36.
36. *Ibid.,* p. 55.   37. *Ibid.,* 57–58.
38. Quoted in Hoffman, *The Poetry of Stephen Crane,* pp. 158–59.
39. *The Sullivan County Sketches of Stephen Crane,* ed. Melvin Schoberlin (Syracuse, New York, Syracuse University Press, 1949), pp. 65–71.
40. *Ibid.,* pp. 51–54.   41. *Ibid.,* pp. 61–64.
42. *Stephen Crane: Stories and Tales,* ed. Robert W. Stallman (New York, Vintage Books, 1955), pp. 286–317.
43. *Ibid.,* p. 315.   44. *Ibid.,* pp. 316–17.
45. For a more deterministic interpretation of this story see Charles C. Walcutt, *American Literary Naturalism, A Divided Stream* (Minneapolis, University of Minnesota Press, 1956), pp. 72–75.
46. *Stories and Tales,* pp. 215–41.   47. *Ibid.,* p. 236.
48. *Ibid.,* p. 233.   49. *Ibid.,* pp. 224–25.
50. Hoffman, *The Poetry of Stephen Crane,* p. 5.
51. *Works,* X, 137–218.
52. Russel Nye, "Stephen Crane as a Social Critic," *Modern Quarterly,* XI (1940), 48–54.
53. Berryman, *Stephen Crane,* p. 54.   54. *Omnibus,* p. 594.
55. Linson, *My Stephen Crane,* p. 21. "OK" was Crane's nickname for Linson.
56. *Ibid.,* p. 69.   57. *Ibid.,* p. 70.
58. The article reprinted in *Stories and Tales,* pp. 167–68.
59. Hamlin Garland, *Roadside Meetings* (New York, Macmillan Co., 1930), pp. 190–91.
60. *Sullivan County Sketches,* p. 8.
61. Robert H. Bremner, *From the Depths: The Discovery of Poverty in the United States* (New York, New York University Press, 1956), p. 167.
62. *Ibid.,* p. 104.   63. *Works,* XI, 191–93.
64. *Ibid.,* pp. 37–45.   65. *Ibid.,* pp. 105–8.
66. *Ibid.,* p. 108.   67. *Ibid.,* pp. 1–36.
68. *Ibid.,* p. 28.   69. *Poems,* p. 96; see also p. 100.
70. *Ibid.,* pp. 106–7.
71. Lars Ahnebrink, *The Beginnings of Naturalism in American*

Fiction (Cambridge, Massachusetts, Harvard University Press, 1950), p. 229.

72. Alfred Kazin, *On Native Ground* (Garden City, New York, Doubleday and Co., 1956), p. 48. See also Granville Hicks, *The Great Tradition* (New York, Macmillan Co., 1933), p. 161.

73. Beer, *Stephen Crane*, p. 58.   74. Quoted in *Ibid.*, p. 205.

75. *Poems*, p. 18.   76. *Omnibus*, pp. 655–56.

77. *Works*, X, 34.   78. *Ibid.*, pp. 157–58.

79. *Ibid.*, p. 159.   80. *Works*, X, 19-90.

81. Beer, *Stephen Crane*, p. 205.   82. *Ibid.*, p. 148.

83. Quoted in *Ibid.*, p. 206.

84. *Stephen Crane's Love Letters to Nellie Crouse with Six Other Letters*, ed. Edwin H. Cady and Lester G. Wells (Syracuse, New York, Syracuse University Press, 1954), p. 35.

85. Nye, *Modern Quarterly*, p. 53.

86. Walcutt, *American Literary Naturalism*, p. 69.

87. *Works*, X, 156.   88. *Ibid.*, p. 189.

89. *Ibid.*, pp. 137–40, 141, 150–56.

90. *Ibid.*, p. 177.   91. *Ibid.*, p. 194.

92. *George's Mother, Ibid.*, X, 19–90; *The Monster, Ibid.*, III, 25–102.

93. Hoffman, *The Poetry of Stephen Crane*, pp. 175–76.

94. Probably late January, 1896, *Love Letters*, pp. 43–45.

95. *Ibid.*, p. 44.   96. *Poems*, p. 30.   97. *Ibid.*, p. 69.

98. *Ibid.*, p. 22; see also Nos. LVII and LVIII.

99. *Works*, III, 37.   100. *Poems*, p. 51.

101. January 12, 1896, *Love Letters*, p. 35.

102. *Omnibus*, p. 680.

103. Harry Hartwick, *The Foreground of American Fiction* (New York, The Macmillan Co., 1933), p. 27.

104. Stow Persons, *American Minds* (New York, Henry Holt and Co., 1958), pp. 333–34.

105. *Works*, IX, 238.   106. *Ibid.*, II, 29–53.

107. Hoffman, *The Poetry of Stephen Crane*, p. 149.

108. *Works*, II, 151–74.   109. *Ibid.*, p. 174.

110. *Stories and Tales*, p. 218.   111. *Ibid.*, p. 220.

112. *Ibid.*, pp. 220–21.   113. *Ibid.*, pp. 233–34.

114. *Works,* Vol. VI.   115. *Poems,* p. 72.
116. Hoffman, *The Poetry of Stephen Crane,* p. 56.
117. Nye, *Modern Quarterly,* p. 52.
118. *Poems,* p. 31.   119. *Ibid.,* p. 54.
120. Hoffman, *The Poetry of Stephen Crane,* p. 76.
121. *Poems,* p. 59.
122. Ahnebrink, *The Beginnings of Naturalism,* p. 98.
123. Introduction to *Works,* I, xvii-xviii.
124. Crane to John Hilliard, July 14, 1900, New York *Times.*
125. *The Red Badge of Courage* (New York, Random House, 1951), p. 9.
126. *Ibid.,* p. 10.   127. *Ibid.,* pp. 12-13.
128. *Ibid.,* p. 16.   129. *Ibid.,* pp. 15-35.
130. *Ibid.,* p. 41.   131. *Ibid.*   132. *Ibid.,* p. 51.
133. *Ibid.,* pp. 64-65.   134. *Ibid.,* p. 79.
135. *Ibid.,* p. 89.   136. *Ibid.,* p. 91.
137. *Ibid.,* p. 106.   138. *Ibid.,* pp. 106-15.
139. *Ibid.,* p. 132. In a similar situation, except that it was in civil rather than military society, George Kelsey refused to go to church because he was sure people would see him for what he really was.
140. *Ibid.,* p. 136.   141. *Ibid.,* p. 195.
142. *Ibid.,* p. 202.   143. *Ibid.,* p. 209.
144. *Ibid.,* p. 213.   145. *Ibid.,* p. 266.

CHAPTER 3

FRANK NORRIS: *The Romantic Rebel*

1. Ernest Marchand, *Frank Norris, A Study* (Stanford University, California, Stanford University Press, 1942), p. 7.
2. The only full-length study of Frank Norris' life, and the source of most of the material in this life sketch, is Franklin Walker, *Frank Norris* (Garden City, New York, Doubleday, Doran, and Co., 1932). Another useful, though brief, account is contained in *Frank Norris Bibliography,* ed. Joseph Gaer (California Literary Research, SERA project 2-F2-132 3-F2-132, n.d., n.p.).
3. Walker, *Frank Norris,* pp. 86-88.
4. Van Wyck Brooks, *The Confident Years: 1885-1915* (New

York, E. P. Dutton and Co., 1952), p. 103. See also Joseph J. Kwiat, "The Newspaper Experience: Crane, Norris, and Dreiser," *Nineteenth Century Literature,* VIII (September, 1953), 99–117, and Henry Steele Commager, *The American Mind* (New Haven, Yale University Press, 1950), p. 56.

5. Walker, *Frank Norris*, pp. 146–47.
6. See *Ibid.*, p. 150.   7. See *Ibid.*, pp. 173–81.
8. *Ibid.*, p. 257.   9. *Ibid.*, pp. 281–82.
10. *Frank Norris of "The Wave," Stories and Sketches from the San Francisco Weekly, 1893–1897* (San Francisco, The Westgate Press, 1931), Introduction, p. 5.
11. Isaac Marcosson, *Adventures in Interviewing* (New York, John Lane, 1920), pp. 239–40.
12. Walker, *Frank Norris*, p. 85.
13. William F. Taylor, *The Economic Novel in America* (Chapel Hill, University of North Carolina Press, 1942), pp. 304–5.
14. Granville Hicks, *The Great Tradition* (New York, The Macmillan Co., 1933), p. 173.
15. Frederic T. Cooper, *Some American Story Tellers* (New York, Henry Holt and Co., 1911), p. 297.
16. *Collected Works of Frank Norris* (10 vols., Garden City, New York, Doubleday, Doran, and Co., 1928), X, 21–26.
17. *Ibid.*, IV, 228–46.
18. Alfred Kazin, *On Native Ground* (Garden City, New York, Doubleday and Co., 1956), p. 74.
19. Commager, *The American Mind*, p. 113.
20. *Works*, X, 148–61.
21. *Norris of "The Wave,"* pp. 163–74.
22. The use of what are ordinarily thought of as male names for females is a common occurrence in Norris' writings.
23. *Works*, X, 198–208.   24. *Ibid.*, p. 90.
25. *Ibid.*, p. 91.   26. *Ibid.*, pp. 72–76.
27. *Ibid.*, Vol. IV.   28. *Ibid.*, X, 80–81.
29. *Ibid.*, p. 81.   30. *Ibid.*
31. An example of the first type may be seen in A *Reversion, Ibid.*, III, 43–50; and of the second type in *Son of a Sheik, Ibid.*, IV, 68–74.

32. *Ibid.*, IV, 185–202.   33. *Ibid.*, X, 115–46.

34. *Ibid.*, p. 119.   35. *Ibid.*, p. 146.

36. Frank Norris, *Vandover and the Brute* (Garden City, New York, Doubleday, Page and Co., 1914), p. 11.

37. *Ibid.*, p. 29.   38. *Ibid.*, p. 30.   39. *Ibid.*, p. 52.

40. *Ibid.*, pp. 204–5.   41. *Ibid.*, pp.213–15.

42. *Ibid.*, pp. 215–18.   43. *Ibid.*, p. 229.

44. *Ibid.*, p. 243.   45. *Ibid.*, p. 249.

46. Frank Norris, *McTeague* (New York, Rinehart and Co., 1950), Introduction, p. xiii.

47. *Ibid.*, p. 21.   48. *Ibid.*, p. 22.   49. *Ibid.*

50. *Ibid.*, pp. 23–24.   51. *Ibid.*, p. 23.   52. *Ibid.*, p. 62.

53. *Ibid.*, pp. 62–63; see also pp. 135, 137, 139–40.

54. *Ibid.*, pp. 208–9.   55. *Ibid.*, p. 65.

56. *Ibid.*, pp. 127–28.   57. *Ibid.*, p. 66.

58. *The Letters of Frank Norris*, ed. Franklin Walker (San Francisco, The Book Club of California, 1956), pp. 45–46.

59. *Ibid.*, pp. 30–31.

60. Frank Norris, *Blix* (New York, Doubleday, Page, and Co., 1905), p. 92.

61. *Ibid.*, p. 109.   62. *Ibid.*, pp. 249–50.

63. *Ibid.*, pp. 327–28.   64. *Ibid.*, p. 108.

65. *Works*, III, 215.   66. *Ibid.*, p. 218.

67. *Ibid.*, pp. 273–74.   68. *Ibid.*, p. 265.

69. *Ibid.*, pp. 260–61.   70. *Ibid.*, IV, 91.

71. *Ibid.*, p. 38.

72. Frank Norris, *The Octopus* (New York, Sagamore Press Inc., 1957), p. 310.

73. *Ibid.*, p. 128.   74. *Ibid.*, p. 201.   75. *Ibid.*, p. 206.

76. *Ibid.*, pp. 276–77.   77. *Ibid.*, p. 319.

78. Marcosson, *Adventures in Interviewing*, p. 238.

79. Norris, *The Octopus*, p. 454.

80. Frank Norris, *The Pit* (New York, Grove Press, n.d.), pp. 244–47.

81. October 17, 1899, *Norris Letters*, p. 44.

82. Norris, *The Octopus*, p. 409.   83. *Works*, VII, 56.

84. *Ibid.*, p. 98.   85. *Ibid.*, pp. 221–22.

86. *Ibid.*, p. 8.　　87. *Norris Letters*, p. 34.
88. *Works*, VII, 22, 66–67.　　89. *Ibid.*, p. 26.
90. *Ibid.*, p. 218.　　91. *Ibid.*, p. 49.

CHAPTER 4

THEODORE DREISER: The Cry of Despair

1. The facts of Dreiser's life can be found in many places. The four standard secondary works are: Robert H. Elias, *Theodore Dreiser: Apostle of Nature* (New York, Alfred A. Knopf, 1949); F. O. Matthiessen, *Theodore Dreiser* (New York, William Sloane Associates, 1951); Dorothy Dudley, *Forgotten Frontiers, Dreiser and the Land of the Free* (New York, Harrison Smith and Robert Hass, 1932); and Burton Rascoe, *Theodore Dreiser* (New York, Robert M. McBride and Co., 1925). Dreiser wrote four volumes on his life: *Dawn* (New York, Horace Liveright, Inc., 1931); *A Book About Myself* (New York, Boni and Liveright, 1922); *A Traveler at Forty* (New York, The Century Co., 1920); and *A Hoosier Holiday* (New York, John Lane Co., 1916). The first two of these were completed after the close of the 1890–1917 period and cannot be used as a source for his thought during the period. Much of the novel *The "Genius"* is also autobiographical. The material for this life sketch has been taken from the above and from a microfilm copy, in my possession, of the Dreiser letters from this period in the University of Pennsylvania Dreiser collection. No attempt has been made to cite factual sources except where the source is directly quoted.

2. See Carl Van Doren, *The American Novel, 1789–1939* (New York, The Macmillan Co., 1940), p. 245; and Matthiessen, *Theodore Dreiser*, p. 4.

3. *Dawn*, p. 9.　　4. *Ibid.*, pp. 371–468.
5. *Book About Myself*, p. 106.
6. Matthiessen, *Theodore Dreiser*, pp. 165–66.
7. *Book About Myself*, pp. 154–55.　　8. *Ibid.*
9. *Ibid.*, p. 197.　　10. *Ibid.*, p. 457.
11. *Ibid.*, p. 458.　　12. *Ibid.*　　13. *Ibid.*, p. 459.
14. Dreiser to H. L. Mencken, February 14, 1916, Dreiser Letters.

15. Matthiessen, *Theodore Dreiser,* p. 59.

16. August 16, 1909, Dreiser Letters.

17. This facet of the novel is emphasized in Charles C. Walcutt, *American Literary Naturalism, A Divided Stream* (Minneapolis, University of Minnesota Press, 1956), pp. 187–92.

18. E.g., the article by Stuart P. Sherman in *The Stature of Theodore Dreiser,* ed. Alfred Kazin and Charles Chapero (Bloomington, Indiana University Press, 1955), especially p. 74.

19. For a concise and convincing statement of this view see David W. Noble, "Dreiser and Veblen: The Literature of Cultural Change," *Social Research,* XIIX (Fall, 1957), 311–29.

20. *Sister Carrie* (New York, Sagamore Press, Inc., 1957), p. 79.

21. *Ibid.,* p. 226.   22. *Ibid.,* p. 225.

23. *Ibid.,* pp. 65–66.   24. *Ibid.,* p. 56.   25. *Ibid.,* p. 283.

26. Noble, *Social Research,* XIIX, 326.

27. *Sister Carrie,* p. 429.   28. *Ibid.*

29. For an interpretation of Carrie as artist see Blanche H. Gelfant, *The American City Novel* (Norman, Okla., University of Oklahoma Press, 1954); and Helen Elveback, "The Novels of Theodore Dreiser with an Analysis of His Other Writings" (Unpublished Ph.D. dissertation, University of Minnesota, 1945).

30. See *Sister Carrie,* pp. 147–52, 222.

31. *Ibid.,* p. 251.

32. *Jennie Gerhardt* (New York, A. L. Burt Co., 1911), p. 16.

33. *Ibid.,* p. 35.   34. *Ibid.,* pp. 78–79.

35. *Ibid.,* p. 93.   36. *Ibid.*   37. *Ibid.,* p. 100.

38. *Ibid.,* p. 126.   39. *Ibid.,* p. 156.   40. *Ibid.,* p. 368.

41. *Ibid.,* pp. 422–23.   42. *Ibid.,* p. 133.

43. *Ibid.,* p. 140.   44. *Ibid.,* p. 133.

45. *Ibid.,* p. 131.   46. *Ibid.,* p. 247.

47. *Ibid., passim,* and especially p. 98.   48. *Ibid.,* p. 99.

49. *Ibid.,* p. 374.   50. *Ibid.,* pp. 238–39.

51. *Ibid.,* p. 430.   52. *Ibid.,* p. 401.   53. *Ibid.,* p. 369.

54. *Ibid..* p. 374.   55. *Ibid.,* p. 76.   56. *Ibid.,* p. 132.

57. *Ibid.,* pp. 93–94.   58. *Ibid.,* p. 306.

59. *Ibid.,* p. 396. This promise of an after-life would also seem

to be the meaning of the final sentence in Dreiser's 1912 short story, *The Lost Phoebe, Free and Other Stories* (New York, Boni and Liveright, 1918), pp. 112–34.

60. Walcutt, *American Literary Naturalism*, p. 199.
61. December 6, 1909; Dreiser Letters.
62. Dreiser to Mencken, December 16, 1909, *Ibid.*
63. Stow Persons, *American Minds* (New York, Henry Holt and Co., 1958), p. 336.
64. *Financier* (Cleveland, World Publishing Co., 1946), p. 244.
65. *Ibid.*, pp. 244–45.
66. *Titan* (Cleveland, World Publishing Co., 1946), p. 189.
67. *Ibid.*, p. 400.   68. *Financier*, p. 397.
69. See *Titan*, p. 138.   70. *Ibid.*, p. 479.
71. *Ibid.*, p. 516.
72. *Financier*, pp. 225–26. It is interesting in this connection that Dreiser, in at least one instance, specifically repudiated violence as part of the battle. When Aileen's father came to take her from Frank, Dreiser made the comment, "No good ever springs from violence." *Ibid.*, p. 290. The intelligent man, of course, would have no need for violence.
73. See e.g., *Titan*, pp. 376–77.
74. *Financier*, p. 302.   75. *Ibid.*, p. 502.
76. *Ibid.*, p. 5.   77. *Ibid.*, pp. 271–72, 435.
78. *Titan*, p. 187.   79. *Ibid.*, pp. 483–90.
80. *Ibid.*, p. 11.   81. *Ibid.*, p. 320.
82. See e.g., *Ibid.*, p. 382.   83. *Financier*, p. 173.
84. *Titan*, p. 470.   85. *Financier*, pp. 271–72.
86. *Titan*, pp. 188–89.
87. Kazin and Chapero, *The Stature of Theodore Dreiser*, p. 236.
88. *Titan*, p. 551.   89. *Ibid.*, p. 552.
90. *The "Genius"* (Cleveland, World Publishing Co., 1946), p. 105.
91. *Ibid.*, p. 161.   92. *Ibid.*, p. 236.   93. *Ibid.*, p. 284.
94. *Ibid.*, p. 361.   95. *Ibid.*, pp. 359–62.   96. *Ibid.*, p. 534.
97. *Ibid.*, p. 680.   98. *Ibid.*, p. 689.   99. *Ibid.*, p. 690.
100. *Ibid.*, pp. 690–708.   101. *Ibid.*, p. 734.

102. It should be remembered that Dreiser started *The "Genius"* before the Cowperwood series but did not complete it until after the writing of *The Financier* and *The Titan*.

103. *"Genius,"* pp. 359–61.   104. *Ibid.,* p. 367.

105. *Ibid.,* p. 285.   106. *Ibid.,* p. 197.   107. *Ibid.*

108. *Ibid.,* p. 286.   109. *Ibid.*   110. *Ibid.,* p. 366.

111. *Ibid.,* p. 308.   112. *Ibid.*   113. *Ibid.,* p. 685.

114. *Ibid.,* pp. 156–57.   115. *Ibid.,* p. 163.

116. *Ibid.,* p. 726.   117. *Ibid.,* p. 118.

118. *Traveler at Forty,* p. 416.

119. *Ibid.* See also *Titan,* p. 11; and Theodore Dreiser, *Hey Rub-A-Dub-Dub* (New York, Boni and Liveright, 1920), p. 273.

120. *Traveler at Forty,* p. 141.

121. H. L. Mencken, *A Book of Prefaces* (New York, Alfred A. Knopf, 1917), p. 137.

122. In this connection see especially *Traveler at Forty,* p. 4.

123. *Hey Rub-A-Dub-Dub,* p. 272. Another expression of man as a combination of good and evil can be found in Dreiser's discussion of Erie, Pennsylvania, *Hoosier Holiday,* p. 192.

124. Mencken, *A Book of Prefaces,* pp. 137–38.

125. *Traveler at Forty,* p. 524.

126. Theodore Dreiser, *The Best Short Stories of Theodore Dreiser* (Cleveland, World Publishing Co., 1956), p. 176.

127. Alfred Kazin and Granville Hicks have suggested that Dreiser did not share his generation's faith in social reform. See *On Native Ground* (Garden City, New York, Doubleday and Co., 1956), pp. 64–65; and *The Great Tradition* (New York, The Macmillan Co., 1933), pp. 227–32. Henry Steele Commager, however, suggests that Dreiser tried to portray the world as so revolting that men would be moved to change it. See *The American Mind* (New Haven, Yale University Press, 1950), p. 116. Charles C. Walcutt has suggested that more than one naturalistic novelist may have been so motivated. See Walcutt, *American Literary Naturalism,* pp. 26–27.

128. *Traveler at Forty,* p. 43.   129. *Hoosier Holiday,* p. 224.

130. *Ibid.,* p. 225.   131. *Ibid.,* p. 226.

132. *Ibid.*   133. *Ibid.,* p. 60.

134. E.g., see *Ibid.,* pp. 325–26, 345; *Hey Rub-a-Dub-Dub,* p.

255; and *Ainslee's*, III (April, 1899), 293. The last reference is to a poem called "Bondage" in which Dreiser described man as a bond slave to God.

135. *Best Short Stories*, pp. 99–115.

136. *Hey Rub-A-Dub-Dub*, p. 272.

137. *Traveler at Forty*, pp. 479–80.

138. *Ibid.*, pp. 41–42. See also *Hoosier Holiday*, pp. 283–84.

139. *Hoosier Holiday*, p. 285.

140. *Moods Philosophical and Emotional Cadenced and Declaimed* (New York, Simon and Schuster, 1935), p. 268.

141. *The Stature of Theodore Dreiser*, p. 120.

142. *Hoosier Holiday*, pp. 230–31.

143. *Ibid.*, p. 182.   144. Rascoe, *Theodore Dreiser*, p. 65.

145. *Traveler at Forty*, pp. 178–79. He also felt there was going to be progress made in the realm of marriage relationships. Society, he contended, must and would open the door of human misery in this area. *Ibid.*, pp. 498–500.

146. *Ibid.*, p. 162.   147. *Hoosier Holiday*, pp. 367–69.

148. There is considerable justification for believing that Dreiser, in exact opposition to the Progressives, moved much further toward a view of progress in the years following World War I. This growth in optimism was paralleled by a greater concentration on the force of the environment in determining man's nature, and the two ideas would seem to have been closely intertwined in his mind.

149. *Twelve Men* (New York, Horace Liveright Inc., 1919), p. 360. The sketch is "W.L.S.," *Ibid.*, pp. 344–60.

150. *Hoosier Holiday*, p. 253.

151. See *Traveler at Forty*, pp. 12, 19, 338–39; and *Hoosier Holiday*, pp. 78–79, 92–93, 128–29, 511–12, 512–13.

152. Gerald Willen, "Dreiser's Moral Seriousness: A Study of the Novels" (Unpublished Ph.D. dissertation ,University of Minnesota, 1955), p. 62.

153. *Ibid.*, p. 221.

154. *Plays of the Natural and the Supernatural* (New York, John Lane Co., 1916), pp. 83–118.

155. See Walcutt, *American Literary Naturalism*, pp. 197–201.

156. This play was not published until 1918, but it was probably

written in 1916. There are several letters from Dreiser to Mencken concerning the play in the latter months of 1916, so it must have been completed by the fall of that year. Hartwick's analysis of this play as an example of the fact that Dreiser's idea of tragedy was Shakespearian rather than Greek, as Mencken had claimed, is interesting and on the whole an accurate analysis. See Hartwick's *The Foreground of American Fiction* (New York, American Book Co., 1934), p. 91.

157. *The Hand of the Potter* (New York, Boni and Liveright, 1918), p. 27.

158. *Ibid.*, pp. 198–99.

159. It is entirely possible to cast Dreiser in the role of reformer in the period after 1920. There are reform tendencies in *An American Tragedy,* and Dreiser himself participated in social reform movements. His final joining of the Communist party was in all probability motivated solely by his desire for reform. But the role of reformer does not suit him in the years before 1917.

160. *The Stature of Theodore Dreiser,* p. 90.

161. *Traveler at Forty,* p. 6.

CHAPTER 5

WINSTON CHURCHILL: *The Conservative Revolution*

1. For publication figures see Alice Payne Hackett, *Fifty Years of Best Sellers, 1895–1945* (New York, Bowker, 1945).

2. See Etling E. Morison, ed., *The Letters of Theodore Roosevelt* (8 vols., Cambridge, Mass., Harvard University Press, 1945), VIII, 958–59.

3. Morris E. Speare, *The Political Novel* (New York, Oxford University Press, 1924), p. 321.

4. John C. Underwood, *Literature and Insurgency* (New York, Mitchell Kennerley, 1914), p. 344.

5. Henry Steele Commager, *The American Mind* (New Haven, Yale University Press, 1950), p. 256.

6. There is no satisfactory study of Churchill's life. The best available is Frederic Brinker Irwin, "The Didacticism of Winston Churchill" (Unpublished Ph.D. dissertation, University of Pittsburgh,

1947). The material for this life sketch is taken from that work plus information gathered from Churchill's family in private conversations and letters. Other studies available include: J. Breckinridge Ellis, "Missourians Abroad No. 11: Winston Churchill," *The Missouri Historical Review*, XVI (1922), 517–21; and Warren I. Titus, "Winston Churchill, American: A Critical Biography" (Unpublished Ph.D. dissertation, New York University, 1957). The most important published studies on Churchill's work are Charles C. Walcutt, *The Romantic Compromise in the Novels of Winston Churchill*, University of Michigan Contributions in Modern Philology, No. 18 (Ann Arbor, University of Michigan Press, 1951); and Richard and Beatrice Hofstadter, "Winston Churchill: A Study in the Popular Novel," *American Quarterly*, II (Spring, 1950), 12–28. Both literary historians and historians of ideas have generally ignored Churchill entirely or have mentioned him only in passing. The monumental three-volume *Literary History of the United States*, Robert E. Spiller et al (eds.) (New York, The Macmillan Co., 1948), which contains bibliographies for practically every literary hack since the founding of Jamestown, has none for Churchill.

7. Quoted in Irvin, "The Didacticism of Winston Churchill," p. 50.

8. My conclusions on Churchill's view of himself are based on conversations with various members of his family and on a series of letters from his younger son, Creighton Churchill.

9. *American Quarterly*, II, 12–28.

10. *Ibid.*, p. 13.   11. *Ibid.*, p. 15.

12. *Rendezvous with Destiny* (New York, Vintage Books, 1958).

13. *Age of Reform* (New York, Alfred A. Knopf, 1956).

14. See David W. Noble, *The Paradox of Progressive Thought* (Minneapolis, University of Minnesota Press, 1958), pp. 103–24.

15. This particular aspect of Cooley's thought is clearly analyzed in David W. Noble, "The Religion of Progress in America, 1890–1914," *Social Research* (Winter, 1955), pp. 417–40.

16. E.g., the character Eliphalet Hopper in *The Crisis*.

17. Underwood, *Literature and Insurgency*, p. 312.

18. Frederick Taber Cooper, *Some American Story Tellers* (New York, Henry Holt and Co., 1911), p. 53.

19. *The Celebrity* (New York, The Macmillan Co., 1898); "Mr.

Keegan's Elopement," *The Century*, LII (1896), 215–27; and "By Order of the Admiral," *The Century*, LVI (1898), 323–41.

20. *Coniston* (New York, The Macmillan Co., 1906), p. 67.

21. *Ibid.*, p. 61.   22. *Ibid.*, p. 221.   23. *Ibid.*, p. 515.

24. As Austen left Flint's home he encountered Victoria, told her everything, and finally proposed. Flint and Austen agreed to disagree, and the lovers were married, much to the delight of the convalescing Hilary.

25. *Mr. Crewe's Career* (New York, The Macmillan Co., 1908), pp. 53, 181–82, 329, and *passim*.

26. *Ibid.*, p. 53.   27. See *Ibid.*, pp. 480–81.

28. (New York, The Macmillan Co., 1910). This suggestion was first made in Hofstadter's article.

29. *The Inside of the Cup* (New York, The Macmillan Co., 1913), p. 18.

30. *Ibid.*, p. 27.   31. *Ibid.*, p. 293.

32. For a direct expression of Churchill's religion of personality see "Modern Government and Christianity," *Atlantic Monthly*, CIX (1912), 12–22; and "The Modern Quest for Religion," *The Century*, LXXXVII (1913), 169–74.

33. *Inside of the Cup*, p. 510.   34. *Ibid.*, p. 511.

35. *Ibid.*, p. 264.   36. *Ibid.*, p. 250.   37. *Ibid.*, p. 260.

38. *Ibid.*, p. 27.   39. *Ibid.*, p. 137.   40. *Ibid.*, p. 289.

41. *Ibid.*, p. 507.   42. *Harpers*, CXXXII (1916), 249–56.

43. *Inside of the Cup*, p. 410.   44. *Ibid.*, p. 403.

45. *A Far Country* (New York, The Macmillan Co., 1915), p. 14.

46. *Ibid.*, p. 164.   47. *Ibid.*, p. 173.

48. "A Matter for the Individual to Settle," *Hearsts*, XXI (1912), 2395.

49. See "Our Common-Sense Marriages," *Good Housekeeping*, LVII (1913), 53–59.

50. *A Far Country*, p. 498.   51. *Ibid.*, p. 365.

52. *Ibid.*, p. 456.   53. *Ibid.*, p. 102.   54. *Ibid.*, p. 362.

55. *Ibid.*, p. 458.   56. *Ibid.*, p. 362.   57. *Ibid.*, p. 459.

58. Irvin, "The Didacticism of Winston Churchill," p. 228.

59. *A Far Country*, p. 496.

60. *Harpers*, CXXXII (1916), 249–56.

61. On this point see "Our Common-Sense Marriages."

62. *The Dwelling Place of Light* (New York, The Macmillan Co., 1917), p. 462.

63. *Ibid.*, pp. 299–300.   64. *Ibid.*, p. 232.

65. *Ibid.*, p. 156.   66. *Ibid.*, p. 46.   67. *Ibid.*, p. 344.

68. *Ibid.*, p. 441.   69. *Ibid.*, p. 422.   70. *Ibid.*, p. 334.

71. *Ibid.*, p. 427.   72. *Ibid.*, p. 427.   73. *Ibid.*, p. 13.

74. *Ibid.*, p. 58.   75. *Ibid.*, p. 102.   76. *Ibid.*, p. 107.

77. *Ibid.*, p. 227.   78. *Ibid.*, p. 278.   79. *Ibid.*, pp. 382–83.

80. *Ibid.*, p. 390.   81. *Ibid.*, pp. 162–63.   82. *Ibid.*, p. 438.

83. *Dr. Jonathan* (New York, The Macmillan Co., 1919).

84. Walcutt, *The Romantic Compromise*, p. 45.

85. Although Churchill's loss of faith in the possibility of meaningful social reform was not the only reason for his withdrawal from political and literary circles in the years after 1918, the other reasons lie outside the scope of this study. As a matter of fact, Churchill never stopped writing; he simply refused to allow the publication of his later work. This whole problem will be explored at length in my biography of Churchill.

INDEX

Aaron, Daniel, 51
Adams, Brooks, 7
Adams, Henry, 7, 19
Adams, John, 9
Addams, Jane, 193
Age of Reform (Hofstadter), 212
Ahnebrink, Lars, 83, 104
Ainslee's magazine, 156
Alger, Horatio, 11
Altgeld, John Peter, 175, 195
American Mind (Commager), 259-60
American Tragedy, An (Dreiser), 191
Arms, George, 48
Army and Navy Journal, 207
Atlantic, The, 20-21

Baker, Ray Stannard, 116
Baldwin, James Mark, 262
Balzac, Honoré de, 155-56
Bass, Altha Leah, 49
Beer, Thomas, 87, 100
Belcher, H. C., 56
Bierce, Ambrose, 64
Black, Jeannette, *see* Norris, Jeannette Black
Black Riders, The (Crane), 65, 68-72, 93-94, 101-3

Blaine, Emma Bell, *see* Churchill, Emma Bell Blaine
Blix (Norris), 115-16, 119, 137; Condy Rivers in, 135-37; Travis Bessemer in, 135-37
Blue Hotel, The (Crane), 74; Swede in, 74-75; Scully in, 74; Johnnie in, 74-75; cowboy in, 75; Easterner in, 75
Borah, William E., 120
Breadwinners, The (Hay), 46
Bremner, Robert, 81
Brooks, Van Wyck, 71, 115
Brute (Norris), 122
Bryan, William Jennings, 21, 175, 195
Burton, Dr. Lucius L., 79
By Order of the Admiral (Churchill), 217

Cawein, Madison, 53
Celebrity, The (Churchill), 205, 207-8, 216-17
Century magazine, 54
Churchill, Emma Bell Blaine, 207
Churchill, John, 207
Churchill, Mabel Harlakenden Hall, 207
Churchill, Winston, 7, 22, 158, 205-51 *passim*, 256-57; comparison

Churchill, Winston (*Cont.*)
with Theodore Dreiser, 202;
early life, 207; becomes managing editor of *The Cosmopolitan*,
207; marriage, 207; moves to
New Hampshire, 208; elected to
New Hampshire legislature, 208;
runs for state governor, 209;
death, 210; compared with W.
D. Howells, 211; and Progressivism, 212-13, 215-16; faith in
aristocratic tradition, 216-17,
225, 248; and leadership principle, 217; as reformer, 225, 238,
251; on individual and society,
225-26, 239; rejects Gospel of
Wealth, 226, 240; and social
Christianity, 226-35, 242, 250;
and the dual nature of man, 232-
33, 236, 241-42; and divorce,
238-39, 280-81; as popularizer of
ideas, 242
Civil War, 9, 20, 212, 253
Clan of No-Name (Crane), 98
Collins, Carvel, 131
Commager, Henry Steele, 2, 120,
206-7, 259-60, 276
"Company" (Howells), 53
Coniston (Churchill), 205, 208-9,
217; Jethro Bass in, 208, 217-22;
Cynthia Ware in, 217-18; Will
Wetherell in, 218; Cynthia
Wetherell in, 218-20; Bob
Worthington in, 218-19; Mr.
Worthington in, 218-19; Mr.
Morrill in, 219
Conrad, Joseph, 67
Constitution of the United States,
13
Conwell, Russell B., 11
Cooley, Charles Horten, 6, 13, 213-
15, 224, 234, 241, 251, 262
Cooper, Frederick T., 119, 217
Cooper, James Fenimore, 2
Cosgrave, John O'Hara, 115
The Cosmopolitan magazine, 21,
156, 207
Crane, Mary Peck, 62

Crane, Rev. Jonathan, 62
Crane, Stephen, 7, 22, 60-111 *passim*, 112, 116-18, 121, 151, 205,
255-57; conflicts in writing, 62;
childhood, 62-63; as reporter, 63,
66-67; literary "creed," 64; and
the "Crane myth," 65; and Cora
Taylor Stewart, 66; and Spanish-
American War, 67; death, 67;
and beliefs about God, 68-74
passim, 102-3; and views of man
in relation with Cosmos, 77-78,
109-10; and reformers, 83-84;
and the heroic ideal, 95-97; and
love themes, 100-1; compared
with Frank Norris, 118; compared with Theodore Dreiser,
163, 203
Crisis, The (Churchill), 205, 216
Croly, Herbert, 240, 262
Crossing, The (Churchill), 205, 216
Crouse, Nellie, 87, 92, 94, 121
Cry of a Huckleberry Pudding, The
(Crane), 74

Darrow, Clarence, 120
Darwin, Charles, 11, 60, 189, 197
Davis, David Brion, 179
Davis, Richard Harding, 67, 114-
15, 208
Dawn (Dreiser), 154
Death and the Child (Crane), 68;
Peza in, 69, 97-98
Delineator magazine, 157
Dewey, John, 16
Dickens, Charles, 64
Dr. Jonathan (Churchill), 249
Doggett, Gertrude, *see* Norris, Ger-
trude Doggett
Doubleday, Nelson, 117
Doubleday, Page, and Company,
117
Dreiser, Paul, *see* Dresser, Paul
Dreiser, Sallie White, 156-57
Dreiser, Theodore, 7, 22, 151, 153-
204 *passim*, 205, 255-57; early
years, 153-54; and sexual rela-
tionships, 154, 169, 178, 181,

187-88; and religion, 155; and literary tradition, 156; marriage, 156-57, 277; conflict over morals, 158, 190-91; view of man in society, 160-65, 171, 191-93, 202; and human freedom, 160, 171, 203; and ethics, 161, 163, 191; compared with Stephen Crane, 163, 202, 204; and "chemic" affinities, 169; and naturalism, 172; and Nietzsche, 172-73; on human nature, 191; as reformer, 191, 194-95, 276, 278; on man and the Cosmos, 191-92, 195-98, 202; on free will, 191, 199-202; compared with Frank Norris, 202; compared with W. D. Howells, 202; compared with Winston Churchill, 202

Dresser, Paul, 154, 156-57

Durkee, Ruel, 208

Dwelling Place of Light, The (Churchill), 205, 242, 250; Janet Bumpus in, 242-48; Claude Ditmar in, 242-45, 247; Lise Bumpus in, 243, 245-47; Leonard Rolfe in, 243, 245, 247; Brooks Insall in, 243-44, 246, 248-49; Mrs. Maturin in, 243-44, 246, 248

Economic Novel in America, The (Taylor), 119

"Editor's Study, The" (Howells), 21

Edwards, Jonathan, 207

Eloquence of Grief, An (Crane), 81

Ely, Richard T., 6, 21, 262

Emerson, Ralph Waldo, 2

Enlightenment, 9, 162

Epictetus, 187

Ev'ry Month magazine, 156

Experiment in Misery (Crane), 82, 85

Far Country, A (Churchill), 206, 235, 239, 241, 250; Hugh Paret in, 235-41; Hermann Krebs in, 235-37, 239-40, 241, 249; Mr.

Watling in, 235-37, 240; Maude Hutchins in, 236-38; Nancy Willett in, 236-38

Financier, The (Dreiser), 172-79; Frank Algernon Cowperwood in, 173-81, 186, 190, 193; Aileen Butler in, 173, 275. See also *The Titan*

Frederic, Harold, 67

"From Generation to Generation" (Howells), 51

Gabriel, Ralph H., 11

Garland, Hamlin, 54, 63-64, 80, 117

Gates, Prof. Lewis E., 114

"Genius," The (Dreiser), 157-58, 172, 181, 188, 193; Eugene Witla in, 181-86, 188-91, 193, 197; Angela Blue in, 181-86; Miriam Finch in, 182; Christine Channing in, 182, 188-89; Mrs. Dale in, 184-85; Suzanne Dale in, 184-85, 187-88

Genteel Tradition, 61

George, Henry, 195

George's Mother (Crane), 86, 94; George Kelsey in, 87, 89-91, 104-5; Johnnie in, 90

Germinal (Zola), 123

Gilded Age, 112

Godkin, E. L., 20

God Lay Dead in Heaven (Crane), 100

Goldman, Eric, 212

Greco-Turkish War, 66, 97

Greene, John C., 4-5

Hale, Edward Everett, 54

Hall, Mabel Harlakenden, *see* Churchill, Mabel Harlakenden Hall

Hand of the Potter, The (Dreiser), 158, 200, 278; Isadore Berchansky in, 200-1

Harlakenden House, 208

Harper's magazine, 21, 53

Harris, Catherine, 84, 91

Hartwick, Harry, 95
Hartz, Louis, 8, 12
Hawthorne, Nathaniel, 20, 262
Hay, John, 46
Haymarket Affair (Chicago), 21
Haywood, Big Bill, 120
Hazard of New Fortunes, A
(Howells), 25, 31-33, 35, 38, 56-
57; Basil Marsh in, 26-32, 35, 37;
Every Other Week in, 25, 29-30;
Jacob Dryfoos in, 27-32, 35-37,
39, 48, 56; Fulkerson in, 27, 29,
35; Lindau in, 27, 32; Conrad
Dryfoos in, 27-30, 35; Beaton in,
27, 35, 37, 39; Colonel Wood-
burn in, 27, 32; Margaret Vance
in, 28; Mrs. Marsh in, 29-30;
Howells' opinion of, 31
Henry, Arthur, 156
"Heredity" (Howells), 52
Hergesheimer, Joseph, 104
Hicks, Granville, 70, 119
Hoffman, Daniel, 71, 100
Hofstadter, Richard, 211-12, 242
Holmes, Oliver Wendell, 20
Homestead Affair, 55
Hoosier Holiday, A (Dreiser), 198
Howells, William Dean, 7, 19-59
passim, 61, 64, 116-17, 147-48,
158, 206, 212-13, 225, 253-57;
as poet, 20, 51-53; as biographer,
20; Consul in Venice, 20; edits
The Atlantic, 20-21; writes "The
Editor's Study" column (*Harp-
er's*), 21; writes "Easy Chair"
column (*Harper's*), 21, 53; opin-
ion of *A Hazard of New Fortunes*, 37; and labor unrest, 55-
56; and religion, 56; opinion of
Stephen Crane, 62; encourages
Stephen Crane, 65; compared
with Theodore Dreiser, 202;
compared with Winston Churchill, 211; on society, 263-64
Huxley, Thomas Henry, 155, 189

Impressions and Experiences
(Howells), 54

Indian Summer (Howells), 26;
Theodore Colville in, 26
Inside of the Cup, The (Churchill), 205-6, 226, 241, 250; Dr.
Gilman in, 227; Asa Waring in,
227; Eldon Parr in, 227-31; Alison Parr in, 227-29, 232, 235;
Nelson Langmaid in, 227-28,
230; John Hodder in, 227-35,
249; Mrs. Goodrich in, 228; Preston Parr in, 228, 231; Gordon Atterbury in, 229; Horace Bentley
in, 230-32; Kate Marcy in, 231-
32; Sally Grover in, 231; Bedloe
Hubbell in, 232
In the Heat of Battle (Norris), 121
Intrigue (Crane), 100

James, Henry, 67
Jameson's Raid, 115
James, William, 16
Jefferson, Thomas, 9
Jennie Gerhardt (Dreiser), 157,
165, 188; Jennie Gerhardt in,
165-72; William Gerhardt in,
165; Mrs. Gerhardt in, 165; Senator Brander in, 165-67, 171; Lester Kane in, 166-71, 197; Vesta
in, 166-67, 172; Robert Kane in,
166-68; Mr. Kane in, 166, 168;
Mrs. Gerald in, 166-67
Johnson, F. H., 262

Kazin, Alfred, 83, 120
Killing His Bear (Crane), 74
Kruger, Paul, 115

Landlord at Lion's Head (Howells), 37, 39; Jeff Durgin in, 27,
37-39, 57; Mr. Westover in, 37-
38; Mrs. Durgin in, 37; Cynthia
Whitwell in, 37; Mr. Whitwell
in, 38
Lane, John, 158
Laughing Gas (Dreiser), 200
Lauth (Norris), 124, 150; Lauth in,

124-25; Anselm in, 124-25; Chavannes in, 124-25
Leiter, Joseph, 117
Life, Art and America (Dreiser), 195
Lincoln, Abraham, 20
Lincoln Republican Club, 209
Linson, Corwin E., 63, 79-80
Literature and Insurgency (Underwood), 206
Little Regiment, The (Crane), 97; Dan Dempster in, 97; Billie Dempster in, 97
Liveright, Horace, 158
Lloyd, Henry Demarest, 21, 262
Locke, John, 12, 253, 263
London, Jack, 95
Louisville *Times*, 116
Lowell, Amy, 70
Lowell, James Russell, 20, 26

McClure's Magazine, 80, 116
McClure, S. S., 116
McTeague (Norris), 114, 116, 119, 129, 147, 150; McTeague in, 129-35; Marcus in, 129-31; Trina Sieppe in, 129-35; Miss Baker in, 129; Grannis in, 129
Maggie (Crane), 65, 78-79, 85, 89, 94; Maggie in, 78, 86-89, 91, 100; Jim in, 78, 86, 89; Pete in, 78, 86, 88-89
"Manifest destiny," 12
Man Proposes, No. V (Norris), 122
Man's Woman, A (Norris), 116, 119; Ward Bennett in, 139-40; Lloyd Searight in, 139-40
Marchand, Ernest, 60-61, 112
Marcosson, Isaac, 116, 118, 135, 143
Marcus Aurelius, 189
Matthiessen, F. O., 153-54, 156
Melville, Herman, 262
Memorandum of Sudden Death, A (Norris), 120
Mencken, H. L., 158, 165, 173, 193, 200, 204
Men in the Storm (Crane), 81

Mr. Crewe's Career (Churchill), 205, 217; Humphrey Crewe in, 208, 222-24; Hilary Vane in, 221-22, 224, 280; Austen Vane in, 222-25, 280; Augustus P. Flint in, 222-24, 280; Job Braden in, 222; Victoria Flint in, 223, 280; Adam Hunt in, 223
Mr. Keegan's Elopement (Churchill), 217
Modern Chronicle, A (Churchill), 206, 226, 238, 250; Honora Leffingwell in, 226, 235, 238; Howard Spence in, 238
Modern Instance, A (Howells), 23, 39; Bartley Hubbard in, 23-25, 27, 37, 39, 56; Atherton in, 23, 25; Ben Halleck in, 25-26, 37, 48, 57; Squire Gaylord in, 39
Monster, The (Crane), 78, 94; Dr. Trescott in, 89-91; Henry Johnson in, 90
Moran of the Lady Letty (Norris), 116, 119, 138; Ross Wilber in, 138-39; Capt. Kitchell in, 138; Moran in, 138
Munroe, Lily Branden, 64

Nana (Zola), 87
Naturalism, 22
"New Year's at San Quentin" (Norris), 121
New York Society for the Prevention of Vice, 158
New York *Times*, 63
New York *Tribune*, 63
Nietzsche, Friedrich Wilhelm, 172-73
Noble, David W., 6, 12-13, 163
Norris, Benjamin Franklin, 112-14
Norris, Benjamin Franklin, Jr., *see* Norris, Frank
Norris, Charles, 118
Norris, Frank, 7, 22, 95, 112-152 *passim*, 153, 205, 255-56; anti-intellectual attitude, 114; and parents' divorce, 114; goes to Harvard, 114; goes to South Af-

Norris, Frank (*Cont.*)
rica, 115; assistant editor on *The Wave*, 115; meets McClure, 116; goes to Cuba, 116; works for *McClure's Magazine*, 116; special reader for Doubleday, Page, and Company, 117; marries, 117; death, 118; compared with Stephen Crane, 118; and naturalism, 119-20, 126; interest in violence, 120; interest in superman, 120, 139; and heredity and circumstances, 122-23, 128, 131-32; on the nature of man, 124, 132-33; attitude toward sexual relationship, 133-34, 138, 146, 149; concept of man in society, 137, 145; and the Wheat Series, 140-46 *passim*; on the novel, 146-48 *passim*; discovers *Sister Carrie* (Dreiser), 156; compared with Theodore Dreiser, 202

Norris, Gertrude Doggett, 112-14, 116

Norris, Jeannette Black, 117, 135

Nye, Russel B., 79, 87-88, 101

O'Connor, Joseph, 95

Octopus, The (Norris), 116-17, 140, 143, 150; Magnus Derrick in, 141-42, 144, 150; Vanamee in, 143; S. Behrman in, 143; Mr. Shelgrim in, 143; Presley in, 143, 146; Buck Annixter in, 144

Ohio State Journal, 20

Ominous Baby, An (Crane), 81-82

Open Boat, The (Crane), 66, 76, 99

Overland Monthly, 114

Paradox of Progressive Thought, The (Noble), 6

Parks, Mrs. Lilli Lewis, 145

Patten, Simon, 262

Persons, Stow, 174

Phillips, David Graham, 7

Pit, The (Norris), 117, 144-45, 150; Laura Dearborn in, 144, 146, 150; Corthell in, 144; Jadwin in, 145

"Plea for the American Tradition, A" (Churchill), 234, 241

Progressive mind, 2, 3

Progressive Party, 209-10

Progressivism, 3, 212, 254, 257-58

Quality of Mercy, The (Howells), 33, 35, 38; J. Milton Northwick in, 33-37; Matt Hilary in, 34-35; Putnam in, 34; Maxwell in, 35; Pinney in, 35; Mr. Hilary in, 36

Rauschenbusch, Walter, 262

Red Badge of Courage, The (Crane), 65-66, 103-4; Henry Fleming in, 104-9; Jim Conklin in, 105, 107

Richard Carvel (Churchill), 206-8, 216; Chartersea in, 216; Grafton Carvel in, 217; Dorothy Manners in, 217; Allen in, 217; Comyn in, 217; Richard Carvel in, 217

Richards, Grant, 158

Rise of Silas Lapham, The (Howells), 23-25; Silas Lapham in, 23-25, 39, 56

Robert d'Artois (Norris), 113

Roosevelt, Theodore, 120, 206, 209, 237

Ross, Charles G., 157

Royce, Josiah, 231

St. Louis *Globe-Democrat*, 155

Salvation Boom in Matabele Land, A (Norris), 120; Otto Marks in, 120

San Francisco *Chronicle*, 113, 115

Saturday Evening Post, The, 117

Schopenhauer, Arthur, 189

Schreiner, Olive, 64

Scott, Sir Walter, 64, 208

Shanghaied, see *Moran of the Lady Letty* (Norris)

Sister Carrie (Dreiser), 117, 156, 159, 163, 165, 171; Carrie Meeber in, 159-60, 162, 164-65, 167; Charlie Drouet in, 159-62; George Hurstwood in, 159-61, 164-65; Mrs. Hurstwood in, 159; Mr. Ames in, 163
Smith, Henry Nash, 12
"Society" (Howells), 51-52
Son of Royal Langbrith, The (Howells), 39; James Langbrith in, 39-40, 42-43; Hope Hawberk in, 39-40, 42-43; Mr. Hawberk in, 39, 42; Mrs. Langbrith in, 39-43; Royal Langbrith in, 39-44; Dr. Anther in, 39-43; Reverend Enderby in, 40-44; Judge Garley in, 41
Spanish-American War, 67, 96
Speare, Morris E., 206
Spencer, Herbert, 6, 11, 60, 69, 111, 155, 189, 197
Spinoza, Baruch de, 189
S. S. *Titanic*, 158
Steffens, Lincoln, 117
Stevenson, Robert Louis, 64
Stewart, Cora Taylor, 66-67
Stewart, Donald, 66
Stewart, Sir Norman, 66
Stops of Various Quills (Howells), 51
Story of an African Farm (Schreiner), 64
Sullivan County Sketches (Crane), 74
Sumner, John S., 158
Sumner, William Graham, 6, 19

Taft, William Howard, 209
Tarbell, Ida M., 116
Taylor, William F., 119
Tent in Agony (Crane), 74
Terra, La (Zola), 113
Third Circle, The (Norris), 122
Thoroughbred (Norris), 121; Barry Vance in, 121; Jack Brunt in, 121; Wesley Shotwell in, 121

Through the Eye of the Needle (Howells), 45, 47-50; Mr. Homos in, 45, 49-50, 56; Mrs. Makely in, 45, 47, 50; Eveleth Strange in, 45, 49; Mrs. Thrall in, 48
Titan, The (Dreiser), 173-81, 195; Frank Algernon Cowperwood in, 173-81, 186, 190, 193; Aileen Butler in, 174; John J. McKenty in, 174; Berenice Fleming in, 174, 178; Mollenhauer in, 175-76; Swanson in, 175. See also *The Financier.*
Tolstoy, Leo, 54
Traveler at Forty, A (Dreiser), 158, 192, 198
Traveler From Altruria, A (Howells), 45-46, 48, 51, 55; Mr. Twelvemough in, 45, 47; Mr. Homos in, 45, 47, 49-50, 56; Mrs. Makely in, 45, 50; Eveleth Strange in, 45, 48; Mr. Bullion in, 46; Mrs. Thrall in, 48
Traveller in War-Time, A (Churchill), 209
Travis Hallett's Half Back (Norris), 120-21
Turner, Frederick Jackson, 12-13
Twain, Mark, 64

Uncharted Way, The (Churchill), 210
Underwood, John G., 206, 216

Van Doren, Carl, 153
Vandover and the Brute (Norris), 114, 119, 126, 128, 150; Vandover in, 125-28, 134-35, 149; Turner Ravis in, 127-28; Ida Wade in, 127-28; Charlie Geary in, 149; Dolliver Haight in, 149
Veblen, Thorstein, 6, 164
Venetian Life (Howells), 20

Walcutt, C. C., 88, 172, 200, 249, 276

Walker, Franklin, 115, 117, 119
War is Kind (Crane), 68, 70-71
War Memoirs (Crane), 96
Wave, The, 115-16
Wealth, Gospel of, 10-11, 13-14, 16, 19, 39, 45, 47, 57, 62, 82, 213, 226, 240, 253-54, 262
Wells, H. G., 66-67
Whilomville Stories, The (Crane), 101
White, Sallie, *see* Dreiser, Sallie White
Whitman, Walt, 195
"Who Are Our Brethren" (Howells), 54-55
Wife of Chino, The (Norris), 123; Lockwood in, 123-24; Felice

Zavalla in, 123-24; Chino in, 123-24; Reno Kid in, 123
Willard, Frances, 83-84
Willen, Gerald, 199
Wilson, Woodrow, 193, 208, 258
Wolf, The (Norris), 117
World, The, 67
World War I, 1, 209-10, 251, 256, 277

"Ye Ages, Ye Tribes" (Dreiser), 196-97
Yerkes, Charles T., 158, 172
"Yvernelle" (Norris), 113

Zola, Emile, 68-69, 87, 111, 113, 119, 123, 149, 156